P9-CMK-441

BELUSHI

a biography

JUDITH BELUSHI PISANO
AND TANNER COLBY

Published by Rugged Land, LLC

401 WEST STREET · SECOND FLOOR · NEW YORK · NY · 10014 · USA

RUGGED LAND and colophon are trademarks of Rugged Land, LLC

PUBLISHER'S CATALOGING-IN-PUBLICATION DATA

(Provided by Quality Books, Inc.)

Belushi Pisano, Judith.
Belushi / by Judith Belushi Pisano and Tanner Colby;
foreword by Dan Aykroyd; introduction by Judith Belushi Pisano.
-- 1st ed.

p. cm.

Includes bibliographical references and index.

ISBN 1-59071-048-7

1. Belushi, John.   2. Comedians—United States—Biography.
3. Actors—United States—Biography.
I. Colby, Tanner.   II. Title.

PN2287.B423B45 2005   792.7'028'092
QBI05-700255

Book Design by
JK Naughton Design

RUGGED LAND WEBSITE ADDRESS: WWW.RUGGEDLAND.COM

OCTOBER 2005

1 2 3 4 5 6 7 8 9

First Edition

DEDICATION

For Dan and Juanita Payne

For Frank and Nancy Colby

*For proving that loving guidance
and encouragement really
do make a difference*

MITCH GLAZER:

He was a force of nature.

MICHAEL O'DONOGHUE:

He was a Gypsy king.

DAN AYKROYD:

He was the only man I could ever dance with.

TABLE OF CONTENTS

FOREWORD
by Dan Aykroyd   xi

INTRODUCTION
by Judith Belushi Pisano   xiii

Chapter 1
HOLY SHIT
a star is born   1

Chapter 2
SWEET HOME CHICAGO
Humboldt beginnings   15

Chapter 3
**SEVEN YEARS OF COLLEGE
DOWN THE DRAIN**
the West Compass Players   29

Chapter 4
EAT A BOWL OF FUCK
a Second City first   41

Chapter 5
DO NOT TAKE THE BROWN STRYCHNINE
a lemming's life   57

Chapter 6
THE PERFECT MASTER
radio days   77

Chapter 7
**I WOULD LIKE TO FEED YOUR
FINGERTIPS TO THE WOLVERINES**
life in New York on Saturday night 95

JOHN'S BIRTHDAY

Chapter 8
AND WE'RE JUST THE GUYS TO DO IT
the worst house on campus   131

Chapter 9
I SEE THE LIGHT
getting the band back together   147

Chapter 10
(I GOT EVERYTHING I NEED) ALMOST
the American Dream   165

Chapter 11
HOW MUCH FOR THE LITTLE GIRL?
a mission from God   181

Chapter 12
FROM THE BOTTOM
the Smokemeister General   201

Chapter 13
SEE IF YOU CAN GUESS WHAT I AM NOW
crossing a great divide   215

BILLY & JOHN '80

Chapter 14
BUT NOOOOOOoooooooooOOOOOOOooooooo
a fight with the neighbors   231

Chapter 15
NOTHING IS OVER UNTIL WE DECIDE IT IS
the spin cycle   247

Chapter 16
DON'T LOOK BACK IN ANGER
a lonesome road   259

EPILOGUE
viking funeral   273

Acknowledgements   276
Notes on Sources and Method   277
The -ographies   279
Cast of Characters   282
Photo Index   288

FOREWORD

by Dan Aykroyd

There has been wave upon wave of revisionist history published since the original years of *Saturday Night Live*, all of it with varying degrees of accuracy. You can be sure that, of all the books written on the subject, this is the one that comes closest to the truth.

Judy Belushi Pisano has collected here the personal memories of dozens of John's close friends. I was one of the closest. When John and I met in Toronto in 1973, we bonded instantaneously. I knew that this was someone who understood me and someone whom I understood. From that moment began one of the great partnerships of the century. John would do anything for his friends, and it was that loyalty and that bond that he prized above all else. He didn't care about money at all. He never had but a crumpled wad of bills at any given time. Never carried a wallet or even any form of ID, and he didn't have to. His word was good and his handshake was honored anywhere he went. He talked his way into the White House and across the Canadian border with nothing but a smile. All the doors of the continent were open to him. He was America's Guest.

And as such, John was a magnet, a lightning rod, a charismatic emissary of generosity and goodwill. To qualify for his friendship—and it was extraordinary once you had it—he had to respect you. You had to have some kind of talent or ability that he could relate to, or you had to be a genuinely good person in a way that he could perceive. It is no accident that the friends and associates he gathered around him are today many of the most successful and talented artists in America. To understand John's relationships with those around him is to understand the man himself, and that is what Judy shows to us here.

As I have said before, ours was a full friendship, no dimension of it unexplored except the sexual one. John and I shared bunk beds backstage at *Saturday Night Live*. We shared the blood brotherhood of Jake and Elwood Blues. We shared many a late night discussing our dreams and ambitions. And yet, page after page, I was staggered by the things this book reveals outside of my own knowledge of John and his life. This is not just a standard show-business biography of John Belushi the actor and celebrity. This is personal and powerful storytelling that brings to life all the fun and excitement of hanging out with the Squazerbeam, which was the private name by which Mitch Glazer and I knew him.

John's death brought an early end to our partnership, but I've been fortunate to have that collaboration continue with Judy. During the years that we all spent together, she was far more that just John's partner in marriage. She was the Blues Sister, a full creative partner in all of our film, television and book endeavors, and she brings all of her skill and meticulous dedication to this project now. Together with Tanner Colby, the writer who has helped her recollect the highs and lows of John's life, Judy has given us a human, intimate and frankly surprising new perspective on this charismatic actor, comedian, rock star, movie star and man who, to me, defined the American Hero.

Dan Aykroyd
John Belushi's partner, 1973-1982
New York City
July 2005

INTRODUCTION

by Judith Belushi Pisano

John and I took a trip to Europe that included a memorable stop in Paris, a three-hour layover between planes during which we made a whirlwind tour of the city. Reps from John's record company quickly drove us past some of the major sights—the Eiffel Tower, the Louvre, the Arc de Triomphe, McDonald's, all the postcard icons. As we raced back to the airport John turned to me and, with his classic Bogart impersonation, said, "Well, sweetheart...we'll always have Paris." Thus ended our brief affair with the City of Lights. At the time, we just took it for granted that life moved that fast.

The life that John and I had was not normal. I couldn't say what normal is, but I know it's not what we had. I can say, however, that our time together was pretty damn great. John opened up my world. His inquisitive approach to things transformed much of what I see and how I see it, even to this day. He took me down many roads I might otherwise have blindly passed by. Ultimately, he showed me how strong I can be.

The fact that John died from a drug overdose left me riddled with guilt. To keep busy, and as some form of penance, I created projects for myself, things I thought he would like. I started a charitable foundation in his name. I produced a *Saturday Night Live: Best of Belushi* video, an MTV special and a video tribute that played on the first anniversary of his death. Along the way, I videotaped interviews with friends, family and coworkers, with the intention of putting together a biography.

But at the same time I was also working to put the past behind me, to move forward. Eventually, both the interviews and my plans for using them fell deeper and deeper into storage, where they sat, gathering dust, for the next twenty years.

Life moved on. In the intervening decades, I've had the good fortune to remarry, to a man who brings me great joy and new life lessons. My family now includes my husband Victor, three beautiful, spirited stepdaughters and a son who is, as his name Lucas portends, a bearer of light. That I found love again is remarkable. That I am a mother is both a delight and a wonder.

So why *now* am I diverting my energies to another "John project"? Because I needed to finish what I started, and I'm lucky enough to have the support of my family to do so. Because the gods put a string of events in my path that led to Rugged Land and Tanner Colby, who poked around the crumbling cardboard boxes in our basement and saw the potential for a great book. And because I once mistakenly gave the key to John's story to the wrong person, and this was a chance to get it right.

No book could capture all that was John Belushi; he was way too big for a nutshell and pretty unwieldy for a book. But with a little help from his friends and contemporaries—an extraordinary group of talented, perceptive individuals—Tanner and I have painted a portrait that holds a mirror up not only to John but also to a unique time in the history of American comedy and entertainment. In many ways, John's story is the story of that generation.

To complete the work I began so long ago, we conducted over a hundred new interviews. The sheer volume of remembrances provided a daunting palette from which to work, well over ten times the amount of material distilled here. John packed so much into his relatively short life that most people still have a hard time putting his story in the context of a man who lived only thirty-three years. It was a challenge to keep a focused story line that honestly explored the many facets of his personality, talents, fears and flaws. John was full of contradictions. While he was troubled and his death was tragic, his life was exhilarating, inspiring, sometimes infuriating, often exhausting and yet always full of laughter, love, joy and good old-fashioned fun. We tried to find the same balance here.

In the end, despite all the blemishes and scars, the impression of John that lingers is still magical and irreplaceable. Often, when I meet people and they discover that John and I were married, they say, "I'm sorry." I understand and appreciate their sympathy, but the time for condolences is long past. When John died, I believed I would never recover, that I would never find happiness again. At that point, the years we had shared marked half of my age. Now, it is less than a third. Today, I can easily say that I have been blessed manyfold. "They," it turns out, were right: time does heal wounds, and love does conquer all.

Twenty-three years after his death, John Belushi's memory is still vivid to millions of people, many of whom weren't even alive at the time that he died. He was one of those rare people so terribly and tremendously famous that his last name alone says it all. Through his humor and his music, he continues to enrich people's lives with his outrageous sense of fun. In a way, he belongs to the public now, to his fans, and for them he can happily live forever. And I think he would like that.

Judith Belushi Pisano
Martha's Vineyard
July 2005

Chapter 1

HOLY SHIT

a star is born

JAMES WIDDOES, *co-star*, Animal House:

I was around for most of the summer and started to hear the buzz. The most interesting thing I heard was not from anybody in show business; it was from an investment banker that I used to play tennis with. One day he said to me, "What's the deal with this *Animal House*?"

"What are you talking about?" I asked. Apparently, in the year since we'd shot the movie, National Lampoon's stock had gone from $2.50 to around $17.

"I dunno," I said. "Maybe it's good."

On July 28, 1978, National Lampoon's Animal House premiered in New York City. It was an offbeat, outcast little movie that no one had ever heard of and that nobody really cared about. It featured a cast of complete unknowns and a guy from a TV show called Saturday Night Live.

As one of SNL's Not Ready For Primetime Players, John Belushi had already achieved a good measure of fame and success. Years of steady and ambitious progress had taken him from the stages of Chicago's Second City to the downtown New York comedy scene to the NBC studios at Rockefeller Plaza. But the cult stardom of late-night TV was nothing compared to the cultural phenomenon that Animal House was about to become. Record-breaking crowds lined up around the block to see it. Near riots broke out in theaters. Toga parties and food fights erupted across the country. That fall, Greek fraternities, practically on life support after years of decline, suddenly watched their membership soar.

Animal House took the country by storm, and riding the crest of the wave was John as Bluto, the impish rabble-rouser, the anarchic everyman, the animal. Director John Landis described Bluto as a cross between Harpo Marx and the Cookie Monster. A closer appraisal would also include a healthy dose of John Wayne

and Elvis. Bluto wasn't just the life of the country's party. Bluto was the guy you trusted. Bluto was your new best friend. And so, by extension, was John.

Just as the Animal House craze was reaching its peak, another of John's inspired creations was also about to explode. Four years earlier, in a dive bar in Toronto called the 505 Club, John and fellow future SNL performer Dan Aykroyd decided they wanted to form a band. They even had a name. At the time, the two men lived in separate cities—separate countries, even—and had known each other for less than twelve hours. But John was never one to bother much with the details, or let them get in his way.

By the summer of '78, the Blues Brothers had gone from personal pet project to full-blown musical and evangelical revival. Amateur gigs at downtown New York clubs had led to a stint as the warm-up band for Saturday Night Live, which had led to a spot as actual musical guests on the show, which had led to a record deal for a live album, which now led to a nine-night stand opening for Steve Martin to sold-out crowds at the Universal Amphitheater in Los Angeles, California. On September 9, 1978, at 8:30 PM, thousands of A-list celebrities and screaming, toga-wearing fans came together to witness…what? A band? A comedy routine? Nobody really had any idea. It turned out to be something closer to alchemy. When John walked into the Universal Amphitheater that night, he was one of the most promising young actors in America. When he walked out, he was something else entirely. If the place had had a roof, the Blues Brothers would have blown it clean off.

Fame is not an exact science. The only readily available explanation for John Belushi's universal appeal is that no one had ever really been John Belushi before, at least not on that scale. He was just an ordinary guy, only extraordinarily so. Most celebrities get put on a pedestal. John got put on a barstool, and everyone in the country lined up to buy the next round. The following month, Saturday Night Live's audience swelled to as many as nineteen million viewers per week, its highest ratings yet. With average ticket prices of around two dollars, Animal House was pulling in over a million dollars a day. The live album Briefcase Full of Blues hit stores the first week of December, sold a million copies before Christmas and racked up two million more before its run was over. Born in a hard-luck ethnic enclave in Chicago, this firstborn son of working-class Albanian immigrants suddenly found himself holding on to a rather large brass ring. And when he woke up on the morning of his thirtieth birthday, January 24, 1979, a mere six months after Animal House premiered, John Belushi had the number-one late-night television show in the country, the number-one selling album on the Billboard charts, and the number-one highest-grossing film comedy of all time. It was a trifecta the country had never seen before—and has never seen since.

SEAN DANIEL, *Universal Studios executive★*:

In the beginning, *Animal House* was this odd little movie that nobody paid much attention to. I'd sit in the screening room watching the dailies that were coming back from Eugene, Oregon, and for the first week or so I was more or less by myself.

After a few days a couple more people began to show up. A week later it got a little more crowded. By the time the shoot was halfway over, the daily screenings were packed. Everyone was remembering their own fraternities, their own days in college. When all the executives started to say, "I knew a guy just like Bluto," that's then I knew we had something.

A few months before it was released, we had our first preview in Denver. It was a nervous time for all of us. John wanted to know how it was going to play, and he was waiting anxiously by the phone in New York.

★*See Cast of Characters index (p. 282) for complete details*

People went crazy. I was shocked. I've never seen anything like it. John Landis and I ran out into the lobby afterwards, found a pay phone and called John. There was maybe half a ring before he grabbed it.

JUDITH BELUSHI PISANO, *wife*:

John just about levitated from his chair when the phone rang. He immediately began drilling them for all the specifics: "Did they laugh when they saw the Delta house?" "Did they boo at the Omegas?" "Did they cheer for the Deathmobile?" And of course, "Did they like Bluto?" John was just so excited. He hung up and did a little "happy dance" around the room.

PETER RIEGERT, *co-star*, Animal House:

I called Landis and asked him how it went. "Listen to this," he said. He played me an audiotape of the screening. You couldn't hear any dialogue; all you heard was laughing, screaming, cheering and whistling.

John and Judy before the **Animal House** *premiere*

IVAN REITMAN, *producer*:

If they could've torn the seats out of the theater, they would have.

JUDITH BELUSHI PISANO:

Right up to the night of the premiere, neither John nor I really had any idea how big it was going to be. John didn't even own a suit. Wanting to do it up right, we went to some place on Madison Avenue and had him fitted for one. Mitch Glazer and Laila Nabulsi came up to our suite an hour or so before we needed to leave. We were all laughing and excited with anticipation. We took a few photos, got in a limo and headed to Radio City Music Hall. It was all very lighthearted and intimate. Then we got to the theater and that was it: the crowds, the photographers, the lights. From that point forward our lives were never really the same.

BERNIE BRILLSTEIN, *manager*:

The New York premiere can only be described as lunacy in an enclosed space. None of us expected it. The hype was generating someplace none of us knew about.

JAMES WIDDOES:

I didn't see much of John at the after party. We went in there and everybody just got completely pulled apart from each other. There was no question that this was John's night, that all the stars had aligned for him.

JUDITH BELUSHI PISANO:

The premiere was not a typical Hollywood promotional affair. It was a real party. John and some of the other actors got up and joined the band onstage. It was all very sloppy, but no one cared. John was the man of the night. People kept hitting him in the arm. *Nice goin', man!* By the time we got back to the hotel, he was complaining that his arms hurt.

MARK METCALF, *co-star*, Animal House:

I went to the premiere in Westwood with Joan Hackett, an actress friend of mine. After the movie I said to her, "It's kind of derogatory toward women, don't you think?"

She said, "Mark, this movie is derogatory toward everybody. It'll be a huge success."

MITCH GLAZER, *writer*:

The night that *Animal House* opened, he got me to drive around with him to movie theaters to see all the mania. When we got to the Sutton we were going in just as people were coming out. All these kids who'd just seen Bluto on the big screen suddenly walked right into him outside the lobby. They went crazy. They were all asking for his autograph; one of them gave him a bottle and asked him to break it on his head. John was so excited about it, in a way that only a kid would be.

SEAN DANIEL:

He used to call me from the Waverly Theater in New York and say, "It's packed in here. I just talked to the manager, and he says he sells out every night!" Then, just to drive the kids crazy, he'd run down the aisle, jump in front of the screen and dash out the exit door.

AL FRANKEN, *writer*, SNL:

One night after *Animal House* was first out, John insisted on getting a limo and going around Manhattan with me and Tom Davis, just to see the lines around the blocks at theaters. At that point I think he took on a little bit of Bluto as his persona.

SEAN DANIEL:

Nobody looked better in a toga than Bluto. People embraced him as this protector and this friend. Bluto was a genuinely good guy who stood up for what was right, who took on straight, dull, rigid America—and was fearless about it. All around the country people spontaneously began to have toga parties. We got beer distributors to sponsor them, but we couldn't keep up; it was all happening on its own. On occasion, John would call a radio station where we knew one of these toga parties was happening, and people would go completely nuts because he was on the air.

JOHN LANDIS, *director*:

Bluto originally wasn't a big part, and isn't a big part. It's a real ensemble piece, and has a lot of fine actors. But it was great for John in that it has terrific entrances and exits for Bluto.

He was like your best friend from high school, just a guy you could have a laugh with. I could always close my eyes and see John as one of those guys from the locker room from when I played sports growing up. Everybody knew somebody like him, or wanted to know somebody like him. John just raised it to an art form.

—Tom Brokaw

Bluto sort of comes on, is charming and funny and gets off. The whole structure of the film centers on Tom Hulce and Stephen Furst, Pinto and Flounder. They carry the story, but John is the one you remember. The script wasn't designed for Bluto to burst through. John burst through.

CHRIS MILLER, *writer*, Animal House:

John and I lived near each other in the Village and one morning we decided to get breakfast at a place called Al and Dan's Luncheonette, this funky, old-fashioned place on Bleecker Street. I met him at some spot near where we both lived. We had to walk about a block and a half to get to Al and Dan's. With all of the fans, it took us an hour.

MICHAEL KLENFNER, *Atlantic Records executive*:

I walked down the street once with Muhammad Ali, and the only thing that was even close to walking down the street with Ali was walking down the street with John. He stopped traffic. It was just pandemonium. People wanted to touch Jake Blues. They wanted to see Blutarsky. They wanted a piece of him. He was an everyman. He was the guy who did what they wanted to do. He could squirt Jell-O out of his mouth, put on a suit and tie, knock out a killer blues song and then dance with another heterosexual man and make it look sexy.

SEAN DANIEL:

He enjoyed the success of *Animal House*. He was happy for the other actors and the writers, because a lot of those guys had come up together. And I think he liked that it was the biggest thing in New York. While on one hand it was getting harder to live the life he might have wanted to, at that moment I think he really liked being king.

JOHN LANDIS:

When we were in Chicago doing press for the movie, he went out with Tim Matheson and the producers to a bunch of blues clubs. John just went all night long. The next morning we had to take the door of his hotel room off its hinges so we could get in, wake him up and get him out to do the press rounds. It was a great time for John, but it was a lot for him to handle. He didn't have much of an off switch.

The first week of September, just before the Universal Amphitheater shows, John and I checked into LaCosta, the famous health spa outside San Diego, so he could relax and clean out. One morning we found ourselves in a swimming pool doing water calisthenics with a bunch of older men. "Arms over your head! Now bend your knees!" John was bored to tears. He couldn't stand it. Then he glanced over at the guy standing next to him in the pool, and it was William Holden, *the* William Holden. John couldn't get over it. He kept asking him to do lines from *Sunset Boulevard*.

Holden had a good sense of humor about it all, and he took a liking to us. We ended up having a few meals together, listening to his stories about what it was like in Hollywood and how he'd handled it. John was captivated. "Don't take it personally," Holden said. "The press will knock you down, but you just have to get back up. Then you'll be a hero all over again. Just take it all for what it's worth. They're good to you when you're on top, but once you start to slip a little they'll try and tear you down. Most of the press are scum. They're vampires. They'll suck you dry, and they'll hate you if you die in your sleep."

"Why's that?"

"Because it's bad copy."

★ ★ ★

LAILA NABULSI, *producer*:

The night of the *Animal House* premiere, Universal had gotten John a suite at the Sherry Netherland Hotel. Mitch, Judy and I were all up there getting ready when John said, "I have a present for you. We're going to do the Blues Brothers—as a real band. We're going to open for Steve Martin for nine nights at the Universal Amphitheater, and we're going to record it for a live album."

And we just sat there like, "We are?"

"Yeah!" he said. "Judy, you're gonna design the whole look of the band and the album. Mitch, you're gonna write the liner notes and the legend of the Blues Brothers. And Laila, you're going to be the president of the band." That's how it all started. It was a way for John to create this little family by giving us all jobs to do. It was pretty funny when you think about it because none of us had any experience whatsoever in the music business.

BERNIE BRILLSTEIN:

Steve Martin was at the height of his career, and his agent, Marty Klein, needed an opening act for this gig. He called me and asked if the Blues Brothers would do it. "Of course they'll do it," I said. The place was already sold out, and I knew Steve would attract the people who wanted to see John and Danny.

"I can only pay seventeen thousand for all nine nights," he said. That was birdseed, but I didn't care. I thought of it as an investment in the future; so did John, who used $100,000 of his own money to record the gigs because the record company's money was too slow to arrive. John and Danny used the $17,000 to pay the band.

LAILA NABULSI:

A lot of people thought that it was kind of a joke. I don't think people realized that John could really pull it off. We knew what we were doing, but nobody else really had any idea.

Plus, we were all TV people, so we weren't really doing it the way it's usually done. We had this very funny sense of "blues aesthetic." When we got to LA, we all had to go to Rent-A-Wreck and get old, beat-up bluesmobiles, everybody had to wear black, everybody had to have blues nicknames, that sort of thing. We were definitely putting on a show.

MITCH GLAZER:

The look and the wardrobe were a nice protective device for John and Dan. They're actors, and to get up as musicians, live, in front of 6,000 people and the cream of the LA celebrity world, well, it took balls.

JUDITH BELUSHI PISANO:

As much as John loved being an actor and a comedian, at heart his fantasy was to be a rock and roll star. The danger of the whole Blues Brothers enterprise, that was the kind of pressure he thrived on.

MICHAEL KLENFNER:

John, in my opinion, was very, very nervous. This was his first time playing with a real band in front of a big audience, and many of the folks at Atlantic Records did not believe in this on any level. They thought it was a novelty, but it wasn't. We had our bandleader, Paul Shaffer, the best musician I've ever seen, period. We had Steve Cropper and Donald "Duck" Dunn, the legendary rhythm section of the Memphis Stax/Volt movement. We had Matt "Guitar" Murphy. We had the entire horn section from the *Saturday Night Live* band, the best studio guys in New York. We'd brought in Tom Scott, the saxophone player, who was a real West Coast gunslinger kind of a guy. And then we had the best fucking drummer in the world. Steve Jordan played the drums like somebody had an electric cattle prod up his ass. Once he was in the pocket you'd need a gun to get him off time.

MITCH GLAZER:

I had just given John a hug backstage. Then Judy and I went out and sat together. In those days the amphitheater was still open, and it was one of those perfect, beautiful, breezy Los Angeles nights. I was sitting there surrounded by every important person in the entertainment business when all of a sudden it occurred to me that this could all go horribly, horribly wrong. But the second they cranked into "Can't Turn You Loose," all of those thoughts just vanished.

JUDITH BELUSHI PISANO:

We looked out over the audience and saw a sea of Blues Brothers hats and T-shirts—and we just kind of laughed. It was like: *they exist now.* John had this dream, and now it was real. When Jake and Elwood walked onstage, it hit me. I was really overwhelmed, and I actually had to fight back the urge to cry.

BERNIE BRILLSTEIN:

After the last rehearsal I had said, "Now, John, don't just casually saunter out to the center of the stage. Universal Amphitheater's really large."

He just looked at me and said, "I make the greatest entrances since Jimmy Durante." That opening night he did three cartwheels out to center stage, and the place went wild. Half of the audience had togas on, half were dressed up as the Blues Brothers, and everyone else had arrows through their heads. It was a time like no other.

DANNY KORTCHMAR, *musician*:

As soon as the band hit the opening tune and the guys came out from the side of the stage—John doing his cartwheels and Danny holding his briefcase—it was all over. It was history. The audience went up for grabs. And nobody knew. As a matter of fact, a lot of people thought they were going to die a terrible death. But it worked because the band was so excellent and the show had been so well rehearsed, and because John and Danny were sincere. It was one of the few times that you knew right away this was going to become an institution. Not just a successful music effort, an institution.

All of the musicians had thought that Danny and John were going to make fun of what they did for a living, make a mockery of it. One night I sat next to Joe Cocker in the third row. He actually looked nervous. Three songs in he turned to me and said, "Oh, okay. He's doing this for real."

—Jim Belushi

LAILA NABULSI:

I think we put to rest any idea that it was a joke. It was the love of the music that was driving John. He didn't want it to be stupid.

MICHAEL KLENFNER:

The first show was so hot they could have just taken that, mixed it and put it out. And each show just got tighter and better. I remember thinking to myself, how the fuck is Steve Martin gonna follow this? They took a very long time with the set change for the audience to cool off. And every night it seemed like they took longer and longer.

ROBIN WILLIAMS, *actor*:

It was a wild night. They tore the place up. Most of the time comics open for bands, but this time the band opened for the comic. It was a pretty dangerous combination to have this huge burst of energy and then send out after them one lone man with an arrow.

DAN AYKROYD, *partner in crime*:

Steve Martin was very gracious. He was really one of the pivotal guys behind getting us started. He loved the act and loved us and gave us his opening venue. It was incredible that he let this powerhouse band go out and blow the audience away and then came on and did an hour and a half of comedy.

DANNY KORTCHMAR:

Everyone was backstage. All the players in town. Everybody I knew that could make that gig made it. They wanted to be a part of it. What made it so fun and different was that it was just as big a party for John and Danny as it was for the audience.

BILLY BELUSHI, *brother*:

I was going to college in California at the time, so I got to go to the first Blues Brothers show. *Saturday Night* was pretty big, so in my world John was a star, but of course that's not how I related to him. It was pretty amazing to be backstage, but the best part was just to see John so happy. Afterwards, I stuck with Judy and the people at their table. John was in so much demand that I didn't really get to spend much time with him.

MICHAEL KLENFNER:

The second night I took Mick Jagger with me. The whole show he kept turning to me and saying, "Fucking John's brilliant. I didn't know he could move like that." And on and on about Danny and the band. Backstage, John and Mick had what was basically a musician's discussion—John had become a credible musician, a blues singer, not just a crazy guy who did these little skits on TV. And that was very important for him.

MITCH GLAZER:

When I look back on that whole week at Universal, it's kind of a perfect, golden moment. But there was also a lot of pressure on John then. That was the same week that the deal for *1941* came down. Every director in Hollywood was lining up backstage at the Amphitheater, mixing congratulations with business, and he was starting to look a little worn from the attention. It wasn't just a celebration for him; it was also the next test.

JIM BELUSHI, *brother*:

Ours was the classic second-generation immigrant family. We really believed in that idea of the American Dream, the ability to succeed on your own terms. John had worked extremely hard for years in order to make it, and in doing so he'd almost completely isolated himself from the family. After I congratulated him, I said, "John, I've handled the family for years. I've been the guy explaining why you never

write and you never call. I've done my part, and now it's your turn."

"You're right," he said. "I'll take it from here." After that night he called everybody in the family and fixed them up financially. He bought Mom and Dad a ranch so high in the California mountains that Dad said it made him feel he was living back in the hills of Albania. John was suddenly back in touch and stayed that way, but the change was so dramatic and forceful that it scared everybody half out of their wits.

BERNIE BRILLSTEIN:

As the box office for *Animal House* climbed, John started getting movie offers. Among the callers was Steven Spielberg. He'd met John during the first season of *Saturday Night Live*, and they'd immediately liked each other. Spielberg's film was *1941*, a comedy spoof about a Japanese military strike on the California coast during World War II. I got a call from Mel Sattler, the head of business affairs at Universal Pictures. He said, "*Animal House* is huge and we've got to have Belushi."

"You don't have him," I said. "There are no options on his deal, and I've got calls for him coming in from everywhere." After *Animal House* I could get just about anything I wanted for John because he'd hit like a fucking rocket, but I figured we'd end up at Universal out of loyalty. They'd brought John to the dance. I said, "Look, Belushi made thirty-five grand on *Animal House*, and you guys are making millions. Now everyone's coming after him. But I'm a loyal guy. You took a shot with him. Here's what I'll do. Send me $250,000 today. Call it a bonus. And I won't make a deal with another studio until you make me a three-picture offer. If I like it, he's yours." Mel messengered the check to my office. It was so easy I figured I should have asked for a million.

John didn't completely grasp how much money it was. Around that same time, he and Judy wanted to rent a brownstone downtown in the Village for $1,800 a month. He asked me, "Do you think Judy and I can afford it?"

"Yes," I said, "I think you can."

Then, in the meeting at Universal with Sattler, I said, "I'm going to walk outside for ten minutes. When I come back, give me your best numbers." I never asked for anything, in part because I really had no idea what to ask for. When I walked back in they laid out the numbers: Three pictures. $350,000 for the first, which would be *1941*. $500,000 for the second. $750,000 for the third. And the $250,000 just for listening, plus per diems and all the usual star perks.

So obviously I took it.

MITCH GLAZER:

We were all sitting in a screening room at Universal watching Kurosawa's *Throne of Blood*. It was a whole bunch of us. Landis had invited us there as a bit of a diversion for John, which he needed. John had some fun grunting along with Toshiro Mifune, but the spirit in the room was subdued. The red phone light blinked and it was for John. There was a brief, muffled conversation. Then, fifteen minutes later, the phone started blinking again. John picked up.

After the movie was over, John and I headed over to a taco stand outside the Universal lot for a chili dog. It was one of those brown, smoggy Los Angeles afternoons. The whole time John had a strange smile on his face. Finally we stopped on an overpass that bridged this rusty little stream. "I got the Spielberg movie," he said. "I think this means I'm set. I mean, I don't ever have to worry about money again." He leaned over the concrete wall, looking down at the stream.

I told him, "It's an old tradition to throw a penny in there for luck."

He reached in his pocket and pulled out a crumpled twenty-dollar bill, arched his eyebrow and smiled. Then he started slowly tearing the twenty and tossing little bits of green confetti out over the ditch. "Thank you, LA," he said quietly. "Thank you, Hollywood." ∎

Chapter 2

SWEET
HOME
CHICAGO

Humboldt beginnings

GUS DIMAS, *cousin*:

You wanted to be American. You were always striving to get ahead and follow that idea of the American Dream. For all of us, coming out of this working-class, immigrant neighborhood, the idea of owning a restaurant like John's dad did, or buying a Cadillac, that was really the big thing.

Above: Marian, Jim and John

J
ohn Belushi was born at the Norwegian American Hospital in Chicago on January 24, 1949, at 5:12 AM. He weighed eight pounds, fourteen ounces and, by many accounts, was already well on his way to sprouting a full growth of beard. At the time, his family lived in a low-rise, industrial pocket of Chicago known as Humboldt Park.

John was a full-blooded Albanian. His mother Agnes had come to Chicago by way of a small Albanian community in Akron, Ohio. His father Adam had come to Chicago by way of a somewhat larger Albanian community in Qyteza, Albania. Upon immigrating to America in 1934 at the age of sixteen, Adam had taken a job as a busboy at the Palm Grove Inn on the South Side, worked his way up to manager, left to serve his time in the army, and then returned to run his own establishment, called the Olympia Lunch. He would go on to own two restaurants of his own, both of which he would call The Fair Oaks, and both of which he would eventually lose.

John was also the firstborn son, and that meant that the hopes and welfare of the family rested very much on his shoulders. By modern, middle-class standards it's a notion that feels antiquated and old world,

but at the time the pressures for someone in John's position could not have been greater. It was a role he neither asked for nor particularly wanted, but no matter where he went in life it was never very far behind.

AGNES BELUSHI, *mother:*

When Adam and I got married we had to move in with my in-laws. It was 1946, right after the war, and housing was pretty scarce. The first year we were married I had Marian, my daughter. Adam's family almost didn't let me come home; they wanted a boy. Boys are important in Albanian families. Two years later I had John and everybody was very happy.

GUS DIMAS:

Humboldt Park was a little northwest of downtown. There were factories right across the street from our houses and everything like that. It was a real working-class area with a very small Albanian community, maybe ten or fifteen families. We were all very close. There was always a cousin or an aunt or an uncle around. You didn't get raised by just one person; you got raised by a community.

JIM BELUSHI:

John was very dark as a kid, and they used to call him Pancho. He was very well liked in the neighborhood. There was a community pool in the park by the house, and he had the privilege of sneaking in during all hours. They had certain set hours for swimming for adults, swimming for girls and so forth. But he would just climb over the fence any time he felt like it and all the lifeguards would say, "Oh, there's Pancho. Let him go swimming."

AGNES BELUSHI:

John was an easygoing little boy, very quiet and well mannered, always very mature for his age. He was like a little man. He'd talk to anybody. By the time he was four he'd just wander up the street, walk into a neighbor's house, sit down and strike up a conversation. People always related to him like an adult, especially since he never really spoke like a child. Eventually I'd just let Marian and John go to the park by themselves. I would take them over and drop them off at the sandbox. John just took care of himself.

We were the first family to move out of the old neighborhood. When Adam opened his restaurant at North and Austin, one of the waitresses who worked for us lived in Wheaton. Her brother had a home there and was selling it to move on to a bigger place. She told us we should take a look at it. We had no money, no way of buying it, but he told us all we had to have was the mortgage. We didn't have to put any money down. He was nice enough to say, "Adam, just pay me whenever you have it."

John was about six when we moved. About the same time, Adam's father passed away, and so my mother-in-law came to live with us. You might say that John had two mothers. His grandmother, Vasilo Belushi, also helped raise him. We all called her Nena. She lived with us for thirty-four years. She couldn't speak any English, but John understood a little

Adam Belushi, father

Albanian and they never had any problems communicating. John used to call her "the soul of the family."

JIM BELUSHI:

Our grandmother was really a huge influence. We used to communicate with her by speaking English and putting a heavy accent on it, thinking that maybe she would understand it better, but it probably only made it worse. Dealing with my grandmother and explaining things to her required a lot of physical communication. A lot of John's work has that quality.

If your parents spoke Albanian in the house it was kind of embarrassing to you, especially in a place like Wheaton. Nobody knew where Albania was, or what Albania was. It's a mystery place. It was even a mystery to us. It wasn't like we got to be German or Polish or Greek, you know? We were Albanian. What the heck is that?

—Gus Dimas

JUDITH BELUSHI PISANO:

Wheaton, Illinois, was a very stereotypical 1950s midwestern town. It was the DuPage County seat, a holdout Republican zone in the midst of Democratic Chicagoland. Very WASPy. Very conservative. When we grew up it was a dry town. It's where Billy Graham went to college.

SUE KELLER, *friend*:

At Whittier Grammar School in Wheaton, we had no black people. We had no Chinese people. We had no people of any ethnic background whatsoever. I think once we had a Jewish person, only we didn't know he was Jewish at the time. His name was Pete Samuels. Looking back now I realize he was Jewish. But he moved.

So when John showed up in sixth grade, people looked at him like he was from outer space. He had dark hair and he was already growing a beard. Everybody kind of stayed away from him at first, but because of his class-clownish demeanor, he won friends very easily.

MARIAN BELUSHI, *sister*:

Starting in his early teen years, John played comedy albums over and over again a million times until you'd go crazy. All you'd hear was Jonathan Winters and Bob Newhart. He'd imitate them in the mirror, for hours, and then he'd make me listen to him act them out just to get my opinion. Sometimes he'd wake me up in the middle of the night to do this. Then he started writing little skits and doing those for me as well.

JIM BELUSHI:

Jonathan Winters was the big influence. John could do all of his characters. He'd also do impressions of my father, my uncle, everyone in the family. That was his big thing. He never actually mimicked my father in front of him. Oh, no. Of course, he probably could have done it right to my father's face and he wouldn't even have known it.

John was usually kind of quiet and intense around the house, but every once in a while he'd really let loose around the dinner table. He used to do this thing with his eyelid where he would flip it up so the fleshy part was showing and it looked creepy. He'd bow his head down and flip 'em up, then he'd look up at everybody. Marian'd yell, "Stop it, Johnny, stop it!" And my mom would be laughing so hard she couldn't breathe. Of course, my dad didn't see the humor in it. He'd just keep eating.

The first time John actually performed for an audience, he played Khrushchev in the junior high variety show. He did a piece from *The First Family*. He just lifted the piece straight from the album and did it in the show.

AGNES BELUSHI:

When he did that Khrushchev bit, where Khrushchev pounded his shoe at the United Nations, he did the whole thing himself. He went to all the trouble of planting kids out in the audience to ask him questions. After the show the principal stopped my husband and I in the hallway and said, "Mr. and Mrs. Belushi, your son is incredibly talented. Compared to most of the kids that come through this school, he's really one in a million."

SUE KELLER:

In the school plays John and I were always the leads. It was amazing to watch the transformation in him from class clown to real actor. One year he played Scrooge in *A Christmas Carol* and he took it so seriously.

EARL SWEARINGEN, *teacher*:

He was, at times, almost too much of a straight arrow. One time, Principal Mitchell and I were in the office with John, who at the time was the sergeant at arms for the mock congress. Some of the kids had been marking up the insides of their lockers with graffiti. John said, "I'll take care of it."

"Okay, John," we said, "you look into it."

Well, the next day we go down the hall after school, and there's John. He's got two or three of these kids with sponges and buckets washing out their lockers. Of course he hadn't told us, or any of their parents for that matter, that he was doing this. I had to tell him, "John, you can't just keep kids in detention without telling anyone."

AGNES BELUSHI:

When he was twelve he got the Best Actor award, the Best Athlete of the Year award and the American Legion award. They had a big dinner for him at the American Legion hall over in Springfield. He came home that day and said, "Mom, today is the happiest day of my life. I found out one thing. If you want something bad enough and you work hard enough, you can get it." I thought that was quite profound for a twelve-year-old.

DICK BLASUCCI, *friend*:

John and I sat next to each other in freshman English. My older brother Lee was a guitar player and he had a group called the Vibrations. They auditioned John on drums and used him for a couple of jobs; then that petered out. But soon, as everybody does in high school, we started another band. We called ourselves the Ravins and asked John to be the drummer. It was a typical high-school band; we played at the dances, after the football games and at the post-prom parties.

We rehearsed mostly at John's. His bedroom was right off the kitchen in this little alcove. It wasn't even a real bedroom. They didn't have the biggest house. We would set up in there with his drums sticking out in the kitchen. John's love for music didn't start with the Blues Brothers. Even in high school, you could tell he was just passionate about that stuff. He loved the Rolling Stones. The day "Satisfaction" came out, John bought it immediately and listened to it over and over and over again so we could learn how to play it. We didn't let John sing much, but he always sang lead on the Stones songs.

DAN PAYNE, *drama teacher*:

John was in one of my speech classes at Wheaton Central High School. He was always head and shoulders above the other kids. We had these variety shows we put on every spring, and whenever John walked out from the curtains the audience was already laughing before he was even halfway to the microphone. By his senior year we'd just tell him, "Okay, we need a comedy routine here, here and here. John, you got two minutes, five minutes and four minutes." We never knew what he was going to do. We just knew it was going to be funny and we let him do it.

MARIAN BELUSHI:

John was always like my big brother. I never felt like the oldest around him. One night we were in the bleachers at a football game, and some guy called me a name. John heard him, and he got really mad, grabbed the guy and hit him. The guy dropped to the ground and tumbled all the way down the bleachers. I was really upset. I said to John, "What did you do that for?"

"Forget it!" he shot back. "No one talks to you like that!"

We went down to the bottom of the bleachers and this guy was just lying there. I picked up his head to see if he was all right, and John goes, "You apologize to my sister right now." The guy's bleeding all over himself, and John's standing over him making him apologize to me. I was a junior. John was a freshman.

He used to drive us crazy because he wouldn't just come in and do the routine. He would always bring a bunch of friends to be in the sketch with him—kids that weren't in the show otherwise. He'd take them out in the hallway and rehearse them and then they'd come in and do the show.

John never made himself the star of these little skits. He just liked having his friends around. These were kids who maybe weren't that popular, and so he'd bring them out onto the main stage.

SUE KELLER:

John was voted most humorous in high school, but he was also voted homecoming king. He wasn't really considered the class clown or just a buffoon. The physical humor that so many people saw on *Saturday Night Live* wasn't his only talent. He would make people laugh, sure, but he wasn't constantly acting like an idiot.

We did this very avant-garde play once, and John had lost a great deal of weight for it. He was constantly fighting his weight, and I remember it was very difficult for him. That play was so important because it allowed him to really act and not just be a comedian. In one show we had to do a stage kiss; he was pretty nervous and self-conscious about it.

DICK BLASUCCI:

John always had a date when he needed one, but he wasn't a guy who had a steady girlfriend around all the time. When he and Judy found each other, it was pretty obvious, you know, that was it.

SUE KELLER:

John and Judy's relationship is really one of those things that you hear about in storybooks. If I hadn't been there, I wouldn't believe it myself. My sister Stephanie was in Judy's class, and one night she and I were talking about John. We thought, well, Judy's got a bizarre sense of humor—let's try and fix them up. It was all schemed from the very beginning.

JUDITH BELUSHI PISANO:

I first met John just before my sophomore year. My girlfriends and I were hanging out at a Little League baseball game and ran into a bunch of the senior guys. John and two friends gave us a ride home. When we got to my house, John stepped out

John and Judy

of the car to let me out. Goofing around, I shut the door, waved to the driver and said, "Thanks for the ride!" They just drove off and left us there. We were both a little surprised and embarrassed because we'd hardly ever spoken. So we stood there and talked for about ten minutes until they returned. At first I assumed he was Italian; I thought his name was "Balucci." I'd never even heard of Albania.

A few days later, my girlfriends and I went to Herrick Lake to meet some guys. I was happy to see that John was with them. We rented two boats, and John and I wound up in the same one. A water fight broke out, and John, in his enthusiasm, brought his oar back to splash someone and accidentally hit my arm. He immediately dropped the oar and grabbed my arm to make sure I was okay. That night he called and asked, "How's your arm?" and we talked briefly. The next night he called again with the exact same question. I laughed and we talked a little longer. He did the same thing every night for at least a week. Finally he changed his question and asked me if I'd like to go to the homecoming dance. I said I would.

John was co-captain of the football team and a candidate for homecoming king. When the king and queen were announced at the dance, John seemed embarrassed that he'd won. The crown was too small. He felt silly posing for photos. It was tradition that the king and queen would dance together and so

Before the homecoming dance

their dates were left to dance with each other. It was my first taste of being with a celebrity, that part where you are somewhat "pushed aside" and left to wait patiently until the commotion is over. As soon as the ceremony and photos were complete, John came and took my hand. He wanted to leave right away.

JEAN JACKLIN, *mother-in-law*:

The first time I met John I had gone with Judy and her father to his family's restaurant. John was a busboy, the most elegantly handsome young character I ever saw in my life. There was a lot of tension. We had the impression that John was horribly embarrassed. For Judy to be dating an Albanian was certainly strange in a place like Wheaton. Meeting with the Belushi family was like going into another world.

JUDITH BELUSHI PISANO:

When I first went over to John's house I was struck by how different it was. The house was small but comfortable. Most of the activity took place in the disproportionately large kitchen. His grandmother, Nena, was a stereotypical immigrant; she wore a housedress with an apron, hairnet and slippers. Although she didn't speak English, it was uncanny how she and John communicated. It was clear from the beginning that she was the one who held the family together.

Dinner with the Belushis was another new experience. The talk was loud and it seemed as if everyone spoke at the same time. The table was covered with large plates of food—more than enough for two whole meals—and as soon as you sat down the race was on to fill up your plate. They couldn't believe how "little" I ate. Agnes and Nena were always trying to beef me up.

In contrast, when John first came to eat at my house he was startled by the fact that my mother served each of us one by one: a little pork chop and a little bit of vegetable and a little bit of potato. John always asked if he could have more, and my mother would give him the "extra" pork chop. He'd eat that and then go home and eat some more.

JEAN JACKLIN:

When he first started coming over for dinner, he was excruciatingly polite. It took me years to realize I was starving him to death.

SUE KELLER:

John's family was very much a mystery to us. My mother always felt bad for him because he seemed to be ashamed of his home. Whenever one of us would go over to pick him up, he would say, "Just honk the horn." We never went inside his house, ever.

DICK BLASUCCI:

In all the years I knew him, I saw John's dad once. We went down to eat at his restaurant and I met him there, but that's the only time I can remember.

JUDITH BELUSHI PISANO:

I don't think either of John's parents was very happy. Deep down he knew that and, like any kid, it made him sad. He found that being funny was a way to make his mother happy, or at least make her laugh. But he told me many times that she'd never be happy, that he'd never be able to solve all the family's problems. And yet, as the oldest son, the golden boy, that's what he felt his parents expected him to do. Agnes turned to John for help more than the other way around. Nena was very nurturing, but she was very much of the old world. Once John was a teenager, I think she symbolized how different they were. She was always cheerful and busy in the kitchen, which was a stable and good part of his youth, but other than that the house felt empty and depressing. I think John's survival instincts told him it was best to get out, and get as far away as possible.

John and I didn't talk a lot during those times. He was in school and then at football practice and then he would do theater. He was gone a lot of the time.

—Jim Belushi

AGNES BELUSHI:

John lived in a world of his own. He was always busy with something. He was rarely with the family, and he never asked for anything. Sometimes it seems to me like he just grew up all by himself.

John, bottom row, third from right, #61

SUE KELLER:

John was always a part of just about every extracurricular activity in school. He wanted to be involved in everything. I never understood where he got so much energy.

JUDITH BELUSHI PISANO:

John loved football. He played middle linebacker, made team captain and honorary All State. When he worked as a busboy at his father's restaurant in Chicago, he rode to work on his motorcycle, a used BMW that he'd bought with his savings. It wasn't much out of the way to stop by Soldier Field to watch the Bears practice, which he often did.

MARK CARLSON, *friend:*

John was a middle linebacker and I was a running back, and we got to be pretty good friends through the football team. John was a very good player when he wanted to be, but I think he always needed some motivation or he needed to be

inspired or be in the mood. He could dog it and loaf a little bit. He was particularly slow and lackadaisical in practice, but he'd always turn it on for the big game.

EARL SWEARINGEN:

I remember the coach talking about John once. He said, "Belushi's terrible at practice, can't get an ounce of hustle out of him. But Thursday night, you put on the practice uniform and he runs through the plays just magnificently, doesn't miss a count, everything goes beautifully. And Friday night he's a gladiator."

John and I were good friends, but I can't say that we were best friends. He was very popular and very well liked, but I can't recall anybody I would say was his best friend; I don't know that he had one.

—Mark Carlson

AGNES BELUSHI:

They used to call him "Killer." One time he got seriously cut over his eye, and he wouldn't quit playing. He wouldn't let them take him out of the game. Maybe it's hard for some to believe, but because he was on the football team, he was always home in bed on time. I never had to say, "John, it's ten o'clock. Go to bed." He was already there. And he would always try and get all the other people on the team to do what was right. "Don't smoke. Don't drink. Get enough sleep." He was always the big brother of the team, trying to get everybody to behave.

MARK CARLSON:

The last Friday night of our junior year, the seniors were having all these graduation parties. We're out riding around on our bikes, it's getting time to get to one of these parties and John says, "Hey listen, come on over to my house. I want to watch this thing on TV."

So we get to his house and he turns on Channel 11, the public television station. It was some kind of *Playhouse 90* thing, you know, *Masterpiece Theater* or something like that. After about two minutes I say, "John, this is *terrible*. This is really, really boring. Let's get out of here."

"Oh, no way. I gotta see this, I gotta watch this, this is really good!" he says. "I'll catch up with you later."

So that was it. I left and went to the party, and he sat home alone on a Friday night watching this acting thing on public television.

JUDITH BELUSHI PISANO:

John's senior year he competed in the state forensics tournament. He'd won districts with his original monologue, and then he won second or third place at state. He played a Nazi summer-camp counselor addressing the kids and ordering them around: "You vill eat and you vill eat until you can eat no more—*and zen you vill have Jell-O!*"

Toward the end of the year, Dan Payne, the drama teacher, cast him in a play called *My Three Angels.*

DAN PAYNE:

There was a play that I'd always wanted to do called *My Three Angels.* It was about three escaped convicts in South

Probably one of the gutsiest things John ever did was the Blue Fairy for the senior men's fashion show. It was completely over the top. If you ever saw a man who did not resemble a woman, it was John. He had a little blue tutu and a little wand. Beyond the costume—which in itself was hilarious—he was totally committed. He danced out on tip-toe and improvised his own interpretations of *pliés*, *arabesques* and *jetés*—all the while singing absurdly in a high-pitched voice. People were laughing so hard they were begging him to stop.

America. I'd always thought the characters were too mature for high school, but when John came along I thought, well, if I can fit some other kids around him, we can do the show. Of course there were a lot of compromises with John, because he always insisted on bringing his friends along to do it with him, but eventually we worked it out.

AGNES BELUSHI:

My Three Angels was the turning point for my husband. We always knew John was good, but when we saw that Adam said, "Now I know he's an actor."

DAN PAYNE:

I knew a director from Chicago, Adrian Rehner, who ran a summer stock theater down in Indiana. I talked to John quite a bit about it, and eventually he agreed to go to Chicago and try out.

I picked him up on a Saturday morning. It was pretty cold and rainy outside. John came out wearing a suit and tie; he

was really taking the audition seriously. But when he got in the car he said, "I'm not sure I really want to do this."

I was a little surprised. Turns out John had an opportunity to get a football scholarship. He really loved acting, but he needed the money for college. He didn't want to get drafted. I reminded him there weren't many five-eight, 170-pound linebackers in the NFL. He agreed to see it through.

Then, on the way into Chicago, he started to change his mind again. He was very nervous about making the wrong choice and going down the wrong road. His dad was never around. He spent weeknights at an apartment over his restaurant, only coming home on the weekends. I think it upset him that his father was gone all the time working but they didn't have any money anyway, forcing him into making tough decisions about college and his future. I finally convinced him that it was just an audition and it wouldn't commit him and he wasn't doing anything else that Saturday anyway.

It was an adult company, but because the director was a friend of mine he said he would let John audition with the

grown-ups. I had to wait in the car; they didn't want me coaching him or anything. So I took him in the house and then waited outside. About half an hour later somebody came out and got me. John was inside entertaining the whole group, cracking them up with comedy bits. They wanted him on the spot. The only problem left was the money situation—there was no money. They could only pay him forty-five dollars a week, but his mother wanted him to make at least fifty. I arranged with the theater to pay the difference myself. He was the youngest paid performer they ever had. He made $50 a week and was expected to mow the lawn and paint as well.

People say that John wasn't disciplined. You hear that forever, and it's just not true. Summer stock is a highly disciplined routine. You can't do six shows in seven weeks—doing one show at night, rehearsing another show in the morning and another one in the afternoon and memorizing the lines for all of them—and be stupid or undisciplined. It can't be done. John was very disciplined; he just made it look so easy.

The night we drove down with Judy to see him, he was in *Murder in the Cathedral,* and I just couldn't believe that it was John. I was amazed. I don't think he was ready for how much hard work it was going to be, but he did an excellent job.

JUDITH BELUSHI PISANO:

John asked the Paynes if they would bring me along when they came at the end of the summer, which they were nice enough to do. He wasn't the lead in the play I saw, but I have photos, and he told me so much in his letters that I feel like I saw them all. The next day, John rode his motorcycle back to Wheaton behind the Paynes' car. That was the end of his summer stock days.

As a final graduation present, just before John went off to college, the Paynes drove us into Chicago to see a show at Second City. I had no idea what improvisational theater was. I thought it was a nightclub. The whole show, John was just mesmerized. He'd enjoyed the work he'd done in summer stock, but when he walked out of the theater that night, it was as if a light had gone on in his head. "This," he said, "this is what I want to do." ■

Summer stock days in Shawnee, Indiana

Chapter 3

SEVEN YEARS OF COLLEGE DOWN THE DRAIN

the West Compass Players

ROB JACKLIN, *brother-in-law*:

I was in grad school at the time of the 1968 Democratic Convention. Demonstrators were everywhere, and Chicago was under siege. On the night they were due to nominate Hubert Humphrey, Mayor Daley promised an all-out offensive against the protestors. I was watching the huge crowds on TV as they headed down Halstead Street. The National Guardsmen had jeeps covered with barbed wire and flamethrowers rigged to fire liquid tear gas. When the crowd wouldn't budge they started firing the gas, and it hit the crowd like water shooting out of a fire hose. I saw the first blast just topple this guy, and I thought, whew, they nailed *him* all right.

About an hour later, the doorbell rang and when I answered it I was almost knocked over by the tear gas fumes. It was John; he was barely conscious. Turns out he was the poor soul I'd seen flattened on TV. I got his clothes off, put him in the shower for half an hour and called Judy.

The incident was very typical of John's way. If he was into something, he was right out on the front lines fighting for it. It was also his first television appearance.

Above: John on a hitchhiking trip to the Pacific Northwest, 1971

When John graduated from high school, Illinois Wesleyan University offered him a scholarship for both football and acting. The coaches arranged for a job that wouldn't conflict with his practice schedule and everything seemed to be in place, with one small exception: his grade point average failed to meet the minimum academic standards required for actual admission. Faced with this small clerical obstacle—and given the fact that he had passed up another scholarship along the way—he turned to a less-than-desirable fallback: the University of Wisconsin at Whitewater, a school with no football team and, at best, an average theater department.

On the road to success, Wisconsin was largely a detour. John spent virtually every weekend coming home to Chicago, either to see Judy or to work as an usher for Chicago's Compass Players, a revived incarnation of the legendary improv troupe that gave birth to Mike Nichols, Elaine May and many others. There he spent his nights at the back of the house studying the actors onstage and learning their craft. Ever since his trip to Second City, school had taken a backseat to his desire to pursue a career in comedy. Perhaps the most telling sign of his utter lack of interest at Whitewater: he

almost flunked his speech class. If anything significant took place during that year it's that John became, in so many words, a hippie. He adopted a radical political stance, grew out his hair, and his wardrobe decisions were increasingly questionable. By spring semester, it was clear that to stay at Whitewater would mean taking out another loan to pay for a second year, something John was hesitant to do. With no real idea what his next step should be, he packed up and moved back home.

JUDITH BELUSHI PISANO:

John was the oldest son and that's absolutely how his life was shaped. It was very much expected that he would go into business with his father and eventually take over the restaurant. Sometime during that first year of college, his dad asked him to be his partner. John said he wasn't interested. His father offered to sign the restaurant over to him. John still said no. His heart wasn't in it.

At that point, though, his heart wasn't in college either. He really wanted to quit school and get out into the world, but there was his draft deferment to think about. When they opened the College of DuPage in Glen Ellyn, a suburb just east of

Wheaton, it was a godsend. First, it provided a much cheaper deferment, and second, it meant our separation was over.

That summer John came back and lived at home. It was a tough time for the family. Adam lost his restaurants and took a bartending job, and Agnes began working at the Wheaton Pharmacy to help make ends meet. John worked with his friend Phil Special delivering furniture in Chicago. On payday he would keep some of the cash for spending and give me the rest to save for him—his entire life's savings was in my piggy bank.

About midway through that first year back, John lost his motorcycle to the repo man. His father had taken out a loan against the bike and couldn't make the payments. Since John had bought it with his own money, he was pretty pissed off. He moved out of the house.

JIM BELUSHI:

John came by to see me one night. We didn't talk much. We all kind of led separate lives in that house. But he turned to me, looked very intensely in my eyes, pointed with his finger and said, "Look, Mom and Dad are irresponsible parents. Just eat and sleep here. Go out for football, for track, for wrestling. Go out for chess club. I don't care what you go out for, but for your own good just stay out of here." He was right. Like a fool, I kept trying to have a relationship with my parents, but they were just

During those years after high school, he'd come by our house late at night and knock on the door, usually anytime from eleven to one, one thirty in the morning. He'd just want to talk. Some nights he'd sleep on our couch rather than go home.

—Dan Payne

too lost in their own dramas. They weren't like parents; they were like siblings, very immature and competitive. Nena really was the love in the family, the conscience of the family. If it weren't for her we'd all be mass murderers, or at least in jail.

JUDITH BELUSHI PISANO:

He stayed with friends for a while and scraped together enough money to buy an old Volvo for a few hundred bucks. It ran well enough, but it was falling apart. John tied the whole thing together with gaffer's tape: the fenders, the door handles, everything. It had a coat-hanger antenna, and you could only go in or out through the passenger door. But it had a good radio.

It was great to have John home again, but we were at odds about a lot of things. His politics were more and more radical; mine were still cautiously liberal. He wanted to have sex; I was afraid to. He was smoking pot and didn't drink; I liked to drink and didn't know he smoked pot. But in spite of all these differences, we shared more: a sense of humor, love of sports, arts, animals, dancing, people, music. We were kindred spirits. We just clicked.

Not long after moving out, John found an apartment about twenty minutes from my house. It was relatively cheap—and rightly so, as it was located in a barn, just down from a stall with some cows. There were two alcoves for beds, so he invited Tino Insana, his friend from DuPage, to share it. Then, to save even more on rent, they invited a third guy to live there. He set up a small tent in a corner to create the sense of a bedroom. Privacy time in the barn had to be scheduled. But schedule we did.

TINO INSANA, *friend*:

The guy who owned the barn got arrested. I'm not really sure what for, but we had to move out and ended up living back at home, the last place either of us wanted to be. So in the

backyard at my house we pitched a tent, strung a bunch of extension cords together, brought out a TV and made ourselves a hangout. It was like a clubhouse, I guess. Pretty soon John wanted to form a comedy group. We wrote a lot of our early material back there. There was a fine line between performing and just having fun together as friends.

STEVE BESHEKAS, *friend*:

In Wheaton, Phil Special's house was where everyone congregated. If you were anybody, you would show up at Special's house at one time or another. While we were all hanging out, John started fooling around, creating these funny bits. He'd do something funny, leave the room and then come back in with some other routine. After a while it evolved into a performance, and John would involve Tino and me in the skits. We didn't know what we were doing, really. We just did whatever John told us.

TINO INSANA:

One day at DuPage they were having a Hootenanny Night, and we decided to go onstage and do our first show. The Compass

Players were a famous improvisational theater group from Chicago. Because we grew up in the western suburbs, we called ourselves the West Compass Players. It was a little pretentious, but we were young. Most of the sketches we did that first night were about cops beating up hippies. Pretty much everything we did in those days was cops beating up hippies, or communists.

After our first night we started playing shows at the DuPage Student Center. It wasn't a real theater, just a room with chairs. We were so young that we were just happy with everything we did. John always surprised me with his powers of invention. The first night he did Joe Cocker was a surprise to everybody.

JUDITH BELUSHI PISANO:

John used to drive around in his beat-up Volvo listening to his car stereo. He'd always crank it up and sing along whenever Joe Cocker came on. With time he sounded more and more like him. One night the guys were doing a first-line/last-line scene—where the audience gives you the lines that you start and end the scene with—and the last line was, "She came in through the bathroom window." And that was when John came out of nowhere with this incredible Joe Cocker impression.

TINO INSANA:

Being a political, satirical comedy group, we were very much a part of the counterculture. John was a true Chicagoan. He loved to satirize Mayor Daley, and he was really into Mike Royko and the big machine politics. We did lots of weird European immigrant characters in our scenes too. We did the Flying Benzini Brothers, a circus act. We did an Italian *Bonanza* called *Petezanza*. Lots of confused poor people walking around in big coats.

In order to make some real money, we started a business as restaurant cleaners where we would go in and clean restaurants after they closed. We worked at a particular smorgasbord restaurant in the western suburbs that became our home away from home. We'd get there after hours, let some friends in the back way, fire up the oven, cook some food and rehearse scenes. That's where we got a lot of our material. Then our friends would leave, we'd put the food away, clean up and go home. Those restaurant owners will never know the contributions they made to John Belushi's career.

JUDITH BELUSHI PISANO:

Once I graduated from Wheaton I went to school downstate at the University of Illinois at Champaign-Urbana. John considered joining me, but it was too expensive, and he wanted to keep his comedy troupe together, so he stayed at DuPage. Still, he managed to visit most weekends.

SUZE ORMAN, *friend*:

Judy and her roommate Carol and I became friends during our freshman year, and we all decided it would be far cheaper if we lived in an apartment together our sophomore year. We crammed into this very, very tiny one-bedroom apartment with three single beds for me, Carol and Judy—with Judy came John. So here, to our surprise, we have this man named John Belushi staying with us. It must have been every weekend, but it seemed like it was all the time.

Eventually his friends started coming down with him and putting on shows at a little place called the Red Herring. John would drive in, do his shows and we'd just hang out all the time eating dinner in this cramped kitchen in our apartment. We were like this little family that had been brought together.

None of us had any money whatsoever. We were all seriously, seriously broke. To say that we had the time of our lives would be putting it mildly.

JUDITH BELUSHI PISANO:

We had no money, but fortunately college life complements that. We didn't drink, and movies on campus were cheap. Our only real expense was pot. John and I were both complete hippies by that point. We smoked a lot of pot, which cost about twenty-five dollars a "lid" and would last about a week. Fortunately, we tracked down a notorious patch of weed growing in a cornfield outside the campus and, on a night raid, collected a few pillowcases full. We stashed them in our dorm closet and doled it out so it lasted most of the year. The

John's ultimate goal was always to get into Second City, but, of course, he did it his own way. He didn't sign up for their workshops. He developed his own company and let Second City discover him.

—Juanita Payne

*The West Compass Players:
John performing with Tino
Insana (bottom left) and
Steve Beshekas (top right)*

College days in Champaign-Urbana

grass was pretty harsh and really lame. We called it Rantoul Rag, named after a town in southern Illinois that we also thought of as lame.

STEVE BESHEKAS:

It was a crazy, fun time. Of course, that was also when the draft was about to be reinstated. Getting the deferments was one of the big reasons we were all still in school. We were all getting those letters from Uncle Sam in the mail. I know John got one.

JUDITH BELUSHI PISANO:

The shit hit the fan for John on December 1, 1969, the date of the first lottery draft since 1942. His number was fifty-nine. Since about thirty numbers a month would be called, John would have to go for a physical sometime early in his sophomore year. Under the new draft law, a college student could postpone his induction only until the end of the current semester. Only a senior could postpone until the end of the full academic year.

By that point the war was out of control in Vietnam, and the debate at home was more and more heated. John said he'd go to Canada before he'd be inducted. A friend from high school pulled a single digit number and had already retreated to the Great North.

About the end of February, John was ordered to report for a physical, mental and moral evaluation to determine whether he was fit for military service. John was a pretty hard-core radical and definitely not fit for military anything, but getting a determination to that effect was becoming difficult. There was a time you could just say you were homosexual or drop some acid during your physical and you'd be rejected, but those days were over.

John knew some fringe people from leftist groups like SDS, the Yippies and the Black Panthers. He collected as much information from them as he could and determined that his best bet was to play up this mysterious seizure that had put him in the hospital as a kid. At the end of the day, miraculously enough, his blood pressure was just a little too high. They said if three independent exams provided the same result, it would make him ineligible for the draft.

The same trail of acquaintances led John to a doctor who allegedly sympathized with draft dodgers. John set up the appointments, and a few days before the first test he started taking a lot of salt. Then, just before the appointment, he took a few laps around a nearby park. But something in John's demeanor made the doctor suspicious; his hippie *bona fides* were just a little too perfect. After the test, the doctor called him into his private office and asked him point blank if he was a narc. Well, imagine John's surprise—and newfound paranoia—when he realized he wasn't going to get any breaks from this guy. The stress alone probably spiked his blood pressure plenty. Ultimately, the plan worked. John was classified 1-Y: unfit for military service.

John Adam Belushi, draft card

TINO INSANA:

The summer of '70, John and I graduated from the two-year program at DuPage and transferred to the University of Illinois in Chicago. They called it Circle campus. We got an apartment in Chicago's Little Italy, safe and low rent—and I'm talking *really* low rent. We were right across the street from Al's Hot Dogs. Everyone at Al's Hot Dogs had a gun tucked up in his belt underneath his apron.

We went looking for a place for the West Compass Players to perform around our new campus and ended up finding this storefront, a coffee house in the Italian neighborhood surrounding campus. We called it the Universal Life Coffee House. We had hooked up with a guy who was a minister in

TINO INSANA:

John and I spent many of those formative sixties moments together. We were sitting around a table in my living room when they announced the position of everyone's birthdates in the draft lottery. We were sweating it.

During the '68 convention, there were thousands of people protesting down in Grant Park. Judy and John and I went down there. We were ten feet away from the incident that set off the riots. A group of guys started tipping over a Chicago police paddy wagon. They were rocking it back and forth and finally tipped it over. Well, the police went berserk. We were right at the very front of this mob, right at the flash point, just inches away from the riot police and their billy clubs. We ran up Congress and down State Street, ducked into a restaurant and watched the melee continue. I went home, but John stayed and got into more of the protests. He was reckless. He had balls.

the Universal Life Church. That way we got a piano at a discount, because we were a church group and not a theater group. It also got us a break on the rent.

My father was a maestro with the Grant Park Symphony, and he played piano for us. With his help we started doing a lot of opera, gibberish opera. Every Saturday night after the show, we'd take the money from the gate and head over to Diana's, this restaurant right across the bridge in Greek Town. John would invite most of the audience to come with us, and we'd treat them with the money they'd just paid us for the show. Usually we'd even end up spending a little more of our own. We'd get there about one in the morning, which was just about the time they were closing, but they'd stay open for us. There'd be a table of twenty-five or thirty people, and we'd eat shish kebab and drink ouzo and dance and smash plates until the sun came up. Then we'd all head back to our cars and go home.

RED FONTANO, *owner, Fontano's Subs*:

I owned a sandwich shop across the street from that church where they used to perform. John was one of the first college

On the Waterfront, *photos taken by John of his television*

kids to come through here. He and his buddies were always in the shop, ordering sandwiches or whatever. My wife would go over and make dinner for them sometimes. They used to goof around in the church, and then at night they'd hang out goofing around on the corner. I belonged to the social club across the street and I'd pass 'em out there most nights when I was headed home. They were not loud, not rowdy. They were good kids.

TINO INSANA:

Universal Life Coffee House pretty much screamed "hippies." Most of the Italians were very friendly to us, but there was a gang called the Taylor Street Dukes that felt very threatened by our presence. One night they came to the theater and started causing trouble. So John said, "Excuse me, but did you pay your one dollar admission?"

And the guy said, "Yeah, man, I paid."

"No, you didn't."

"Yes, I did. Who are you, *God*?"

Push came to shove, shove came to slug and then there was a huge fight. John and the leader of the gang went outside and suddenly the neighborhood exploded with members of this gang. A rough estimate would be about a million of 'em. It was an all-out *West Side Story* rumble. We locked the theater to protect the women and children inside. The university police came and the Chicago police came and finally everything settled down. John and the gang leader were questioned, and the proper people were arrested. John came back in the theater with a black eye and broken nose and finished the show. The next week we found a bullet hole in the side of our building. We closed the theater and decided to tour after that.

RED FONTANO:

John bought a truck from me once. There was a young lady from the neighborhood who got married, and on her wedding night her house burned down. All they had left was this old, paneled delivery truck, the kind with no windows on the sides. Her husband eventually committed suicide by pulling this truck into the garage and suffocating himself. Now the girl was really in a bad way. She needed money. She came to me and asked if I wanted this truck. I didn't need it, but I paid her seventy-five dollars for it just 'cause she needed the money. I parked it out front of the store, painted a big lemon on the side and put a sign on it that said "Fontano's Italian Ices"— and never used it.

John and his crew were across the street all the time and one day he came over and said, "Red, who owns that truck? It just sits there all the time."

I said, "That's mine."

"We wanna buy it. How much would you sell it for?"

"Well, I paid seventy-five dollars, so I want seventy-five dollars. I just want my money back."

"Done," he said. "We'll all pitch in and buy it."

"Fine. What the hell you wanna buy this thing for anyway?"

"I'm going to Hollywood."

"You're going to Hollywood? In that truck? Well, I wish you *bon voyage* 'cause you're out of your mind if you think this piece-of-shit truck is going to make it to Hollywood."

"No, no, no," he said. "Just sell me the truck."

So they scraped together and they bought it. And that was the last I seen or heard of John Belushi until one day I'm watching television and a commercial for this *Animal House* comes on. I just stared at the TV and I said, "I'll be a son of a bitch. He made it." ■

Chapter 4

EAT A BOWL
OF FUCK

a Second City first

DEL CLOSE, *director*:

John said to me once, "Del, do you know why I'm so comfortable onstage? It's because it's the only place in the world where I know what I'm doing."

Above: With Harold Ramis (right)

In the late forties and early fifties, the University of Chicago was a breeding ground for theatrical talent—this in spite of the fact that it had no theater department. In 1953, forced to find their own creative outlet, the students opened the Playwrights Theater in a converted Chinese restaurant in the Old Town section of Chicago. With director Paul Sills at the helm, they put on innovative stagings of Brecht, Chekov, Shakespeare and original plays.

But more exciting than the plays was what was going on offstage. Sills was a devoted believer in improvisation, drilling his actors in the art at every rehearsal. Improvisation as a training exercise was nothing new. Putting improv up before a live audience as a form of satirical commentary, however, would prove to be groundbreaking.

In 1955, the Playwrights Theater closed (ostensibly for fire code violations; possibly for leftist-pinko sympathies) making way for the Compass, where comic improv as we know it today was born. Drawing their ideas from audience suggestions and the day's newspapers, the Compass Players donned black suits and ties and put together a nightly revue that poked fun at the social and political norms of Eisenhower's America. In doing so, they developed a set of arcane and actorly precepts about trust and intelligence, rules that gave improv its guiding principles and underlying structure.

The Compass closed after only eighteen months, but it was reborn in spirit on December 16, 1959, with the arrival of Second City, a small cabaret at 1842 North Wells Avenue, once again in the heart of Old Town. Sills, now collaborating with co-owners Howard Alk and Bernie Sahlins, hoped to create a slightly more stable, upscale venue for their artistic venture. In a few short years, their small theater was the toast of Chicago, featuring such new talents as Alan Arkin, Joan Rivers, Avery Schreiber, Del Close, Robert Klein and Fred Willard. Packed to capacity every night, it was the hippest room in town.

By the end of the decade, however, the revues at Second City had grown, not stale, but comfortable. The performers were a bit older, the humor a bit softer. Outside in the streets, the country was in the midst of a great social, cultural and political upheaval. Inside Second City, however, what had been the revolutionary vanguard of Chicago's comedy and theater scene was now firmly established as a nice place to go for a couple of drinks and an evening of reliable entertainment.

In 1969, Sahlins and producer Joyce Sloane sought to remedy the situation with a complete overhaul of the cast. The older generation was soon replaced with The Next Generation, a younger, greener crew

In improv, you get people whose presence immediately establishes, "This is who I am," and that governs everything else in the scene. In most cases that's sufficient unto itself; the outcome of the sketch is almost predetermined. But what John was able to do—and there isn't a person who worked with him who won't admit this—was to take that reality and say, "This is mine and I'm moving it and I'm steering it." He was totally unique.

—Fred Kaz

that included such fresh faces as Brian Doyle-Murray, Jim Fisher, Eugenie Ross-Leming and Joe Flaherty—not to mention Harold Ramis and his remarkable head of hair. In capturing the revolutionary attitudes of the sixties, the new cast was a big step in the right direction, but the transformation wasn't quite complete. Then, in February of 1971, the company auditioned an uncommonly talented young man from the western suburb of Wheaton. For Second City's Next Generation, the missing link—in every sense of the word—had finally arrived.

JOYCE SLOANE, *producer*:

I was out at the College of DuPage seeing the director of student activities about booking the Second City touring company to play there. He said, "We don't need Second City. One of our students goes down, sees your show, comes back and does the whole thing for us."

"Oh, really?" I said. "I'd like to meet him."

"Well, as a matter of fact," he said, "he's right over there." And there John was, playing foosball in the student center. The director took me over and said, "John, there's someone here who would very much like to meet you."

He told John who I was, and I said, "I understand you're doing our material here at DuPage."

"Well, you know," he said, "I've got my own group and we're working on a lot of stuff. Why don't you come see us sometime?" I said I would. A few months later he came bounding up the stairs at Second City—he never just walked into a room—and handed me a flyer. His group was performing in a church someplace, and he wanted me to come and see them.

Several months later, the main troupe was leaving to do a series of shows at the Plaza Hotel in New York, and we were looking for a replacement company. We had been auditioning and auditioning. Finally I said, "I know who." I called John and he came in. Of course, he didn't come in alone. He'd

been invited to audition by himself, but he brought in Steve Beshakas, Tino Insana, his whole group.

BERNIE SAHLINS, *owner/director*:

John was, and still is, the only actor I've ever auditioned whom I not only immediately fell in love with, but immediately put into the main company. No serving time in the touring companies or any of that. He had something that you can't learn in school. Call it charisma, call it magnetism, he had it.

AGNES BELUSHI:

He just called me up one day after three years of college and said, "Mom, I'm gonna quit school. I know you're gonna be upset, but I've got a chance to go to Second City, and I have to take my opportunity while it's here."

Other than acting, there was never anything John really wanted to do. And he didn't really know what he was going to college for in the first place. So I just said, "Okay, if that's what you want, that's all right with me."

JUDY FLAHERTY, *cast member*:

John and I joined the replacement company at the same time. He had this wild hair and intimidating look. I immediately thought, oh no, what's this going to be like? So it was a real surprise when I found out he was such a delight to work with. I went home and told my husband Joe, "There is this guy in the replacement company who's so talented. Wait till you see him."

JOE FLAHERTY, *cast member*:

He was kind of strange looking. He didn't have a typical face; it was that exotic Albanian look. The first time I saw him I thought he was some sort of auto mechanic who'd wandered into the theater.

Chad Bumford

JUDITH BELUSHI PISANO:

Initially, Bernie suggested that John change his name. He insisted that "Belushi" was too difficult to remember. So John set about for a few weeks trying on new ones. He'd call me and say things like, "Belwish? John Belwish? Whaddaya think?" Then for a while he thought about just John Bell. Then I said, "How about John Chadworth?" Then for a few days he'd only answer the phone as Chad Bumford. Finally he said, "Fuck it, I'll just make sure they remember my name."

BRIAN DOYLE-MURRAY, *cast member*:

I was on a commercial shoot that went late one night when I was supposed to go onstage. I called Second City and told

them I wasn't going to make it. They said, "Oh, that's okay. We've got this kid." John replaced me that night, and when I got back to the theater everyone was talking about him, how he already knew all my parts and what a great job he'd done.

JUDITH BELUSHI PISANO:

When John went into the replacement cast, most of the roles he was given had been created by Brian Doyle-Murray. John watched the show a few times before they left for New York, absorbing every detail of Brian's performance. Later, when Brian returned, they became fast friends. Although they were very different performers, John learned a lot from studying Brian's roles and then working with him after they got back from New York. Brian influenced his pacing, taught him the value of subtlety, and showed him how to make a powerful character out of small gestures and moments. It was good training for John since his talents were pretty raw when he first showed up.

BERNIE SAHLINS:

John was the first of his generation who really hit us and I learned an awful lot from him. He was *the* symbol of the 1960s. For the people who grew up in those times, with the Vietnam War and so on, there was a certain attitude, a certain cynicism or irony that he exemplified. This is a form that's actually run by the actors and by the perceptions of the actors and the audience. John freed it up a bit, made it a little more daring, a little more risky. Second City changed a lot because of John.

JIM FISHER, *cast member*:

When we came in as a company in 1969, our first show was called *The Next Generation*, and we were supposed to be this breath of fresh air. We were the first ones not to wear the traditional black suits, white shirts and ties. Our first reviews basically said, "They're more 'with it' than the previous company, but they're not quite there yet."

And by being this *new* Second City, what we were really trying to do was be the *old* Second City in terms of freshness and originality. It wasn't until *43rd Parallel*, the third revue that we did with John, that we finally started getting the reviews that said, "*This* is the old Second City." John had a lot to do

The company (from left): Joe Flaherty, John, Harold Ramis, Jim Fisher, Eugenie Ross-Leming and Judy Morgan

with that. He was the missing ingredient that put us over the top. Most of your typical Second City audience was the white, liberal University of Chicago crowd. John connected with more of "Da Bears" crowd, the average, blue-collar folks.

HAROLD RAMIS, *cast member*:

For Bernie, John represented some inevitable cultural change that he didn't fully embrace but that he appreciated and understood. John brought a street element onto the stage. It cut through the intellectual pretense of the theater. Second City always prided itself on a really high level of reference, whether it was intellectual, literary, political or whatever. John countered that by bringing street language and vulgarity into the mix. He brought rock and roll to the show. It was like what was happening with the whole generation.

The Chicago Seven conspiracy hearings were going on at that time and Abbie Hoffman was coming by the theater a lot to play with us onstage. Since John was already playing Abbie Hoffman, Abbie Hoffman played Julius Hoffman, the judge in the trial. Things were happening, and we felt like we were very cutting edge. Second City was always outrageous, but when John came that kind of solidified it. He took us even further than we had previously dared to go.

EUGENIE ROSS-LEMING, *cast member*:

John established the frontier. He was on point for the rest of us. He could go insane up there, and then we would know what side sanity was on—it would be just south of John. And you could push him. If you upped your level of insanity, he'd go you one better.

JIM FISHER:

Up until then you were not allowed to use any charged words onstage. No "shit." No "fuck." I think we were allowed one "shit" per show. If you had to curse that was considered a cheat. You were just using the word to get the laugh. But John fought against that over-intellectual attitude. His attitude was, "This is how people talk." We created a sketch called "The World's Most Obnoxious Houseguest," basically as a device for John to be as tasteless as possible. We figured it would help get it out of his system and also sort of contain it within the show.

EUGENIE ROSS-LEMING:

In "The World's Most Obnoxious Houseguest," I played the daughter who brings this boy home to meet her parents, who are like, "Ugh, ick, what are we going to do about our daughter dating this guy?"

THE BIBLE

JIM FISHER:

We were watching *Dark Shadows*, which was this soap opera about vampires. And we sat around saying, "They're running out of material for soap operas. What could possibly be left for them to make into a soap opera?" And the answer was obvious: the Bible. So we came up with a sketch where Mary has to tell Joseph why she's a pregnant virgin.

The first day we did the bit, John was late to rehearsal. John was always late. And we had all grabbed what we *thought* would be the choice parts. I took Joseph. I mean, you can't go wrong with Joseph. By the time John showed up, it was like, "Oh, what's left? Well, I guess there's the angel who delivers the message. John, you can be the Angel Gabriel."

HAROLD RAMIS:

To play the angel John took this leather World War I flying cap and goggles and these little paper wings from backstage. He had learned that if he walked a certain way, very delicately, he could make those little tiny wings flap. So he made this very long, slow entrance. It took forever for him to cross the stage, making these little wings flap with every step, and the audience was howling all the way. It was hysterical. That's when I understood the incredible magnetic power he had.

JIM FISHER:

That was it. He came on, gave one line and got off—and he took the whole scene.

And the daughter says, "C'mon, he's not that bad. He's just a little rough around the edges."

Then John comes out and—you know the gesture guys make when they're exaggerating about the size of a fish they've caught? Well, John comes out and says, "Man, I just laid,"—holds out his hands—"the biggest turd of my life in your toilet. C'mon, I left it in the bowl so you could check it out."

None of us were prepared for it at all, but he did it with such poise and confidence that it was hilarious. Every night he'd change the entrance line and every night it was a challenge for him to see how he would out-gross himself. It was a challenge well met. The audience just collapsed under the sheer weight of how gross it was, and they laughed. They had no choice but to laugh or run screaming from the building.

HAROLD RAMIS:

I had come back in '72 to do the show after a sabbatical, and by then John was a very popular member of the company. I had been playing the long-haired guy, the hippie, the freak, the radical. But when I came back, John was in the spot, and he genuinely *was* all of those things. At first I was a little threatened, and then I really liked him.

This sounds kind of pathetic, but before John showed up I really felt like I had a big following at Second City. Then the first night I saw him improvising onstage I thought, God, I will never take chances like that. I don't have that kind of courage. I admired it, feared it and realized it would take John really far and would always inhibit me. But there was always something safer and more comfortable about being me than there was about being him.

EUGENIE ROSS-LEMING:

He would hurt himself. He'd walk into a wall to get a laugh, and if, God forbid, you were standing next to that wall you might get whacked. It was like an ER when John was onstage. He could take the pain, so he genuinely did not understand how the concept of caution might be a priority for someone else. He was manic and yet utterly calm and controlled in his mania at the same time. He didn't care about the pain because the prize on the other side of the pain was a laugh.

JUDY FLAHERTY:

Literally the second John walked onstage he grabbed everyone's attention. People were dying to see what he was going to do next. What was so impressive about it was that *it just happened.* He didn't do it on purpose. If anything, he tried to tone himself down so he wouldn't dominate the scene. It was hard on the other actors. Sometimes you'd be in the middle of a great scene and people would be looking offstage to see when he was coming on next.

FRED KAZ, *musical director*:

When John came onstage, everything else was just dressing for him.

HAROLD RAMIS:

John could steal a scene just by raising an eyebrow. Plus, he had kind of an odd body anyway, very short legged, so he just looked really funny. Also, in 1972 every counterculture guy walked around dressed like he was going to be on an album cover, and John was the worst.

John introduced a whole new language to the stage with the classic line "Eat a bowl of fuck." I still don't know what it means.

—Harold Ramis

DICK BLASUCCI:

John used to dress horribly onstage, just horribly. Torn-up jeans, ratty shirts. It got so bad that Bernie finally said, "John, either you get a new wardrobe or you're not going on." So John went out to the store and came back the next night with these big red platform shoes and these awful checkered pants— and not as a joke. This was really his idea of what Bernie meant by "nice clothes." Joe Flaherty said it was the loudest outfit he'd ever seen anybody wear. Joe's greatest gift onstage was causing trouble, and that night he was merciless. Every time John entered, no matter what was happening in the scene, Joe would just scream in horror at the sight of this outfit. It was the last night John ever wore those clothes.

EUGENIE ROSS-LEMING:

John's dominating the stage eventually became something of a problem. Everybody was giving him little hints backstage that he was getting excessive, but he didn't take them. So everybody decided to band together one night and fuck with him. When you're out on that stage you're naked. All you've got besides your raw talent are the alliances you form with the other performers. It's a foxhole mentality. A basic improv rule is that you accept whatever you're given and you build on it. But that night we didn't follow any of his leads and left him all alone. We figured we'd give him an object lesson in team playing. It really confused him because it was such a unified effort. Finally, Joe had to take him aside and talk to him about it.

JOE FLAHERTY:

You always have to be careful in group scenes, because you have to share the focus with everyone else. At one point in the scene when John wasn't the focus, he decided that he was going to tie off his arm, shoot up with heroin and pass out in the corner. He wasn't trying to steal the scene; he was just looking for some stage business to do. But of course everyone in the audience immediately fixed on John, as they always did.

Well, it kind of wrecked the scene and everyone was a little pissed. After the show I went to John and I said, "Look, you're good. You're really good. But what you have to do is you have to be aware of the give and take with the actors around you. Let everyone participate."

"I know, I know," he said. "It's just that I'm having so much fun up there that I get carried away." He was genuinely humble about it. I really liked him, and so I was never really upset with him. Once we had that talk everything was fine.

It was the first time I came up against anything that I would call star power, whatever that is. He just had that quality. John was younger than the rest of us, too. He was really into the music scene. Everything was about the music to those kids, and in that sense John was much more of a hippie than the rest of us were.

Fred Kaz, our musical director, was great, but musically he was very jazz-oriented. So whenever Fred was on vacation, my brother Paul would sit in, and that gave John the chance to really do some of his rock and roll stuff.

PAUL FLAHERTY, *musician*:

John and I hit it off very well. I was a guitarist in a band, and John always had that side to him that wanted to be a rock star. But there was no one for him to collaborate with and learn from until I sat down and started working and playing with him.

EUGENIE ROSS-LEMING:

After the shows on Saturday nights, we'd be too wired to go home and John, Paul and I would go jam. We had a little warehouse storage space where we'd go around three o'clock in the morning, not the safest time or place, but we'd just unlock the freight elevator, go into this warehouse and play. I was a bad bass player, John was a bad drummer and Paul was a good guitar player.

JOE FLAHERTY:

He loved doing his Joe Cocker. He was always looking for ways to sneak it in, sometimes without rhyme or reason. He'd

With Eugenie Ross-Leming

be in the middle of an office scene and say, "Well, after work there's going to be this big concert, see…" And then all of a sudden there's Joe Cocker in the middle of the office. Eventually it became so much of a reach that that became the joke.

FRED KAZ:

Over and above everything else, what he had was a natural talent for creating characters. One of the reasons people like John reach the level of fame that they do is that they create these characters that everyone can identify with, characters that are funny because of their reality, not because of punch lines.

THE FUNERAL

JIM FISHER:

Joyce Sloane had brought the cast to the funeral of a friend of hers. We were all sitting in the back, something struck us as funny and we were trying not to laugh. When we got back to rehearsal, Joe suggested doing something based on that idea of being at some solemn occasion and trying to stifle a laugh. Then Del Close said, "You know, I've always wanted to do a sketch about a guy who dies with a gallon can of Van Camps beans on his head."

"Great!"

So we decide to do it that night. We divvy up parts, and John's playing the son of the dead guy. It was one of those golden moments that was perfectly set as it was improvised that first night out. Every beat was great. It never really changed after that and has gone on to become one of the great sketches in the history of Second City.

EUGENIE ROSS-LEMING:

The scene starts out with John and his mother and the priest. Judy Morgan does the grieving mother totally straight through the whole thing, and every time a guest shows up he or she says, "I just heard about Bill's passing. How did he die?"

And you see John start to squirm as his mother tells the story of how his father died: getting his head stuck in a family-sized can of Van Camp's pork and beans. It's such an ignoble death that every time she tells the story, John goes into these contortions—banging his fist, pulling his hair out—because he's so embarrassed. But he has to be respectful and he can't tell her to shut up.

The whole point of the scene, as the characters, was to stifle the urge to laugh in this widow's face. But you're onstage looking over at John, who's just eating the scenery, and it keeps getting harder and harder, as an actor, not to burst out laughing at what he's doing. And as more and more of us get onstage and take our places in the pew, you have that contagious group thing of everyone trying not to laugh, and the audience is laughing because they can all identify with that idea of being in a place where you're not supposed to laugh—and the whole thing just feeds off itself. Then it ends with the mother standing up for the eulogy and saying, "I can still remember his last words: 'I think there's a little bit more left at the bottom. I think I'll look.'" At which point John goes completely insane.

But John would change it and escalate it every night. He'd tear his clothes off, try to hang himself. You never knew what was coming. And that's what made the sketch work. Our whole task as actors in that sketch was not to laugh, but you couldn't help but laugh at John.

JIM BELUSHI:

At Second City there were a lot of "left side of the brain" people, as Del Close would call them. Very intellectual, very witty, couldn't move worth a damn. Couldn't do any kind of physical humor. But John was a behavioralist. He was a great mimic; he would just observe people and then bring it all onstage. In that way he changed Second City. All they used to talk about was Descartes and Kant, moral dilemma and free will. And John would come in and play this hippie off the street who'd lost his memory from smoking too much pot, and the audience loved it because it was like a real person speaking.

JOE FLAHERTY:

John did a lot of drug humor. And the audience wanted a lot of drug humor; they ate it up. Those were the times we were in. Drugs were a part of our life, especially with Del Close as an inspiration saying that they enhanced your artistic vision. Everyone was experimenting with the grass and the LSD. It was even encouraged to a certain extent. The only difference was that John could perform on most of them. He could go onstage and you couldn't tell.

HAROLD RAMIS:

Our generation saw drug use as a kind of psychic experiment. People were validating it as an exploration of consciousness and all that. You could kid yourself for a long time.

EUGENIE ROSS-LEMING:

John and I did this particular pharmaceutical one night, one that neither of us had ever done before. It was amazing. The top of my skull unzipped, opened up and pieces of my brain floated away. This was early on a Saturday night, which meant we had two regular shows and an improv left, and we had no idea how we were going to get through them. We couldn't remember our entrances, our cues. We clung to each other, both physically and psychologically, just to make it through the night. And we did. Everything turned out okay.

After the last improv set, we went out in the street and just wandered around. We were so embarrassed. John was such an excessive person. He'd eat to excess, he'd hurt himself to excess. But when I saw him the next day, it was the one time I ever heard him say, "I went too far. I got too close to the edge." We had a show to do that night, and we were very worried, like we might have done some kind of permanent damage. Then we had the exact same thought. I said, "I'm really, really scared. What if—"

"—I can't be funny any more."

He finished my sentence for me. Now, I was worried about brain damage on a whole bunch of levels, but for John, the mere idea that he wouldn't be funny anymore was simply terrifying. I had never seen John be afraid of anything, but the look of sheer horror on his face said, "If I can't be funny then…what am I going to do?"

We both felt horrible. We made a deal, a pact, we said, "God, if you let me still be funny, I will *never* do this again." We went back onstage that night, and we were still funny. We were so grateful. But things go on. They return to normal, and eventually you forget that deal you made with God.

PAUL FLAHERTY:

Judy was a great influence on John. She was rock solid, and she always brought him back down to earth. When she came to visit he would suddenly become more organized, less scattered, more focused. His routine would change. As wild and talented and impulsive as he was, whenever some sort of order was imposed on him it had a good effect. And he knew that about himself. When Bernie used to crack down on him, John would say that he could feel himself performing better onstage. And Judy did that for him, too.

JUDITH BELUSHI PISANO:

It was clear early on that John liked to be part of a close-knit group. The Second City community was very tight. He liked the family-like setting, and the schedule and commitment provided a comforting routine.

After the shows we usually hung out with friends, smoked pot and listened to music or watched TV. If we were watching a movie we thought was great, John would call Joe and say, "Hey, are you watching this?" And they'd start plotting out a parody. They were all very focused on doing the show and keeping up on current events.

HAROLD RAMIS:

We would meet midday for breakfast at Lum's, this coffee shop on the corner of Wells and North Avenue, and just look through the papers, see what was happening and if there was any material in it. We would kind of check in with each other on where the media and the culture were going, and then characters would emerge.

PAUL FLAHERTY:

John and I wound up being roommates at his apartment a couple of blocks from Second City. After the show he'd be up for hours. Somewhere around two o'clock in the morning he'd always want to take a walk down to the all-night restaurant and grab a bite, which took some getting used to. John was an extremely bright guy, which certainly belies the image of Bluto that people have of him. Sure, it was not the neatest apartment in the world, but he read all the time. He was particularly interested in Napoleon. He was almost a fanatic about him.

JUDITH BELUSHI PISANO:

I always found John's quirks very amusing. During his Napoleon period, I would catch him striking poses, say with his hand in his vest, or with a smug, self-satisfied expression. There was a walk he occasionally fell into that I just knew was Napoleon, a purposeful stride, hands locked behind his back, head held high. He even woke me up once in the middle of the night when he blurted out in his sleep, *"I will ride at the head of my men! I will ride a white horse!"*

HAROLD RAMIS:

It wasn't a real wild and crazy time. There weren't any big misadventures, mostly just a lot of hanging out at the theater and putting the show together. We were all married. I was married at the time to my first wife, and Joe Flaherty was

married as well. John and Judy weren't officially married, but they were together.

JUDITH BELUSHI PISANO:

The summer before my junior year of college, I secretly lived in Chicago with John without telling my parents. They thought I was in summer school. When I transferred from Champaign to the Chicago Circle campus at mid-semester, to live with John, I finally had to tell them.

JEAN JACKLIN:

One night we got a call from John and Judy asking if they could come talk to us. They came over and John walked in very, very serious. We were watching television, and John said, "Could you turn the television off, please?" We thought we knew what was coming: they wanted to get married. John settled down on the couch and looked at us very intently. "Mr. and Mrs. Jacklin," he said, "Judy and I would like to live together."

That one really stumped us. I mean, Judy hadn't even finished college yet.

JUDITH BELUSHI PISANO:

When I saw my parents' expressions I started crying, but John was great. He took my hand and said, "Judy and I love each other and want to live together. I'm making good money now, and I can take care of us." Of course my dad suggested marriage, and John gave the rap on not needing a piece of paper. Considering the situation, my parents were pretty accepting. In time they came to respect and appreciate the fact that John had the—in their words—"gumption" to come and ask for their blessing.

SUZE ORMAN:

John got arrested. He had some unpaid parking tickets, a lot of them. He went in to renew some license and they threw him in jail. They were broke, and Judy's parents didn't know she was living with John yet, so she called to ask me to ask my father for twenty-five dollars to bail John out of jail. The only way John could pay my dad back was by giving us free tickets to see him at Second City. I still didn't think

JUDITH BELUSHI PISANO:

By the second summer of working at Second City, John was restless. The repetition and the long hours grew tiresome for both of us. I would see him after the show for a few hours and then on Mondays if he didn't have extra work. Even though he hadn't really been onstage there that long, he felt it was time to move on. He wasn't sure how to make the next step in his career, or even what it was. So we kind of went the other way, completely dropped out and moved to Colorado to be hippies alone in the wilderness.

A friend of ours had a cabin in the middle of nowhere that he said we could use. It was an hour outside of Boulder and a twenty-minute drive to the nearest civilization. We had about six hundred dollars and no car, but my brother lived in Aspen and agreed to drive us out there. We got there and pulled over to get out. John had been sleeping in the back seat and was a bit groggy. He opened the door, stepped out without really looking and plunged about thirty feet down into this ravine. He pinched a nerve in his back, but we didn't realize how bad it was until my brother had already gone and left us there alone the next day. John couldn't walk and spent most of the next three weeks on the couch while I did my best to keep things together. Finally, we ran out of money and had to call Joyce and ask her to buy us plane tickets home. John went back onstage, and that was pretty much the end of our great hippie experiment.

he was going to make it, but Judy adored him, absolutely adored him. She stuck with him when most of us were like, "What are you doing with this guy?" But the thing was, there was only *one* John. If you let him go, odds were you'd never find another.

HAROLD RAMIS:

One day we helped John and Judy move out of their apartment. They were cleaning out all their stuff when John found an old checkbook from a defunct bank account. He wrote me out a check for a million dollars. I still have it. We used to joke about John's ambition. If there were a producer or some scout in the house, John would be the first one out there.

BERNIE SAHLINS:

At the end of each evening the big applause was always for John. This is when he was onstage with people like Joe and Harold, people with a lot of talent and a lot more experience. John never had any arrogance about what was happening to

Second City offered him stability. It kept him level and in touch with reality for a while. John was always excessive and always wanted to do more and more and more. He didn't have a lot of patience. He always wanted to move on, and he knew he was gonna make it; there was no question in his mind that he was gonna make it.

—Joyce Sloane

him. He always respected the other people, and he learned very quickly because he never felt like he knew it all.

DICK BLASUCCI:

John was already becoming, in local terms, a bit of a celebrity. He was so good in the Second City revues that he was being hailed as the star of the shows and getting a lot of good press.

JIM FISHER:

He used to carry his reviews around in his wallet. One morning we went to the local KABC TV station to do a promo for the upcoming revue. Dick Cavett had come in from New York and he was the main guest. While we were there John walked over to him, stuck out his hand and introduced himself. Then he pulled out his reviews and handed them to him as if to say, "Hi. I'm John Belushi, and here's what people are saying about me."

JOE FLAHERTY:

One night Cliff Robertson came to see the show, as many celebrities often did. He came backstage and congratulated us, singling out John and saying he might like to work with him someday. John was ecstatic. He really thought this was big. So Harold and I hatched a scheme. We left a message at the box office that said, "John, call me at once. Have a movie I want you to be in. Cliff Robertson." John went nuts.

He was just bursting with ambition. From the time he showed up I was wondering how long it would be until he took off. To see what he was like as a person when he was right on the cusp of being famous was fascinating. When you're young like that you're so eager to learn, and you don't have the ego thing going as much. You're just finding your way through life. And that's the way I remember John best, from the Chicago days. After he got famous it was different, more of the Al Capone thing, like, "Oh, yes, anything you want, Mr. Belushi!" But

before that he was still young and drinking everything in and having a good time.

JUDITH BELUSHI PISANO:

Peter Elbling, who'd been in the replacement cast with John, phoned and told him about a new *National Lampoon* off-Broadway show called *Lemmings*. The whole second act was a musical parody of Woodstock. If there was anything John had ever wanted in his life, this was it. He went after it with a vengeance.

DICK BLASUCCI:

I was in the bar at Second City the day he got *Lemmings*. He said, "I auditioned for this New York show. I think I'm gonna take it." That show was perfect for him. It had music. It was subversive. It was right up his alley. It wasn't surprising that New York found him. You kind of knew it was only a matter of time. We knew that in high school.

AGNES BELUSHI:

John called and said, "Mom, you're not going to like this, but I'm going to New York to work with the *National Lampoon*."

John thought I'd be ashamed of him because it was a risqué magazine, but I didn't even really know what the *National Lampoon* was. I said, "Listen, you're not going to do that all your life. If it's a stepping stone to where you wanna go, go ahead."

Just before he hung up he said to me, "I can't help you and dad right now." Our financial problems were quite severe at the time. "This could take a long, long time. So if you don't hear from me, or I don't call you, it's because I can't help you. I have to think about myself and my career now, and then when things are okay and I can help you, I will."

"That's okay," I said.

And that's what he did. ∎

Chapter 5

DO NOT TAKE THE BROWN STRYCHNINE

a lemming's life

TONY HENDRA, *director*:

If there were any way to eviscerate the sacred cows of the Woodstock generation, to bring the savagery of the *National Lampoon* to the stage, John Belushi was the guy to do it. His intense, chaotic presence reached across the footlights and grabbed you by the eardrums. He was the medium and the message rolled into one ferocious package.

In 1969, a small-time magazine publisher and former Diners Club executive named Matty Simmons hired a couple of kids from the Harvard Lampoon to start a new humor magazine. From its first simple, unsophisticated issues, the National Lampoon would go on to boast a staggering array of talent and dominate American comedy for an entire decade. By 1972, two years of steadily increasing success yielded the magazine's first comedy album, Radio Dinner. It was written and performed largely by Lampoon editors Tony Hendra and Michael O'Donoghue, and by a very young Christopher Guest. The album's sales were moderate, but the publicity surrounding it helped to sell magazines. And so, in late summer of that year, Simmons charged Hendra with producing a follow-up.

The Lampoon had made its name by gleefully and viciously attacking the tent poles of American culture. In the realm of music, the obvious target was the live concert album. In the realm of live concert albums, the obvious target was Woodstock. It was not only a concert album but also the defining moment of a movement and a generation.

The gospel preached from Max Yasgur's upstate New York farm had been quite simple: that the spirit of sex, drugs and rock and roll would tear the establishment down and bring us to some higher plain where there would be lots of world peace and communal farming. Much

like the Vietnam War itself, an idea better in theory than in practice. The sex, drugs and rock and roll proved to be so much fun on their own that nobody really got around to any of the world peace. Or, for that matter, very much farming.

In 1972, most of the flower children were still happily riding the Magic Bus to Fantasyland, lost in a psychedelic haze. But that October, in spite of all the sit-ins, love-ins and bed-ins, Richard Nixon was cruising to a breezy reelection. Unlike the civil rights revolution, the much-ballyhooed rock-and-roll revolution had been less about revolution and more about royalty checks. Janis and Jimi weren't so much martyrs for the cause as they were just very, very dead. Among the caustic, cynical Lampooners, a certain amount of disillusionment was beginning to set in. Simply put, the 1960s were ripe for a good beating, and they were about to get it.

SEAN KELLY, *writer*:

After *Radio Dinner* it was determined that the *Lampoon* should do another album. And the question was the laugh track. How do people know it's funny? Rather than put a laugh track in, Tony and I had this notion: what if we did it in front of a live audience? That way we'd have real laughs, even if we sweetened them in the mix. That's why the cast recording was done so early in the run—there wasn't supposed to *be* a run. It was just supposed to be a couple of weeks, maybe, to get an album with real laughs on it. That's part of the reason everything was so chaotic.

TONY HENDRA:

A live rock concert was the best means for us to throw many different performers together, but simply to parody Woodstock didn't seem quite enough, or very easy. There hadn't been anything very despicable about Woodstock itself, except perhaps the self-importance of its performers. But the hopes it had embodied were crumbling daily as the criminal in the White House headed toward another four years of sleaze. What was going wrong? What was our generation's character flaw?

Our answer was self-destruction: Woodstock as a celebration of mass suicide, a generation hurling itself off the cliff by every available means. We called the concert Woodshuck—A Festival of Peace, Love and Death, and wrote songs that would reflect the myriad ways our generation had chosen to opt out of life—to become politically ineffective, culturally impotent, personally self-obsessed or just plain dead. In a word: lemmings.

CHRISTOPHER GUEST, *writer/performer*:

Jerry Taylor, one of the publishers of the *Lampoon,* was a friend of my family. He called me in 1970 and asked me if I wrote.

"Sure, yeah, I write," I said. I'd never written a word.

"Great! Why don't you come in and meet me at this new magazine we're starting."

So my friend Tom Leopold and I wrote an article for one of the first issues. What I really wanted to do, though, was music. Sean Kelly and I worked together very closely on songs and sketches for *Radio Dinner,* and I brought in Bob Tischler and Paul Jacobs, a producer and a musician I knew, to work on it as well. When the idea for a stage show came up, we started writing songs for that. Then when we started to cast the show I brought in Chevy, who I had gone to school with.

CHEVY CHASE, *writer/performer*:

I knew nothing about acting on a stage. I was hired because they needed people who could play two instruments and also

It was a show about death, in essence.
—Alice Playten

be funny, and I could play the drums and the piano. I was pretty bad really, but I got better as the show went on.

JUDITH BELUSHI PISANO:

When Peter Elbling called John about *Lemmings,* we didn't know anything about the *Lampoon.* He told us to check out *Radio Dinner.* On the whole, it wasn't our sense of humor, but hey, at least they'd made an album. Peter knew the fellow who would be directing the show and told him about John.

John couldn't sit idly by hoping the *Lampoon* would call, so he borrowed someone's old reel-to-reel to make an audition tape. It was so low tech. We recorded it in the apartment—I think at one point there was a meow in the background—and had no editing capability. Everything was straight to tape. It was raw, but we thought it was pretty funny and it showed John's range of characters.

TONY HENDRA:

I'd been told there was a young kid at Second City named Belushi who did some musical stuff. I didn't even need to call. In my office the next day appeared a tape, mailed from Chicago. The tape contained a series of impressions, mostly of Brando and Truman Capote, all very tedious—and an absolutely brilliant takeoff of Joe Cocker. John really wanted the job. He called the next day. I told him I loved the Cocker and didn't like anything else. He urged me to come out to Chicago and check him out.

EUGENIE ROSS-LEMING:

The night that *National Lampoon* came to check John out, his eyeballs were spinning in his head. He wasn't nervous; he was just enormously psyched. I think he felt like he had it in the bag.

JOE FLAHERTY:

We knew that Hendra was going to be there that night so we worked it out that the show would be a showcase for John, fitting in Joe Cocker, as many musical things as we could, because we knew the *Lampoon* thing was going to be a musical.

TONY HENDRA:

What I saw at Second City was outrageous. John inserted himself into practically every sketch in a two-hour show. If he felt like entering a scene, he did it without rhyme or reason, with irrelevant characters, listening to no one, taking the action wherever it would leave him front and center. After a while I stopped trying to gauge his talent, which was clearly enormous, and just sat back to enjoy the audacity of what he was doing. A generation of hallowed, culturally acclaimed satiric theater was hanging over his head, but he didn't give a damn.

MATTY SIMMONS, *publisher*:

Tony went to Chicago, and he called me after the show. "This guy is unbelievable. Just fantastic. He ripped the place apart."

"Make sure he can play music," I told him. So Tony went to his house that night and asked John to play something. John took a guitar and played a song. It was okay; it wasn't great. Tony said, "Good. Can you play anything else?" And John played the same thing over again. Turns out he'd asked Paul Flaherty to teach him a song, and that was the only one he knew how to play.

JOE FLAHERTY:

Hendra called a couple of weeks later, made the offer and John was gone.

TONY HENDRA:

When he got to New York, it was not what he expected. I don't recall how long he was here before Judy joined him, but

> **SEAN KELLY:**
> Tony phoned and told me he'd gone to Chicago and made this terrific find. That was John. He was very excited about that. And then he phoned me and said, "I've got another guy that Chris Guest recommended. He's a pain in the ass but he has teen appeal." And that was Chevy Chase.

I spent a lot of time with him keeping his spirits up. He was very lonely, and very depressed about being lonely. This brazen, bushy-haired monster whom I had met in Chicago seemed suddenly to be a very young kid, which indeed he was.

ALICE PLAYTEN, *writer/performer*:

He had a very sad, puppy dog quality about him that made us all think we needed to take care of him. He'd been in New York for a couple of weeks, and it was Thanksgiving and he had no place to go. I invited him to come over to my folks' for dinner, but he wound up going home to Chicago to be with Judy.

GARY GOODROW, *writer/performer*:

John had a certain working-class feel to him that I shared and felt a great affinity for. After that first rehearsal he turned to me and said something like, "Let's get the fuck out of here and go get a cigarette." We got along instantly. He spent a few days on my couch while he looked for a place.

JUDITH BELUSHI PISANO:

I stayed in Chicago to pack us up and clear out our apartment. Money was tight and phone calls were expensive, so John would call every night to talk and we'd try to keep the time down. He was thrilled to finally be in Manhattan. He'd talk all the

time about Brando and Dylan and all these people who'd made it in New York.

He was clearly nervous about the show. There wasn't a feeling of camaraderie like there'd been at Second City. He was feeling alternately up and down, and he had an overwhelming sense of loneliness. He wanted me to get there as soon as possible. But he'd had one cool new experience. Someone had given him a hit of cocaine, and it was fantastic.

PAUL JACOBS, *musician/performer*:

The first day John came into the *Lampoon* offices, he was wearing a green army jacket and he had long hair and a beard. He had a teddy-bear voice, very much an "I'm a nice guy" voice. John used to joke with me that he and I were the only two real hippies in the show. We definitely looked the part a little more than the rest of the people.

JUDITH BELUSHI PISANO:

John got on with Alice, Paul and Gary right off. Chevy and Chris were harder nuts to crack. They had more of a private-school, put-down kind of humor, and John was an easy mark. He was from the Midwest, he was overweight, he hadn't graduated from college, he was ethnic—no, even better—he was *Albanian*. This was all good fodder.

TONY HENDRA:

The problem between Chris and John was instant. Chris had seen *Lemmings* very much as his baby, and in some ways it was. He was officially the music director of the show and had written several of the songs. But he also thought that he was going to have a lot of input into the comedy, which would be the Chris Guest kind of comedy—cool and calculated and very laid back. But the minute—and I mean the minute—Belushi came into the room, his raw energy took over. I could just see Chris wilt. There was always this tension between them, which in some ways was a very useful tension. If the show had been all Belushi or all Guest, it would've been very tedious.

CHRISTOPHER GUEST:

I don't think there was a conflict between John and me. I grew up in New York City and just had a slightly different attitude, I suppose. But I wouldn't say our relationship was difficult. I think John was extremely insecure, and when he came to New York he was just overwhelmed. I can't say whether he was intimidated by me, per se, but he certainly was intimidated.

TONY HENDRA:

John was not intimidated in the least. He said he was, but he wasn't. He thought he could handle anything.

The cast (from left): Mary Jennifer Mitchell, Alice Playten, Gary Goodrow, Chris Guest, Chevy Chase (at piano) and John

JUDITH BELUSHI PISANO:

The move to New York City was rough. Manhattan was overwhelming: high energy, loud, cold and endless. Eventually we were able to move down to a walk-up apartment on Third Avenue and Thirteenth, but for the first month, *Lampoon* put us up at the Roosevelt Hotel in midtown. It was the holiday season, which meant the streets were teeming with people, self-absorbed, fast-walking Manhattanites brushing each other aside with bags stuffed with presents. The neighborhood was expensive, and we were a good distance from the theater.

It seemed like a foreign land, and we were very alone. Early on, the cast members might have a drink after rehearsal, but in general everyone went their own way. The contrast with Second City was striking. Second City provided a home for the cast. Here it was cold and impersonal. The working environment was uncomfortable. Everyone was very competitive, and the show totally lacked direction.

CHEVY CHASE:

Tony had never directed anything before, or since. John actually wound up helping him work out some of the improv exercises we used. To me they were very foreign, the kinds of strange things people do in acting classes. It wasn't as bad as "be a chair," but it was things of that nature. I don't remember John ever "taking charge," but he just had confidence. He was somebody you could look up to for doing it the right way. He never seemed to be tight. He was always loose, but he was always in command. I was very relaxed and loose too, but not as disciplined. I would overplay.

SEAN KELLY:

John would play with something until he had it, and then it locked. He would do that the same in every performance. Not everything, mind you, but if he knew something worked, then it worked. Whereas Chase never trusted the material. He always had to prop up the joke. He'd pick his nose in the middle of the joke and get the laugh on the nose pick but blow the joke. Very much not John's style.

ALICE PLAYTEN:

There was no script, and wherever you left off the day before was not where you picked up the day after. I came out of much more of a straight acting background. I'd done several plays on Broadway, starting as a child, and so I kept waiting for a script to arrive. It never did.

TONY HENDRA:

One of the consequences of putting on a live show for this live album was that, on top of everything else, we had to mount a full-blown off-Broadway revue with ticket sales and advertising and everything else. We would also have to assemble far more material than would normally be needed for a comedy album.

John was very frustrated at first because he didn't think the work was going well, and he was right. I'd been given a mandate to use material from the magazine as a basis for the show. While everybody said they loved the *Lampoon*, its humor was actually very extreme. The improvisation and so forth was not working. To the degree that it was scripted, it didn't work either. It just didn't work. Actors don't talk like magazines.

SEAN KELLY:

We wrote a long sketch for the first act that was based on the *1964 High School Yearbook Parody*. The big joke there was John dancing with Chevy while Chevy wore a bra with falsies. The high-school yearbook worked so brilliantly because it was a parody of a form. It did not lend itself to the stage.

One thing that Tony and I were really keen on in the first act was this parody of *Jesus Christ Superstar* that we'd written. It was called *Jackie Christ Superstar*, and the premise was Jesus as a Borscht Belt standup comic. It was extremely blasphemous. Hendra and I had both been fucked over by religious maniacs for a long time, and we tended to drift in that direction.

John played Pontius Pilate in this thing as the Godfather. We needed Chris Guest to play Jackie, but Chris didn't get it at all. The bit was supposed to be Jackie Christ coming out and

doing his routine, something like, "Now, I don't want to say my parents were poor…but I was born in a stable. Nay, verily. Take the meek, please. Bless you very much!" And then John would come out as Don Corleone and crucify him.

But Chris hated it. And the audience never got it. Half of them didn't know what the hell we were doing, and the other half were deeply, deeply offended. It was the definition of a bomb.

TONY HENDRA:

The cast was incredibly impatient with doing improv. On the one hand you had Chris, who wanted everything scripted and planned. On the other hand you had Belushi, who was bored with improv because that's what he'd done all his life. And on yet a third hand you had Chevy, who sabotaged everything anyway. But the minute they let themselves go on the subject of rock and roll, they discovered new territory. It was their common language. John created the character of the Woodshuck emcee, a wonderfully persuasive hippie Satan urging the masses to self-immolate by any conceivable means, from electrocution to cannibalism.

JUDITH BELUSHI PISANO:

When John first got his script, the second act was made up of the lyrics to ten or so songs with names like "Papa Was a

MATTY SIMMONS:

John came to me three days before we were supposed to open and said, "I've gotta leave. I've gotta go back to Chicago."

I said, "What are you crazy? We're opening in three days. You can't go anywhere!"

"I really can't help it," he said, putting on this big, sorrowful routine. "Judy's so unhappy here. She doesn't like it in New York. She's got nothing to do."

"What does she do?"

"She's an artist."

"Well, now she's working in the art department at the *National Lampoon*." And we brought her in. I found out later that he'd planned the whole thing. That's exactly what he'd wanted me to do.

Jackie Christ Superstar

Running-Dog Lackey of the Bourgeoisie," which was essentially the Communist Manifesto set to a Motown groove. In between each song, it simply said "Emcee." So John began to work on the character and came up with all the transitions between the songs. The most famous line from Woodstock was the emcee telling everyone not to take the brown acid because it'd been laced with strychnine. So, naturally, John told the lemmings not to take the brown strychnine because it'd been laced with acid.

Up until a few days before the opening, John was frustrated because he hadn't worked in his Joe Cocker. He only had one song, "Megadeath," an acid-rock, high-voltage, blow-out-the-speakers number. So one night he sat down and started thinking about how Cocker looked when he performed, like someone with muscular dystrophy. That seemed like the right hook. He wrote his own lyrics, called Paul and got together with him for the music.

PAUL JACOBS:

When it came to putting together John's Cocker parody, "Bottom of the Barrel," we just got together at the Village Gate, I sat down at the piano and we improvised the melody. It happened almost instantaneously.

SEAN KELLY:

Two nights before *Lemmings* was to open, Tony, as he invariably does, came down with colitis. And at this point the first act was still over two hours long. John, Chris and I went to this Italian restaurant around the corner from the Village Gate. We had this heap of sketches and we just started throwing things out. Lose this, lose that, kill this. By the next day, the first act had no ending of any kind, but at least it wasn't two hours long.

The show opened, and for the entire first half the audience sat there cringing while Chevy danced around in a bra with

falsies. On top of that you had this Jackie Christ thing that the audience either didn't understand or hated, and there was also some kind of Beatles song that Tony and Chris had written that the audience didn't know was supposed to be a Beatles song. It was grim.

Then John came out wearing this weird tie-dye shirt, and he said, "I got an announcement. I got an announcement. From now on this is a *free concert*."

And everybody was like, "What the hell is this?" It seemed real. It *seemed* like a mercy killing of the first act. And people started to laugh. I had been sitting there through this first act thinking, *Oh Jesus oh God oh Christ, what a fucking catastrophe.* And then the second John took the stage as the emcee, it was like the plane never even ran down the runway—it just took off. It was fabulous.

PAM JACKLIN, *sister-in-law*:

When the show ended, there was a real high in the audience. John's impact was very powerful, this ability he had to anchor the whole thing. Everyone was good, the cast was really terrific, but John had created this magnificent persona, which was the glue that held it all together. It showed how a seemingly small role could make all the difference in the success of the big picture, something he proved again in *Animal House*.

SEAN KELLY:

The actual emcee at Woodstock was that supercilious Englishman. Later, when John went on the road for the tour and Peter Elbling came in to do the emcee, I went back to the original script that I'd written for this British guy. It was, in a way, better parody, but it was much less effective theatrically.

John, you see, was dangerous onstage. Part of why *Lemmings* worked, and a lot of why *Saturday Night Live* worked, is that although John was very professional, he gave you the impression that anything could happen. That keeps you on your toes. John was not about to jump into the audience and hit somebody, but you always had the impression that he *might*. If one goes to a play, the only real moment of theatricality happens when a door jams on the stage or somebody blows a cue. After that, the audience is alert. It's really happening. And when John was onstage, you couldn't just sit back and be entertained. You were completely engaged.

TONY HENDRA:

When it came to the performance, his talent was just staggering. Unfortunately, we really did have to hide the fact that he wasn't a very good musician.

SEAN KELLY:

John was not a good musician, but he was a funny drummer, like Animal from the Muppets. Part of the fun, of course, was that everyone kept switching instruments. John would sit down at the drums, Chevy would get up from the drums and sit down at the piano, Paul Jacobs would get up from the piano and pick up the Fender. It was a nice little piece of showmanship, and it made the audience go, "Wow! What a talented cast!" But, in truth, you don't have to be very good in order to look very good when you're switching things up like that.

CHEVY CHASE:

John couldn't play the bass at all. It was awful. Chris Guest tried to teach him, but for the most part Paul would play bass notes on the piano. Then, when John got on the drums it was like listening to a high-school rock drummer. He could really sing, though. When he did Cocker, he sang great.

SEAN KELLY:

When John did the Joe Cocker thing, he came out doing these hilarious contortions, and it was funny. Then it was funny again because of the way John and Paul Jacobs worked together. John would be spazzing around. Then he'd start to flag and

lose steam. He'd look over at Paul, and Paul would play *harder* and give him this look: *"More! More!"* So it went from, "Hey, isn't that funny. Joe Cocker is a spaz," to "Oh my God, he's a puppet in the hands of this monster." Then John would finally collapse at the end of the number, do a James Brown thing, get back up, fall back down, climb up the microphone and then do it all over again. It was no longer just a parody; he'd actually created a character. It wasn't just a satirical premise; it was a piece of theater.

CHEVY CHASE:

When he did Cocker, he would spin, spin and go down—Whack!—and it was two hundred pounds hitting the floor. He'd spit beer up in the air, get himself covered with it. He didn't care too much. John and I were both very physical, but John, I found, was more willing to hurt himself. Whenever John took a fall, he hit his head. I think he even knocked himself out once. He really went all the way for something.

TONY HENDRA:

It was a tiny stage, and Chris had these very valuable guitars that had to be left onstage for the whole show. They were always up for the next number, and there wasn't room to store them anywhere else. And when John would do his Cocker bit, he was all over the stage. You could see that Chris was just terrified that John was going to crash into this guitar—which he actually didn't. John was very precise with his movements. But it was a nightmare for Chris. And since John never did anything the same twice, it was a new nightmare every night.

JUDITH BELUSHI PISANO:

At the time, most of the cast and crew were potheads, which was difficult for Chris, who didn't smoke or do drugs. Apparently there were also times when there was some coke around, although I don't remember ever seeing any. But John was always up to try anything, and the different attitudes he and Chris had about drugs caused a great deal of friction.

John Belushi as Joe Cocker

Director Tony Hendra (seated) and cast

TONY HENDRA:

One night, John was playing with Chris's guitar in one of the numbers and he was so stoned he fell off the stage holding the guitar. Chris was just mortified.

CHRISTOPHER GUEST:

Fortunately, he landed on his feet. It was a twenty-thousand-dollar guitar. It was hard. John didn't do many shows, if any, straight. It was virtually every day. I said to him one night, "Can't you just give me the two hours straight?" But that didn't happen. It did become a point of friction. It wasn't that I didn't like John, or didn't respect his talent. It's just that this was going on every night of the show.

TONY HENDRA:

John would come in and say, "Guest gets up my nose. I can't stand it. I don't want to be onstage with him." And Chris

*Overleaf: A series of **Lemmings**-era headshots*

would come in all the time and say, "I'm not going on with Belushi. He's stoned out of his mind." He wasn't necessarily stoned out of his mind, and anyway John could actually function when he wasn't too stoned. There were nights when John was fine. He was usually fine, but not always. When there was someone famous in the audience, he really pulled himself together for that. He was very ambitious. But Chris would complain about it all the time.

CHRISTOPHER GUEST:

Drugs were rampant during that time. And he wasn't the only one that was stoned. The show was a hotbed of that stuff, which was unfortunate. I took it personally. With the work that we were doing every night, eight shows a week, it wasn't fair to the other people.

TONY HENDRA:

There were drugs around *Lemmings*, especially in the dressing rooms. The reason was simple: one of the cast members lived with a dealer. Every other dressing room off-Broadway boasted similar luxuries; the difference with *Lemmings* was that a considerable message in our show was that drugs were part of the ongoing destruction of our generation. As the show became a bigger and bigger hit, some of the cast became more and more like what they were parodying. They really thought they were a rock group called Lemmings, and thus were entitled to the same kind of self-destructive lifestyle.

MATTY SIMMONS:

They all did drugs. You'd walk into the editorial office at the *Lampoon*, and you'd get high just smelling the air.

SEAN KELLY:

Tony would go to Matty and say that he needed some walkin'-around money to buy marijuana for the cast. And Matty would think, "I'm a swingin', Matty kinda guy," and peel off a couple bills.

TONY HENDRA:

I did indulge the rock dreams on a few occasions as a reward to the cast. Twice I asked for money from management to give to the cast to do with what they liked. I'm pretty sure management knew quite well that the money—not much among seven people—would probably be spent on illegal substances, but these were people who preferred grass to champagne and roses. They'd worked hard, they were a hit, and if that's what they wanted, they deserved it.

PAUL JACOBS:

People talk about John doing all these drugs, but I happen to know that he cleared $211 a week doing *Lemmings*. That's how much we got paid after taxes. And his rent was $450 a month. That left him with about $400 a month to live, buy groceries, take the subway and so forth—and on top of that buy all of these drugs. A gram of coke in those days was about $85, so you can do the math. I think a lot of it is greatly exaggerated in people's memories.

As far as John being too messed up to perform, I don't recall it happening much. It was never really an issue. But even if he was, it was the era and the type of show where it didn't much

TONY HENDRA:

I do think that there was something very sad at John's core. There was some deep dissatisfaction that poisoned him, and that he just had no way of filling. He never talked about it. I just sensed it, mostly during that first month or so when we hung out quite a lot. He talked about very little in terms of his childhood; it was hard to get things out of him as far as the background stuff.

John was also one of those people—and it was incomprehensible to me—who just embraced danger. It either meant nothing to him or he actually got a high off of it. I suspect it was the latter.

This is typical Belushi: The first summer in New York, he and Judy came out to my house in New Jersey a couple of times. They had nowhere else to go, and it was a cool place to come, in every sense. Even though it's in New Jersey, it's very picturesque. It has this little mountain stream that runs through it. It's a narrow, rocky little stream, but when it rains—which it does in the summer, torrentially—it becomes a lethal sort of mini Colorado.

John and I had been fooling around in the stream in these tires. The next day we woke up at midday after some revelry the night before and found that it had been raining all night and all morning. The stream was now about ten feet deep. It was incredibly dangerous. There were trees coming down, all kinds of shit. John blearily got up, went down to the river, got in one of these tires, jumped into the river—and disappeared. I mean, within seconds he was gone. It would have been madness to go in after him. Judy and I ran down the stream trying to find him, and we couldn't. And I was terrified, because there was every chance that this guy had drowned. And then, about a mile or so downstream, he sort of reeled out from under the side of the riverbank. "Wow!" he said. "Man, that was great!"

"John, what happened?" we said.

"I don't know. I guess I must have banged my head on the bank and passed out for a second...Hendra, you chickenshit, why didn't you follow me?"

matter. Non-functionality was a performance in and of itself in those days.

JANIS HIRSCH, *writer:*

He just didn't have limits, with anything. If you gave him a loaf of bread, he'd eat the whole loaf of bread. If you gave him a bag of drugs, he'd do the whole bag of drugs. If you put four cats on him, he'd play with all four cats. It didn't really matter what it was.

One of the curious things about John was that the self-confidence he exuded onstage was not a façade. There's nothing more important to getting people to laugh than being confident of what you're doing. You have to be massively committed to being funny, and John was. Everything about John was massive. Yet, at the same time, he also had a massive vulnerability.

—Tony Hendra

SEAN KELLY:

John told me once that he'd found this wonderful thing: Quaaludes. And I said, "Well, what's the deal? What do they do?"

He said, "It's like having had eight beers."

"But the part about having eight beers that I like is having the eight beers," I said. "The feeling I have after I can live without."

But he was all excited about it. I always thought of John as raw id—and vulnerable the way an id is. If you don't have the ego and the superego protecting the id, it gets kicked around a lot. And it takes a lot of energy to be id all the time. I think that was part of the medication with John. I don't think he had any shell.

My experience of seeing him with my kids, who were then very young, was always very good. When he'd come to my house for dinner, he wasn't this wild man sitting on the other side of the table. He was a very amiable, warm person. Over the years one has some lunatics in one's domestic life, and you go, "Oh Jesus, the sooner this guy is gone the better." But I never had that impression with John.

John may have been self-medicating, but he did not give any indications of being unhappy. Sometimes he was pissed off, but there were sort of objective correlatives to being pissed off. He was pissed off because he missed his girlfriend and he wanted to get her to New York. He was pissed off because he felt that he was being underpaid and badly treated, and he certainly had a case there.

TONY HENDRA:

By the summer John was making a lot of noise about a raise and more responsibility. At one point, it became loud enough for me to be told to get rid of him, which I refused to do.

SEAN KELLY:

Although John created material for the show, he wasn't being paid for it. He was being treated as if he were merely an actor in an off-Broadway revue, when in fact he was also a musician and songwriter. There were no Dramatist Guild contracts or anything like that. Nobody signed anything. The music publishing and so forth, Matty kept it all. It was a fuck you of major proportions. But you're young and you think, oh, I'd be doing this for free anyway, and you never realize that you're getting bent over.

CHRISTOPHER GUEST:

Matty Simmons called Chevy and John and me into his office. He didn't want to give us a raise, and so he called the three of us in and said, "You guys are a dime a dozen." That's verbatim. And I just thought, nobody says that. I mean, not for real, nobody *actually* says that. It's like, "You're never going to work in this town again." Nobody really says it. But he told us we were a dime a dozen and basically to stop making trouble or he was going to fire us.

SEAN KELLY:

John hated Matty. Hated him. Of course, you ask Matty nowadays and he'll say John was like a son to him.

MATTY SIMMONS:

John was like a son to me.

JOHN vs. CHEVY

CHEVY CHASE:

John and I had two big moments together in *Lemmings*. We did a takeoff about a guy who sold drugs and a guy who wanted to buy 'em. I was the dealer. I had two motorcycle helmets, and I told him I had something that would give him a real rush.

"Oh, what's that?" he says.

I tell him to put the helmet on and he puts it on and stands there, and then I say, "No, no. Bend over. Get down like you're a lineman on a football team." So he gets down, and then I put on my helmet and as fast as I can run across the stage full steam and—wham!—I hit him in the head and

knock him for a loop. We both go down in a total daze. It was actually a pretty good hit—and we did it every day for a year and a half.

The other bit was one where I played a drunken Hell's Angel *à la* Altamont. Some peace freak had put his fingers all over my bike, and, enraged, I barged out onstage with a chain and a beer can spewing a slew of swear words that was unbelievable. And John was always—whoosh—out of the way just in time, like a ballet dancer. I'd start falling around, threatening him and just being drunk. But I never touched him, never even got him wet. He didn't look that lithe and that agile, but he was.

TONY HENDRA:

The eventual solution was to give John two salaries, one as a performer and one as a director, and let him put together his own company for a tour. So *Lemmings* split up into two groups for the fall. One stayed at the Village Gate, the other went out on a short-lived and extremely ambitious tour as the road company. That was Simmons's belated answer to the Stigwood disaster.

SEAN KELLY:

Matty called Tony and me into his office and said, "You know who was just in here? Robert Stigwood." Robert Stigwood was the BeeGees' producer. He did *Tommy*. He did *Saturday Night Fever*. He was huge at the time, and he wanted to bring *Lemmings* to Broadway. Tony and I were like, "Wow! Robert Stigwood wants to bring our show to Broadway?"

"Yeah," Matty said, "and I told him, 'Get the hell out of here, I'll do it myself.'"

Matty was a piece of work. Of course, he never made any money either. Michael O'Donoghue used to say that Matty was living in a fool's purgatory.

MATTY SIMMONS:

I got a lot of requests. But I didn't do it, because I felt that Broadway wasn't ready for the *National Lampoon* at that time.

TONY HENDRA:

It could've been magnificent with a lot of money, much more like Woodstock itself. But Simmons wouldn't hear of it. So he sent them out to play at some colleges, stay in the Howard Johnson. It wasn't properly executed at all. It was just awful.

RHONDA COULLET, *writer/performer*:

There was an ad in *Backstage* for the road company of *Lemmings*, and I just went down to audition. I did a piece for John and, to my surprise, he hired me. I was a real hippie when I showed up, straight out of the cast of *Hair* in Los Angeles, and so the show was a real shock to me. It was tearing down everything that hippies believed in. We didn't know James Taylor was shooting heroin. We just thought of him as this sweet, happy folk singer, but here they'd written a whole song about it. I had never done improvisational comedy before, either; I didn't even know what it was. But John just said, "You'll do fine." Our very first stop on the tour was Ole Miss, and John had to play George Wallace in one of the skits. He was terrified. He thought he was going to get shot.

CHEVY CHASE:

We were really sort of thrown together when we went on the road. We'd get on a plane—Ozark Airlines or something—and we'd go to Kansas City, we'd do the show. Then we'd be on another plane, we'd go to Mississippi, we'd get into a motel and get ready and do the show, and so on. John became the director and I was the music director, which is pretty funny for a guy who can't read music.

TONY HENDRA:

The touring company was very expensive to keep on the road. Not only did they have to have an identical stage set-up, they also had to have money to live and travel. To make things worse, by the fall of '73, the OPEC embargo was in full swing which meant it was impossible to get gas for the bus hauling the stage and sound equipment from city to city. John was very unhappy with everything—shitty hotels, lousy dressing rooms—and called me constantly to complain.

RHONDA COULLET:

John hated being alone. He missed Judy the whole time. We were always dead tired after the shows so we'd go back to the hotel and just hang out. I was on the road with my husband so John would just come into our room and fall in the middle of the floor and stay there and watch TV.

Chevy used to come and hang out too. The funniest bits he and John ever did were these underwear ads. They'd just come into the room and start doing these fake, ridiculous poses like you used to see in a Sears or Montgomery Ward catalog.

CHEVY CHASE:

Suddenly John and I would appear in our jockey shorts, John on one knee waving, you know, and me pointing and holding a briefcase. When there was free time, it was often filled with raiding the other guys' rooms and throwing wet toilet paper at them or trying to promote shaving cream fights, sort of like college kids. We just did odd things that were funny. We both really laughed a lot at each other. I had struck up a relationship with a girl in Philadelphia whom I really fell for. She'd given me an eight by ten, and I'd put it in a frame and taken it on the road. One night I opened it up and put it on the motel nightstand. John came into the room and he said, "Oh. You got that picture too? I got the one with the donkey dick in it." ■

Chapter 6

THE PERFECT MASTER

radio days

BRIAN DOYLE-MURRAY:

One day John and I were walking down Bedford Street in the Village. We were on our way back to his apartment after breakfast when a freak snowstorm hit. We had these hooded sweatshirts on, and we were running in the street with our heads down. All of a sudden John yelled at me, jumped over and threw me sideways, out of the path of this huge delivery truck that had come out of nowhere. But the truck slammed into him and sent him flying several feet. Then he landed with a perfect tuck and roll over to the curb and just hopped right up, ready to dance. They came and took him to St. Vincent's, but there wasn't a scratch on him. It saved my life; if that truck had hit me, I wouldn't be here now.

In 1972, the offices of the National Lampoon were at war. Writers Tony Hendra and Michael O'Donoghue were the principal combatants, and, like so many good wars, this one began over a woman. The indiscretion itself was fairly ordinary. Michael was quite smitten, she was an open-minded girl, and Tony should have known better. But the consequences of what transpired are somewhat staggering.

O'Donoghue's temper was legendary, and Irish. He accused Hendra of betrayal, severed all communications, drew lines in the sand and insisted that everyone at the Lampoon choose sides. In the middle of the fray stood publisher Matty Simmons. On the one hand he had Hendra, a smart, capable editor whose extracurricular activities were none of the magazine's business, and on the other he had O'Donoghue, a smart, irreplaceable writer whose demands for satisfaction were increasingly disruptive.

Though the two men had collaborated successfully on the Radio Dinner album, Simmons determined that Hendra should be sent off to produce the next album on his own—from which followed the off-Broadway revue Lemmings. Hendra's exile to below Fourteenth Street did ease some of the tension around the office. Lemmings' sudden success, however, did not.

As a child, O'Donoghue had been pulled out of school and bedridden for over a year with rheumatic fever. He emerged from his illness with a sickly constitution, a pronounced inability to play well with others and a great love for radio. Simmons, seeking to mollify his star writer, offered the idea of a National Lampoon radio show. O'Donoghue jumped at the chance. A fully functioning studio was installed in the Lampoon's Madison Avenue offices. It was christened the "Radio Ranch," decorated accordingly, and from it emerged a rather odd and brilliant creation that mixed the savage posture of the Lampoon with the grand sounds of the Golden Age of Radio.

On November 17, 1973, The National Lampoon Radio Hour debuted in some eighty-four markets with such absurd creations as "The Mystery Primal Scream Contest," "Bob the Rapist" and "No Eyes: Blind Detective and His Seeing-Eye Duck, Boneless." Studio engineer Bob Tischler was brought in to oversee production, and the magazine's writers were lining up to contribute to the exciting new medium. But O'Donoghue could keep his temper in check for only so long. Less than five months later, he walked out on the magazine, the radio show and everything to do with National Lampoon.

With his career-making performance in Lemmings, John had established himself as the Lampoon's greatest asset outside of the *magazine. Simmons tapped him to run the* Radio Hour *and to develop the organization's next theatrical revue. Retreating from the chaotic nightlife of the Village Gate, John took the job and embarked on what would be one of the most stable, productive and creative periods of his career. He set about recruiting the best and the brightest talents he could find for his new radio and stage projects. In doing so, he helped assemble what would become, in effect, the farm team for the greatest comedic endeavors of the next quarter century.*

Before Lemmings *and the* Radio Hour, *the* National Lampoon *was already home to the greatest comedy writers in the country: Henry Beard, Doug Kenney, P.J. O'Rourke, Anne Beatts, Chris Miller, Christopher Guest and O'Donoghue himself. Now, thanks to a small romantic indiscretion, you could add to that list the still-unknown talents of Chevy Chase, Gilda Radner, Bill Murray, Harold Ramis, Ivan Reitman, Billy Crystal, Joe Flaherty, Brian Doyle-Murray, Richard Belzer, Paul Shaffer and, of course, John himself.*

JUDITH BELUSHI PISANO:

When the *Lemmings* tour ended, John joined the teeming ranks of unemployed New York actors. It didn't take him long to worry that he "would never work again." About the same time, I transferred from the *Lampoon* art department to the newly created radio show, but because of this feud with Tony, Michael wouldn't use anyone from *Lemmings*, at least not someone that Tony had discovered. He'd never seen *Lemmings*, but he didn't like "them" and "they" were no good and this and that. I suggested John for several things, and Michael's response was always an abrupt no. But I could tell my persistence amused him.

During the pre-launch recording sessions, we had to do a scene that called for a Peter O'Toole impression, and at the last minute the actor canceled. There's a scene from *Lawrence of Arabia* in which Peter O'Toole—ragged and sunburned from fighting his way across the desert—defiantly walks into a "whites only" officer's bar with an Arab comrade and demands, "We want two large glasses of lemonade!" Well, John would do that bit all the time, and it was a real crowd pleaser. So I said to Michael, "John does a great Peter O'Toole."

He took a long pause and looked at me like, if this doesn't work I am so going to enjoy giving you hell about it. Then he said, "Okay, if he can come in today he's hired."

John came up to the studio and did his "two glasses of lemonade" bit. Michael thought it was great and we sent him into the studio. Turns out he couldn't do Peter O'Toole at all. He could only do that one line—and so much of the impression was just in capturing O'Toole's physical presence that it didn't translate to radio anyway. But Michael was in good humor that day, and John turned the session into a personal audition, going off as Capote and Brando and showing what he could do. At the end of the day, Michael realized that John could be a great addition to the *Radio Hour.*

ANNE BEATTS, *writer:*

The rough part for John was that Michael was big on typecasting people, and in the beginning he only saw John as a performer and not as a writer who could come up with his own material.

MICHAEL O'DONOGHUE, *writer/performer:*

He tried to write, but he couldn't physically write. Part of being a writer, you know, is actually being able to form the

John and Judy posing for a **National Lampoon** *photo spread*

little letters and consonants, which he just couldn't do. In the beginning he tried to get a job at the *Lampoon* as a writer. He wrote a piece on some crumpled-up napkin and he came in and said, "Listen, I got this piece here, and…wait a minute. No, wait a minute…wait, this…wait a minute. No, no, this is…wait a minute. This is it. No, wait…" And no one, including himself, could actually read what he'd written. It looked like a ransom note from Bruno Hauptmann.

JUDITH BELUSHI PISANO:

For weeks John tried to get his original material on the show but wasn't having much luck. All of the magazine writers were lined up in front of him, even though they were all print people and didn't get how to write for actors or for radio. It drove John crazy. Then one day he and Chris Guest went into the studio and improvised for half an hour with their dueling Truman Capote impressions. It wasn't the greatest sketch they ever did, but it made Michael and Bob Tischler realize just how much potential was there.

ANNE BEATTS:

Putting the show together was so demanding that eventually Michael was desperate for material. Once he realized how well the improvisation worked, he was grateful just to have anything that he didn't have to write or edit himself.

HAROLD RAMIS:

Once John started bringing improv to the radio show, he began to think of how to get Second City people involved. The first person he brought to New York was Brian Doyle-Murray, several months before the rest of us.

JUDITH BELUSHI PISANO:

When Brian moved to town, it was the beginning of a new era. John and I had been mostly on our own for all of *Lemmings*, but the arrival of an old Chicago friend was the start of building a new family for John in New York.

BRIAN DOYLE-MURRAY:

I moved to New York and slept on his couch for three months. This was at the place on Bleecker Street with Judy and their two fuzzy cats. We started writing and performing together for the *Radio Hour*. We had quite a few adventures. We'd go to boxing matches and rock concerts, go to clubs and hear music and sit around just thinking up ideas. We took some audition classes at HP Studio with a wonderful teacher, Aaron Frankel. After we presented a scene one day, he took us aside and said, "You two guys should really stop taking classes and get out and get some work."

JUDITH BELUSHI PISANO:

John hated auditions because he wasn't good at reading cold. He actively avoided them and instead poured his efforts into getting more and more work with the radio show. He saw that he and Brian needed to generate scripts in order to make a bigger impact. I used to come home from work and find them sitting at the dining room table, working. They'd read me what they'd written that day, and it always made me laugh. It was just a really sweet, simple time.

BRIAN DOYLE-MURRAY:

We were real fertile; we wrote down half of whatever we thought of. John was on my ass constantly. If I left the house without my notebook, he would make me go back and get it. Every day we'd get a *Post* and a *Times* and a *Daily News* and just scour through them writing down anything that made us laugh. Mostly, I held the pencil and he walked up and down a lot. Then we'd head up to the *Lampoon* studio and, within a couple of hours, be recording whatever we'd come up with. After a few months it dawned on me that I was living in New York and I'd better get a place.

ANNE BEATTS:

John and Brian wrote a whole show about capital punishment called "Welcome Back: The Death Penalty," which Michael of course loved because it was about death. That's when Michael really sat up and took notice, and John became an integral part of the show.

But then, on that Easter Sunday, Michael was supposed to be finished with the *Radio Hour* so we could go out for dinner with some friends. I came in and Matty had given my desk to his son. I got really angry. I told Michael that I wanted my piece taken off of the show that week, which would have meant hours of work taking apart the show and putting it back together. Michael called Matty at home, they had an altercation and Matty told him, "If your girlfriend doesn't like it, she can quit. And if you don't like it, you can quit too." So Michael quit, not really thinking that Matty would take him seriously. But Michael had been a pain in the butt for a long time, and Matty, who I think was only looking for an excuse, said okay.

BOB TISCHLER, *producer*:

When Michael left, we needed another creative director. It was pretty much my choice, and the obvious choice was John.

JUDITH BELUSHI PISANO:

John loved working with Michael, considered him a friend and learned a lot from him. But when Bob asked him to take over, he didn't hesitate for a second.

ANNE BEATTS:

I was bracing myself for the ultimatum that we weren't going to be able to see John and Judy anymore, because Michael was going to be so pissed off about being replaced. It never happened. Michael was just too fond of John.

JUDITH BELUSHI PISANO:

Shortly after the *Radio Hour* job came through, Matty also named John the director of a new stage show. He told him to hire a cast and be ready to tour in the fall. John lined up Brian, Joe Flaherty, Harold Ramis and Gilda Radner from Second City Toronto. Shortly before everyone arrived, something went askew, and Matty told John that the show wasn't going to happen for several months. John was furious; his friends had all quit their jobs and were moving to New York on his word. He went to Matty and insisted they be taken care of. Matty, to his credit, agreed to hire them as the *Radio Hour* troupe until the stage show came through.

BILL MURRAY, *writer/performer*:

John was an icebreaker for a lot of people. He was the first one to go from Chicago to New York, and he got everybody out. He was the force; people gravitated to him.

JANIS HIRSCH:

John could eat a chef's salad with his hands, but he also had a sweetness to him that most people can't imagine. He was late once for a recording session, and people were getting really irritated. "Where the hell is John?!" So Judy called the house. What had happened was that their cat, Chubbs, had fallen asleep in his lap, and she looked so cute that he couldn't bring himself to get up and leave. And because he was John, that was the only excuse he needed.

NAT... LAMPOON™

10022   JOHN BELUSHI
                     ...AN DOYLE-MURRAY

635 Madis...

Bob

SAY MOM

Say, Mom, you know summ...
know what that means!...
Insect Bites.   Burns,...
maladies, lock your...
...them out in the...
...radged...

(25)   WELCOME BACK: THE DEA...
                ALL WRITTEN...
                      BRI...

:07)	:03	~~...~~. OPENING	MARTY HARVEY - FR...
	1:40	WINCHELL	PETER WALDREN
	:30	STALLING #1	J.B & B.D-M.
	:13	SEG-1-LAST WORD	SEAN KELLY
	1:13	SHOPLIFTING	LYNN LIPTON, AM...
		...N CREEK	ANNOUNCER & PETER W...

...& B.D-M

B. DOYLE-MURRAY BE...
J. BELUSH,

CAPONE

John

3

WILL   THE   DEFENDENT   PLEASE   RISE

MR. CAPONE, ~~...~~ I HAVE DECIDED
TO SHOW LENIENCY AND NOT SENTENCE
YOU TO DEATH. HOWEVER, I HEARBY
SENTENCE YOU TO A DOSE OF SYPHLIS.

DRYDE...

"...

VOICE...

Shoplifting

1:26

OUR HIDDEN CAMERAS CAUGHT MRS.
...LEN GROUSE OF COLUMBUS, OHIO
...T OF SHOPLIFTING AT AN A
...C ASKED OTHER SHOPPERS
...RE DETERRED FROM SHOP
MRS. GROUSE BY KILLI...

JALTY

BEL...
E-M...

M°CON...

AN, (

RIA

SHOPLIFTING

1st Announcer:
Our hidden cameras caught Mrs. Helen Grouse of Columbus Ohio in the act of shoplifting at an A & P Store. We asked other shoppers if they would be detoured from shoplifting if we punished Mrs. Grouse by killing her . Let's listen

2nd Announcer:

Shopper:
Have you ever shoplifted?

Announcer:
Well... Yes I have. On ...
salmon or a jar of ...

Well ...

YOU CAN HANG ME BY THE NECK
OR NAIL ME TO A TREE J.
IT WAS GOOD ENOUGH FOR CHRIST
...'S GOOD ENOUGH FOR ME.

In the studio (from left): Michael O'Donoghue,
Bob Tischler and John; Harold Ramis

DAN AYKROYD:

I met John at Second City in Toronto. He'd come up to
see the show and grab people for his radio endeavor down in
New York. After the show, he came back to the 505 Club,
an after-hours establishment I was running. We took an
immediate liking to each other, instant, hung out together all
night. After that it was clear that a friendship was forged. I
didn't go and do the radio show, though. I had Second City
duties and this after-hours place and a children's television
show I was on at the time. I was making more money than
the prime minister of Canada, so I stayed with that. But John
grabbed Gilda and Harold and Billy and the others, and there
you had the essential struts, pillars and crutches of the
American comedy industry as we know it today. John was
one of the cohesive forces bringing it all together. I missed
out on that at first.

HAROLD RAMIS:

The day I arrived in New York, I walked right into the
studio and went straight to work. One of the editors had
written *Moby!*, a musical version of *Moby Dick* as performed
by the Little Worth Community Theater in Sabbath Day Lake,
Maine. They put floorboards in the recording studio to make
it sound like we were on a stage. Tony Hendra was Ishmael,
John was Ahab and Brian was Starbuck.

BRIAN DOYLE-MURRAY:

John was great as Ahab, sang like a bird.

JUDITH BELUSHI PISANO:

Once John put the troupe together, the *Radio Hour* really
just went to another level. Michael's vision and unique style
were unfortunately lost, but now there was a cohesiveness to
the writing and acting that hadn't existed before. The troupe
worked like the writers on the old Dick Van Dyke sitcom—
just a bunch of fun, happy people putting a show together.

JANIS HIRSCH:

They were very serious about the way they worked. They'd
get together at this little coffee shop called Sandalino's in the
Village and sit at the table and throw out ideas. They would
generate a whole bunch of scenes and bits and premises, and then
Gilda would go home and type it all up, because she was the girl.

BOB TISCHLER:

Sometimes we wrote things on paper, but mostly we
improvised. The way we worked was we would run tape for
as long as we wanted to, and then I would cut an hour of tape
down to five minutes. John loved to go in and improvise for
hours, especially with Chris Guest. They were not terrific
friends, but they improvised well together.

HAROLD RAMIS:

So much talent came through that room. It was the most amazing thing to watch. John and Chris Guest and Bill Murray could sit at the mic and do forty-five minutes as different characters, and it would all be hysterical. I've never seen anything quite that good.

Traditionally, you think of writers sitting down with a pen and paper. John could do that, but not with great discipline. He never finished college or anything, and there were those of us who were just more schooled in it or more practiced in it. John's contributions weren't necessarily on paper but he could create volumes of great stuff just participating in those "yes, and…" discussions around the table.

BOB TISCHLER:

John's sense of humor did not go in a straight line at all. In other words, you couldn't even begin to imitate him. He would go way off on a tangent, and you'd go, "Where the hell is he going?" And then it would come around and all of a sudden make sense.

ANNE BEATTS:

John would come over to your house and, while conversational balls were being batted back and forth, he would just kind of sit there quietly. Then at some point he would pick up the ball and run with it. He would go into some

At the office (from top left): Brian Doyle-Murray, John and Harold; Harold, Joe Flaherty, Bob, John and Christopher Guest; Gilda Radner; Michael and Bob

incredible monologue in which he would stand up, go all over the room and act out all sorts of parts while everyone else in the room rolled on the floor in fits of uncontrollable laughter. Then he would sort of subside, sit down and—once people were able to start breathing again—the conversation would resume. That was an evening with John.

BOB TISCHLER:

John loved having the studio. It was right there, always at our disposal. If you thought of something, you could immediately go in there and put it on tape. Everybody would hang around the office in case they were needed for a part, and also because it just wound up being the cool, fun place to be.

CHRISTOPHER GUEST:

It was fun because we had complete control. We were left to our own devices. We would hang out at those offices, and there was this incredible feeling of arrogance that everybody had, including myself. You were just kind of floating on air, thinking, wow, I can come up here, I can do what I do, we can make record albums, we've done this successful stage show, we have this successful radio show—and they pay me.

HAROLD RAMIS:

Like Second City, the *Lampoon* gave us an empty stage. They trusted our process and said, "Here's the studio. Get in there." We were all doing fairly well. No one was getting rich, but we didn't have to hustle; no one had to take second jobs, and everyone felt it would only get better. We really felt that we were in the presence of genius. What I've always told students is to find the most talented people around you and stick with them. Don't leave them. That's how this sort of thing happens. You see someone as talented as John or Gilda and you go, "Wow! Hey, what are you doing next?"

The greatest thing was that everyone liked everyone else. There were no assholes. John and Judy had a very warm household, a really nice apartment in the Village. They would always host the Thanksgiving dinners and so forth. It felt like they were more settled, in a way. We all enjoyed each other's company, and we had this great gig. We were going to work on Madison Avenue for the *Radio Hour* in the daytime and hatching this material for the *Lampoon Show* at night. It was productive, it was good, and everyone was happy.

RICHARD BELZER, *writer/performer*:

We spent a lot of time together in those early days, just laughing and having a good time. We were like children. One day John and I were walking down Broadway, and we passed one of these so-called massage parlors. We had never been in one before and so John says, "Let's check it out." So we walk up the stairs and into this Turkish whorehouse with all these tacky chandeliers and maroon curtains, and out come this man and this woman. He's wearing a suit, and she's got this slinky negligee thing on. They start talking to us in all these absurd euphemisms, basically trying to sell us sex without actually saying it. So John asks her, you know, "What can we get?"

She looks at him seductively and says, "You can get anything you want."

"Anything we want?"

"*An-y-thing you want.*"

"Great. Can I get a roast-beef sandwich?"

They threw us out.

JANIS HIRSCH:

When Danny Aykroyd first came to visit New York, I was living with two guys, one of whom was, and still is, very gay. He had this big, fluffy, curly hair and always wore pink-tinted Erica Jong glasses, Marilyn Monroe T-shirts and short shorts. He was the dope dealer.

So Danny gets into town and he wants a little pot. John tells him, "Okay, I'll take you to this connection, but I've gotta tell ya, this guy is a *motherfucker*. Keep your head down. Don't make eye contact. Have exact—do you have exact change? Are they crisp, clean bills? Do not give this guy old, crumpled—do not *fuck* with this guy, Danny. Do you hear me? Just give him the money, and he'll give you the pot, and then we *leave*. Got it?"

"Uh, yeah...sure," Danny says.

So by the time they get to our apartment, John's got Danny so scared of this menacing dope dealer that he's literally quaking with fear. They open the door. Danny timidly steps into the apartment, and across the room prances this flaming gay man in short shorts going, "*Hey!*" Danny almost shit himself. It was brilliant.

BILL MURRAY:

When I first got to New York, they were doing the *Radio Hour* and getting ready to go on the road with the tour, so they wanted to hire some guys to do the radio show in their place. So Belushi and Tischler had this meeting with me. John said, "Now, Bill, we understand that, you know, you're a little aggressive and that you've got some violent tendencies and stuff like that. You're kinda wild and you can't control yourself. We want you to be real serious."

I just stared at him like, "Who the hell are you talking to?" I'd known John at this point for about five years. This was a guy who went down the stairs on his head just for fun, but he was acting very serious and very professional because he was supposedly in charge of the whole thing. It was all for Tischler's benefit.

Finally John said, "Okay, well, I guess it's okay. You'll be working here starting 9 AM tomorrow." And the job turned out to be a zoo, of course.

At play (from top left): Gilda Radner and Richard Belzer;
Joe Flaherty; Bill Murray and Christopher Guest;
Brian Doyle-Murray and John; Harold Ramis and Bill Murray

JOE FLAHERTY:

We'd do the radio show during the day and get together and flesh out the stage show at night. John was on this big kick, a very *Lampoon* kick, of grossing out and insulting the audience. "They love it," he said. I always had a hard time with that, but the show was very in your face with regard to subject matter. We attacked the right, the left, any kind of traditional institution. It was just a scattershot of insults aimed at everybody.

IVAN REITMAN, *producer*:

I had always wanted to do comedy movies. I had done a small, low-budget comedy/horror movie with Eugene Levy and Andrea Martin called *Cannibal Girls*. I also had this show on Broadway called *The Magic Show*. I looked up Matty

John and Gilda Radner on tour

Opposite: A Lampoon Show *publicity still*

Simmons's name on the masthead of the magazine, called him and said, "I'd like to do a movie with *National Lampoon*." And he was actually nice enough to see me.

We hit it off. He saw that I had some Broadway experience and said, "A lot of people are calling me about making movies, but I have this stage show called the *National Lampoon Show*, and I don't have anybody to produce for me." At that point the show was on tour, and they were hoping to bring it to New York.

I said, "You got it."

JOE FLAHERTY:

It was a good show, but they booked us into really bad places. They booked us into bars and pubs. It was rough. In London, Ontario, we played this biker bar. That was a tough night. Comedy wasn't that big back then. So when people saw that we were a comedy revue and not a music show, they'd boo and hiss. They were all drunk, hostile, young guys. And of course it didn't help that our first number was all of us coming out with underwear on our heads singing "You're the Pits!" to the tune of Cole Porter's "You're the Tops." That pretty much slammed the audience right from the very front of the show. Toronto was the worst.

HAROLD RAMIS:

Matty Simmons had warned us to have two shows' worth of material. He said, "These places are not theaters, they're nightclubs, and in the smaller venues the audience might not leave after the first show." But we had one show of good material and we thought that was all we needed.

JUDITH BELUSHI PISANO:

There was a famous book in the sixties by a writer named Carlos Castaneda who wrote about his experiences with a desert shaman named Don Juan. Don Juan was supposed to be a master of "plant magic," meaning they took a bunch of peyote and mushrooms together and had all sorts of visions. The stories were charmingly bizarre and good fodder for humor. So every night John would interview Richard Belzer as Castaneda and they'd take questions from the audience. It was kind of a Mexican Dear Abby on mescaline.

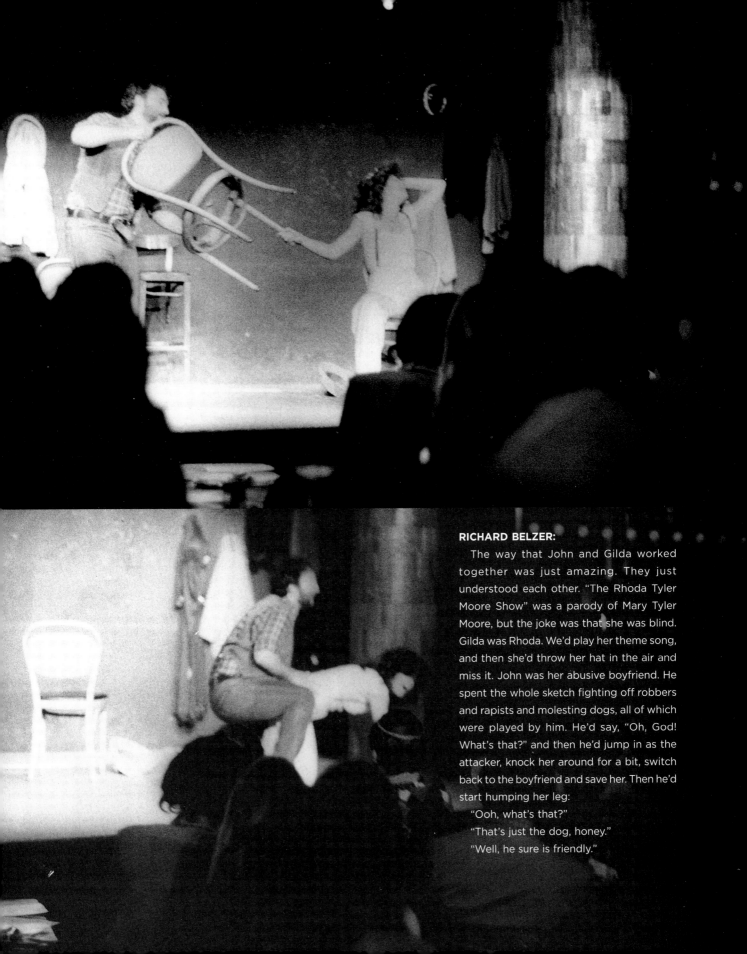

RICHARD BELZER:

The way that John and Gilda worked together was just amazing. They just understood each other. "The Rhoda Tyler Moore Show" was a parody of Mary Tyler Moore, but the joke was that she was blind. Gilda was Rhoda. We'd play her theme song, and then she'd throw her hat in the air and miss it. John was her abusive boyfriend. He spent the whole sketch fighting off robbers and rapists and molesting dogs, all of which were played by him. He'd say, "Oh, God! What's that?" and then he'd jump in as the attacker, knock her around for a bit, switch back to the boyfriend and save her. Then he'd start humping her leg:

"Ooh, what's that?"

"That's just the dog, honey."

"Well, he sure is friendly."

IVAN REITMAN:

I caught up with them in Toronto at a club called the El Macombo. I knew that I'd made a very good decision after I saw the first show. I said, "Wow, these people are just amazing." And the center of the show was John. He was the energizer of the whole thing.

They knew I was there as this potential producer, and so they were kind of friendly to me, in their own particular way. They normally did two shows a night, and in most of the venues the audience would empty out and a new one would fill back in. I happened to be backstage when they found out that virtually no one from the first show had left.

There was a general panic backstage. "What are we going to do?"

And either Harold or John—I can't remember which—said, "Well, let's do the same show over again and just change all the punch lines."

Then they get out there for the second show and put on one of the most spectacular examples of thinking on your feet and cleverness you could possibly imagine. I've never seen anything like it before or since. Basically I was watching them do a completely new improvisation based on another improvisation that they'd just done not an hour before. About five percent of the audience was really drunk, and they started yelling, "What the fuck are you doing? We heard that before!" And then, slowly, they all came to the realization of what they were witnessing. It was remarkable. It was a tour de force.

HAROLD RAMIS:

Ivan really liked the first show, and then when he saw us improvising the second show, he was just amazed. He came to us and said, "I want to produce this in New York, and I'd love to do a *Lampoon* movie." He just liked everyone involved.

He and Matty made a deal that they would co-produce the first *Lampoon* movie with Ivan producing the stage show. After Toronto we went back to New York. Brian decided to leave the show, and so we brought in Billy to work with and then ultimately replace him. We got a rehearsal studio and started pulling the show together.

IVAN REITMAN:

I rented some rehearsal space in midtown Manhattan and showed up the very first day—they let me sit in the back. At some point John and Bill were arguing about something. I sort of spoke up and said, "Well, don't you think it would be better if…"

Then suddenly everything stopped, and these six formidable comedic geniuses slowly turned to me like I'd made a bad smell in the room. They just looked at me for what seemed like the longest, most soul-chilling moment. Then Bill slowly walked over, put his arm around me like he was my best friend,

One night John and Billy just switched parts and did each other's bits for the whole show. That's when I realized what geniuses they were.

—Rhonda Coullet

picked up my scarf, wrapped it carefully around my neck, led me out the door and said, "So why don't you come on by some other time."

I came back the very next day. You had to learn to be brave with these guys. I thought the show needed a little sharpening. Because I didn't know any better, I brought in Martin Charnin, who was the director and co-writer of *Annie*. *Annie* was, at that time, the most successful show on Broadway. They wouldn't pay him any attention. He would be like, "Okay, cast, you do this, and you go there, and you hold for applause and let's run this one more time." They'd just look at him like he was from outer space and then do whatever it was they'd wanted to do in the first place. In the end, it was really Belushi who organized it.

John was clearly in charge. He took it upon himself to be the administrative captain as well as the creative director. He was strangely, given his later reputation, the most professional of the group. He became the cast spokesperson. He was always the one to call and say we need this or let's do that. He'd complain about the marketing, how we needed to buy better ads, and so forth. He was the most focused on doing the thing right. And then onstage he was the emcee of the show and certainly the one in charge there as well.

RICHARD BELZER:

I came in as a replacement for Harold Ramis shortly after the show came to New York. When John found out that I wasn't getting paid the same as the rest of the cast, he threatened to quit. I got the raise. There were a lot of big personalities in the room in those days. I don't know if ringleader is the right word, but he was a kind of guiding energy. Eight out of ten times he'd say what we were going to do and we'd end up doing it, just because he was that persuasive. He was the number one cheerleader for having a good time, and he was very compelling.

BILL MURRAY:

If John was supposed to enter, say, thirty seconds behind you, you'd be ready to go on and John just wouldn't be there. You'd hear your cue and be like, "But there's nobody behind me to go on next." You'd walk on, say your line and then the door would burst open and it would be him. It was scary, but exciting. John had really perfected his technique. He knew exactly what he wanted, and he understood what was the right thing to do in every medium he was in.

IVAN REITMAN:

He was a substantial man who could just move beautifully. In a crowd of extraordinarily talented people, he was the electrical force that held it all together and gave the show its focus. When he later became more famous for his drug use, I'd have to tell people, "No, you don't understand. He was an actor as fine as Brando." He had that same kind of power on the stage. As good as he was in the movies, he actually had a much stronger effect live.

JIM BELUSHI:

The night that I went to New York to see the *National Lampoon Show*, Doug Kenney was sitting in the audience with me. We were looking up at the stage, and he said, "Brian, he's got a great face for the screen. Billy, he'll always work. Gilda, everyone will love Gilda. But your brother," he said, "your brother's gonna be a big star." ■

Chapter 7

I WOULD LIKE TO FEED YOUR FINGERTIPS TO THE WOLVERINES

life in New York on Saturday night

MARK METCALF, *co-star*, Animal House:

During the summer of 1975, I was at the Delacorte Theater in Central Park with John Heard, the actor, and our respective girlfriends. We'd come early with a blanket and a bunch of potato salad and fried chicken to sit in the grass and have a picnic. We were sitting there eating when along came this guy that Heard knew from Chicago. He introduced him and asked him to sit down and have some wine and a little chicken.

As he sat down he started telling us about a meeting he'd had with this guy named Lorne Michaels to do a live, late-night comedy show on TV. He talked a lot about how terrible TV was and how if he did it he'd be stifled and locked into the system and all that. We got pretty wrapped up in his story about jumping up on Michaels's desk and launching into a tirade on the horrors of television and the evil sucking sound it made as it pulled you into its mechanism, so much so that we didn't notice that he'd been helping himself to a healthy portion of our dinner. We just sat there on the grass laughing and talking for about twenty minutes. It felt like a conversation, but in retrospect he was doing most of the talking. When he was done he just got up, said thanks, and wandered on his way—at which point we realized that most of the potato salad, and all of the fried chicken, was gone.

There is much to say about the early years of Saturday Night Live, and most of it has already been said over and over and over again. The birth of the show is one of the most well documented in history, surpassed in coverage only by those of democracy, aviation and Christ. To recap: Johnny Carson ordered NBC President Herb Schlosser to stop running repeats of the Tonight Show late-nights on Saturdays. Schlosser charged producer Lorne Michaels with filling the gap. Michaels had a vision that shifted the earth's axis, aligned the planets and changed the face of comedy as we know it.

But in the summer of 1975, all of that was yet to be written. John had wrapped up the National Lampoon Show at the Palladium Theater and gone to California to film an episode of Supervision, a television show that Harold Ramis was creating for PBS. In the episode, John played the leader of a band of scrappy revolutionaries. They take over the headquarters of the most powerful television network on earth, threatening to destroy it if it does not meet their demands: stop poisoning the airwaves with offensive, mind-numbing programs.

Above (from left): Chevy Chase (kneeling), Laraine Newman and Dan Aykroyd (standing), Jane Curtin, Gilda Radner, host Ron Nesson, John, Garrett Morris and Lorne Michaels (on bed)

In the end, however, the revolutionaries become so seduced by the power of the new medium at their command that they are sucked into and become a part of the system they had hoped to tear down.

While John was in California, many of his contemporaries—Michael O'Donoghue, Anne Beatts, Gilda Radner, Chevy Chase—had been hired to work on a scrappy, revolutionary late-night comedy show that was going to tear down the offensive, mind-numbing programs that were poisoning the airwaves. Things proceeded from there about like one might imagine.

By the fall, John joined this unlikely crew of orphans in occupying the NBC studios and offices in Rockefeller Plaza. The other performers were Laraine Newman, Dan Aykroyd, Garrett Morris and Jane Curtin. Among the other writers were Al Franken and Tom Davis, Marilyn Suzanne Miller, Tom Schiller, Rosie Schuster and Alan Zweibel. The performers were paid only $750 a week. Many of the writers, less than that. The show itself was one part vaudeville, one part rock and roll and one part grade-school Easter pageant. For many months it was held together by little more than spit, duct tape and adrenaline. And yes, it did in fact change the face of comedy as we know it.

John and Lorne's relationship was complicated. There was a great deal of affection on both sides. Also fear.

—Anne Beatts

For John, it would be the intermediate step to realizing all of his ambitions, a lucky break given that he initially didn't want the job—and almost didn't get it. After months of resistance, Michaels had only agreed to hire him on the basis of a cold audition, an audition that consisted mostly of John walking around in a bathrobe with his hair tied up in a knot while not saying a word.

JUDITH BELUSHI PISANO:

John came up with the Samurai at home, so I watched the development of that one up close. There was a samurai film festival on PBS. John had heard about Toshiro Mifune, who was famous for these intense Japanese samurai films, and he was really excited to see them. These movies ran all day. He watched them…and watched them…and watched them. It was as if the TV was this force drawing him in. He'd get closer and closer to the set, watching Mifune and talking along with him in a deep, guttural tone. Suddenly he was up and moving around the apartment, imitating Mifune's gestures.

I'd seen enough to know he needed a sword, so I gave him this five-foot pole that was in the back of a closet. Big mistake. The next thing you know he's all over the room, swinging his sword, attacking everything in sight. The cats were running for cover, and I was grabbing up all the lamps and vases before he could destroy them.

LORNE MICHAELS, *producer*:

I'd seen John in the *National Lampoon Show* with Gilda, whom I already knew was going to be in the cast. He sort of dominated the show. I thought he was funny, but I think maybe because I was there he was working really hard, playing to the back of the house. That tends to work better onstage than in front of a camera. I wasn't knocked out; let's put it that way.

But Michael O'Donoghue and Chevy were both big fans and strongly endorsed him, and so I agreed to meet with him. At our first meeting he said that he didn't do television. It was all terrible and so forth. And I couldn't afford that kind of attitude. In my mind, we had this very small window in which we'd be able to get this show on and do it right before the network started to crack down. So I needed a group of people who were going to be disciplined and focused and really passionate about what they were doing. I think, looking back, what he meant to say was that he didn't do television, but he'd heard that I was different. But he came across the wrong way. I thought he could be trouble. We moved on for a couple of weeks, and then Michael and Chevy revisited it. They kept saying, "You're wrong on this."

ALAN ZWEIBEL, *writer*:

Lorne was hesitant to hire him. He was a little afraid of him. John hated television, and he made that known. That's why he did *SNL*, because it wasn't going to be television; it was going to make fun of television.

ANNE BEATTS:

Lorne said he was trouble, but we were like, "What? He's a sweetheart. Are you kidding?" And the way that John had exploded onto the stage in *Lemmings* was kind of amazing. It was the nexus of rock and roll and comedy, just as *SNL* was going to be. We just thought that if you were going to hire anyone, John should be at the top of the list. We really lobbied for it.

CHEVY CHASE:

It was a question of having to convince Lorne that there was a place for this kind of guy in the cast. Michael O'Donoghue and I were the only ones who knew John from having worked with him. I told Lorne, "Look, he's funny, he's got edge and he can make you laugh." I don't think it took much more than the Samurai audition to convince Lorne that John certainly was funny and had ideas.

JUDITH BELUSHI PISANO:

John decided he wanted to do the show. After being so adamant that he wouldn't do television, he became convinced that this was going to be different, outrageous, and he had to do it. But he would have to audition, which was very upsetting to him. John was never that adept at auditioning, and he was afraid of blowing it. So I suggested that he do the Samurai character he'd been working on. He liked that idea. I gave him a rubber band to pull back his hair, and he grabbed his robe, took the pole and off he went.

TOM SCHILLER, *writer*:

The auditions for *Saturday Night Live* were held at the Nola sound studios on Fifty-seventh Street. John was there swinging his samurai sword around for three hours in the audition hall, waiting to go on. Finally I said, "Someone better hire him before he kills somebody." But then he did the actual audition, and it was just the cutest thing. He walked in like he was going to kill someone, then took the samurai sword and started pretending to play billiards with it, which endeared him to all of us. It was a wonderful character. From that very first audition I started wondering how I could use the Samurai in a sketch.

LORNE MICHAELS:

He did what was referred to in the seventies as a "nonverbal audition." He just sort of made sounds, played pool and grunted. It was tremendously impressive.

JUDITH BELUSHI PISANO:

The first days at *SNL* were pretty exciting. Everyone believed they were involved in something new and bold. The writers all had assignments, and everyone was busy; John felt a little left out in that regard, but everyone was into throwing around ideas and trying to make each other laugh. He'd go up to the office about midday and stay until one or two in the morning. It became all consuming almost immediately.

The fact that the show was at Rockefeller Plaza was the real jolt that he'd made it to a new level. The lobby is very grand, a lot of art deco sculptures and mosaics and gilded carvings. For a while we always walked through quickly, thinking someone was going to spot us and kick us out. That's how out of place we felt. Even after John was a full-time employee of NBC, the elevator guards always hassled him. The fact that John never carried any ID with him didn't help.

The battle for the show began immediately. The whole idea that it was going to be "live" was very exciting. John assumed the Not Ready For Prime Time Players would be the main feature, that it was a sketch comedy show. But for the first show, the host, George Carlin, had two long stand-up bits; plus, there were two musical acts, two guest comedians and a short film from Albert Brooks. And then there were the Muppets. Everyone in the cast was pretty disappointed by how little airtime they had. John, as usual, was probably the most vocal.

ANNE BEATTS:

There was always quite a bit of friction between Lorne and John from the start. Just before the show began, Lorne fired him. I'm not sure why. John stormed off in a huff, went across the street and disappeared into the Pig & Whistle, this dive bar on Forty-eighth Street.

I tracked him down, had a beer with him and said, "No, no, this is crazy. This is a big opportunity for you. You've got to go back there and apologize." I kind of dragged him back up to the seventeenth floor and pushed him into Lorne's office and shut the door. I don't know what happened after that, but obviously he stayed on the show. I don't know if that was a good thing or a bad thing. Later on I thought maybe I should have just left him in the Pig & Whistle.

BERNIE BRILLSTEIN:

The day before the show, the set still wasn't finished and the sound system didn't work correctly. I went backstage and ran smack into a commotion. John, already dressed for the show's cold opening, was arguing with a producer, who was panic stricken. He needed Belushi to sign his contract. "You can't go on the air unless you do," he said.

I didn't understand why John was having a problem, but he ran up to me, waved the papers in my face and said, "He insists that I sign this contract."

"So sign it," I said. "What's the big fucking deal?"

"What do you think?" he said. "Would you sign it?"

"Listen, kid. I helped devise this contract, so of course you should sign it. It's very fair. It's really okay. Besides, you're going on in five minutes."

With Michael O'Donoghue in "Wolverines"

"Tell you what," he said. "If you manage me, I'll sign."

"You got a deal."

Belushi grabbed a pen and scribbled his name, then took his place on the set. I figured I'd never see him again. And then it hit me: he was pretty smart. He knew I managed Lorne, and who better to represent you than the boss's representative? He instinctively saw an opportunity and played it brilliantly in two minutes flat.

MICHAEL O'DONOGHUE:

John and I did the very first sketch on the very first show together. It was something I'd written for him in which he played an Albanian who was trying to learn English. I was a professor, a rather stern professor, strong on discipline, and I said to him, "Repeat after me: I would like to feed your fingertips to the wolverines."

And then John, in his pathetic Albanian accent, said, "I would like to feed your fingertips to the wolverines."

"We're out of wolverines; would you accept a badger in its place?" And John repeated that. And then, "'Gee,' Ned exclaimed. 'Let's boil the wolverines…'" Or something. I forget this stuff. But anyway, then I had a heart attack and then John had a heart attack and then Chevy Chase—or "a giant garden slug," as I liked to call him—stepped out and said, "Live from New York, it's *Saturday Night*." And the legend was born.

ROSIE SCHUSTER, *writer*:

The most lasting sketch from the first show was probably the slightest. "Bee Hospital" was just this little melodrama I'd written, this little slice of life. It really wasn't anything at all, and so I was astonished that Lorne wanted to put it on over and over again. I guess he just liked the surrealist idea of the whole cast dressed in these crazy outfits. The bees were on every show for a while, and John just felt it was so beneath him. I was one of the girl writers and still, legally, technically, Lorne's wife. But the fact that I was the one who put him in the dreaded bee costume was probably the nail in the coffin of our relationship.

AL FRANKEN, *writer*:

He hated being a bee.

©1976 Edie Baskin

With Laraine Newman and Dan Aykroyd in one of the dreaded, innumerable bee sketches

ANNE BEATTS:

He loathed being a bee.

RICHARD BELZER:

He despised being a bee.

CHEVY CHASE:

The fact is the network hated the bees. After we did the bees on the first show, they said, "One thing we don't want is the bees." And so the first thing Lorne did was have a new bee sketch every week. I just think John didn't like looking like a bee. He always wanted to be a little more handsome than he felt he was, and he just didn't think he looked handsome as a bee.

FRANNE LEE, *costume designer*:

The bee costume was his nemesis. He'd say to me, "I hate all this padding! It's too hot!"

"So then don't wear the padding," I'd say. "You're fat enough. You don't need it." Well, that guaranteed that he put on the padding. A lot of his performance in that costume was so good because he hated it so much. He felt that it was so humiliating, and all of that really came through in the character.

JUDITH BELUSHI PISANO:

The problem with the bee had more to do with what happened during the first weeks of *Saturday Night*. It was more about the fact that the Not Ready for Prime Time Players were not the main focus of the show, and for John the bees became a symbol of that. Other than the "Wolverines" sketch, pretty much all John did in those first few shows was be a bee.

But because *Saturday Night* was the kind of show where you took your anger and used it, he was able to turn that around into a scene in the third show where he went off on Rob Reiner about how much he hated it. As much as he hated the bee, he figured a way of ever so slightly moving his head so that the antennae darted and bobbed precariously above his head and looked really funny which, of course, endeared the bee to people even more.

With host Buck Henry in "Samurai Delicatessen"

LORNE MICHAELS:

The Samurai sketch on the seventh show was really the breakthrough for John. Richard Pryor was the host. He knew me pretty well, but he didn't want to come to the offices and be around a large group of white people whom he didn't know. So I went over to his hotel room and worked with him there. I kept telling him about John's Samurai. Then I had John come over. He did it for Richard, and Richard was like, "I gotta do that." Then Tom Schiller wrote it up as "Samurai Hotelier."

TOM SCHILLER:

When you work on a comedy show, your brain is always trying to figure out funny things to do. One day I was walking along Sixth Avenue with Chevy Chase, and out of nowhere I said, "Samurai Hotelier."

And Chevy said, "Yeah! That's a great idea." So I took it back and wrote it and passed it in. Lorne changed it to "Samurai Hotel," because he thought "hotelier" was too intellectual for people to understand.

LORNE MICHAELS:

When Buck Henry came on to host the tenth show, he asked if we had thought about doing the Samurai again, which John was ambivalent about. He said he didn't want to repeat things, but we went ahead and did it, and they came up with "Samurai Delicatessen."

BUCK HENRY, *host*:

John was always the one who said, "No, no, I don't want to do anything twice." Well, he and I did ten of them together. I don't know how many he did in all. So that notion was easily dispelled. But it was such a great part for him. It was a perfect idea, and I always thought that I was particularly good at doing it with him because I always understood what he was saying in Japanese.

TOM SCHILLER:

After "Hotel," all the Samurais were taken over by Alan Zweibel. I made a whole list of ideas and Alan added to it. He took it over from then on.

ANNE BEATTS:

The first Blues Brothers bit on the show was actually the two of them in bee outfits. The bees became one of those things that just pursued him—like smashing the beer can on the forehead as Bluto—whether he wanted it to or not.

BUCK HENRY:

I remember thinking, when I saw the "King Bee" number, what are they doing? What is this about?

But then, I often felt that.

CHRISTMAS '75

ALAN ZWEIBEL:

When they say I "wrote" the Samurais, what the fuck does that mean? "John throws tomato up, grunts, slices it." Yeah, great writing. The fun of it was in writing Buck Henry's part. Buck comes in with the *New York Times* under his arm, talking about the Super Bowl—"You know, I think if Pittsburgh gives Franco Harris the ball..." "Hakutokotah?" "Yes, I do want mayo."—and just blithely accepting the fact that this guy, this Samurai, has a deli. That was the fun of those sketches. Writing John's part was its own fun, but it was mostly just stage directions. I didn't write the grunts.

There were never any laughs in read through for the Samurai. Buck would read his parts, and John would grunt in the appropriate places. He was basically just going through the beats of the scene. He'd save it all for the performance.

After a while, it became a challenge to give John more moves. He had the big sword and the little sword and he grunted. So to give John more moves, we had to draw from the environment. In "Samurai Optometrist," John takes a

Above: Judy, Christopher Guest, John, Harold Ramis, Laila Nabulsi and Brian Doyle-Murray; Tom Davis, Michael O'Donoghue, Al Franken, Gilda Radner and Bill Murray; Paul Shaffer, Danny and John.

turtle, tosses it up and carves out a set of tortoise-shell glasses. If there were no such thing as tortoise-shell glasses, we would not have done "Samurai Optometrist." The settings dictated the jokes.

JUDITH BELUSHI PISANO:

The Samurai was a big breakthrough for John and one of the first things on the show that made him feel like he was getting somewhere. But then, after that first six months or so, Chevy became famous for his "I'm Chevy Chase and you're not" bit that he did during the news. He was definitely the star of the show, whereas when John walked down the street, people would hang out of their car windows, point to him and yell, "Hey, it's the bee!" It wasn't exactly what he'd dreamed his life in television would be like.

BOB TISCHLER:

Doing *The National Lampoon Radio Hour*, we always considered Chevy the least likely to make it. He just didn't have the same training and skills. And then on *SNL*, John watched Chevy all of the sudden zoom up and he was not comfortable with it at all. It was just a big surprise.

THE LAST VOYAGE OF THE STARSHIP ENTERPRISE

JUDITH BELUSHI PISANO:

At first John was very distraught, because he didn't think they were going to cast him as Captain Kirk. Michael O'Donoghue told me he wasn't sure who he wanted to cast. Then finally he waffled and asked, "Do you think John could do it?"

"Of course he can!" I said. "He does it all the time." John had just been through a period where he watched a lot of *Star Trek*.

MICHAEL O'DONOGHUE:

John said that he could do Bill Shatner. And then all through the rehearsals he couldn't do Bill Shatner. At all. It was awful. He just *said* he could do Bill Shatner. Just before airtime, I told him, "Boy, you really stabbed me in

the back with this Bill Shatner claim." Then he went on the air and did a flawless Shatner. It was the only time he ever did it. He did it for ten minutes on air, and never before or since.

JUDITH BELUSHI PISANO:

John was so into it that he actually shaved his sideburns in that pointed shape that they did on the show. And then for all the scenes before that, he put makeup over it so it looked like he had normal sideburns. Then when the *Star Trek* sketch came, the other guys had to paint their sideburns on, and John's were real. He was so proud of that sketch. That was the last show of the season, so for the next two weeks he walked around with those pointed sideburns just so he could talk about it some more.

PENNY MARSHALL, *actress/director*:

He'd go on his tirades and sulk. There was a lot of, "How come Chevy's in more stuff than I am?" He'd come over to your hotel and start moping about how he wasn't in enough sketches, that he was talented and why wasn't he doing what Chevy was doing. His insecurities would come out massively at that time.

CHEVY CHASE:

John didn't talk to me much. He did not throw himself into the group, didn't come into the office and discuss sketches. I spent most of my time in the office with Lorne, putting things together. John seemed to have other things to do. For one reason or another, he never particularly sought me out.

I think maybe he was sort of surprised that I was there at *SNL*. I don't know if he ever knew that I was instrumental in helping to convince Lorne to hire him. I think his feelings had to do with his real desire to be a star and to make it. I always knew he would, but there were clear-cut reasons why—whether I was good or not—I would be recognizable faster

John and Chevy

than John. I was saying my name every week, and people probably couldn't pronounce his. But apparently it did affect him a great deal, though I wasn't aware of it at the time. John was always petulant and cantankerous anyway. That was just his nature. He was also very soft and an easy pushover.

ROSIE SCHUSTER:

He wasn't pleased with the material he was getting. One time I heard him say, "They throw me bones a dog couldn't chew on." Another one of his favorite phrases at the time was, "I go where I'm kicked."

LORNE MICHAELS:

Chevy was thirty-one. I was thirty. Michael was probably sixty. We'd all been around and been part of other scenes. John was twenty-six. Danny was twenty-three. And that five or six years of age difference was significant, almost generational.

JUDITH BELUSHI PISANO:

On a certain level, John just felt like an outsider. There was always a group around Lorne, those who fit in. Part of John's problem with Chevy was that Chevy was foremost among them. He and Lorne had become friends before the show, and they worked together a lot. John was jealous of that.

Lorne was also a bit of an enigma to John. He couldn't quite relate to him as a contemporary because he seemed older and wiser. He really wanted to be friends, but it always seemed that a line was drawn, a line that said, "I'm your boss," or "We're too different," or "Please don't hurt me." Something was in the way, and John didn't understand it. He couldn't break into the inner circle, and he felt it affected his ability to get the results he wanted with the show. It was a lot like the social scene in high school, except in this case the result affected your grade.

RICHARD BELZER:

I think on a certain level Lorne had a bit of a crush on Chevy. But everyone who was there always felt that John was the funniest guy on the show. It was just a question of finding the right part to showcase his talents and make a name for him with the people watching. When he and O'Donoghue came up with the Weatherman, that really nailed it.

"But nooooooooooooo…"; as the Weatherman, with Chevy Chase

ALAN ZWEIBEL:

The Samurai came before the Weatherman, but the Weatherman was the first time he really engaged people as John Belushi—this pent-up, angry, average guy who gets himself so worked up he falls over from a heart attack. John's appeal didn't come from delivering the best punch lines, though he certainly could. If you watch some of the shows, John will look at the camera for a second with the eyebrow and then go right back into the scene, as if to say, "Look where I'm going next." And that took the viewer for a ride. That's what made his relationship to the people at home so powerful. There was an attachment, an identification that was made.

I was standing next to Lorne watching the monitor one of the first times he did the Weatherman, and Lorne said, "It's Gleason." And he was right. When you think about it there was a lot of Jackie Gleason, a lot of Ralph Kramden there. There was something so blue collar about John. He looked uncomfortable in a suit. Whenever he had to wear a suit on the show, he looked like some guy off the boat who'd been dressed up by his relatives to go for a job interview. Look at the Samurai: a guy who can't speak English, who's stuck in all these lowly jobs and is so put upon he tries to commit suicide.

When immigrants come to America, they're outsiders and they have to assimilate: change their names and lose their identities. Most of the Jewish and ethnic entertainers before John had done that. He didn't. He didn't blend in. He did it on his own terms. He was the angry, rebellious voice they all identified with. It's little wonder a nation of immigrants embraced him.

DAN AYKROYD:

That summer, after the season wrapped, John and I took a cross-country trip together. We went to Jann Wenner, who suggested that we write a *Rolling Stone* piece about it. He really set us up. John took the Chevy Caprice that we rented from Hertz and had a three-thousand-dollar Nakashima sound system put in it: CB, radio, all paid for by *Rolling Stone*. And we hit the road.

John used to love the gas stops, going in to chat with the guys behind the counter there. There were lots of cigarettes, continuous tapes being shoved in, listened to and discarded, John getting really mad at me for driving too fast. The two of

us in the Bluesmobile in the movie was basically the two of us on those trips. He had so much to say, so much to object to, and it was my job as the driver to take it. That was the early gestation of life as the Blues Brothers.

In July of '76 the American Legion had a convention at the Bellevue-Stratford hotel in Philadelphia, and they suffered a few deaths due to bacteria polluting the air conditioning water, hence Legionnaire's Disease. So of course when we went through that's where we stayed. We just walked around the hotel in gas masks having all sorts of fun. We stopped at the Democratic Convention in Atlanta where Jimmy Carter was being nominated. We visited a friend of mine in New Orleans. It was just the two of us, which was great. There were no entourages then. Neither of us had our staff with us, because there was no staff.

JANN WENNER, *publisher*, Rolling Stone:

One night, while they're on their trip, I'm sitting in my house around two in the morning. I get a phone call from a guy who identifies himself as Sheriff Leander Perez from some parish in Louisiana, and he says he's got these two guys in custody, a Mister Don A-kroid and a Mister John Bool-oosh-ai, and they've just killed somebody driving a car that's registered to *Rolling Stone*. He's getting me really whipped up about how he's got

them in jail and the victim's family is there and on and on. And of course it was them. They loved to do that kind of stuff.

DAN AYKROYD:

Halfway through we pulled over at the University of Arkansas in Little Rock. John wanted to stop on the college campuses to see what the penetration of the show was, to see if it was punching through to the audience that was going to mean something to our careers in the next ten years. I don't think we got recognized at all, anywhere. We certainly didn't get laid, that's for sure.

If John and Danny spent their journey to California totally unrecognized and sexually unfulfilled, the same could not be said of Chevy Chase. Chevy left for Hollywood with a great deal of recognition and went straight into the arms of his fiancée, a woman so beautiful that she enticed him to quit the hippest show on American television. That fall, Chevy announced that he was leaving SNL to produce and star in several prime-time specials; lucrative movie deals were pending as well. He appeared in the first handful of shows that season, helping the cast and the audience to make the transition. He then moved to Los Angeles for good, marrying just a few weeks later. Chevy would later regret his decision to leave. John would not.

With the breakout star of the first season gone, John was there, eager and able to take his place. The Samurai became the show's biggest

recurring character. The Weatherman's exasperated "but, noooooo…" became the show's next trademark catchphrase. John's ascension to the spotlight started to catch the attention of the national press, including the eye of a young writer named Mitch Glazer. Glazer worked for Crawdaddy, an upstart challenger to Rolling Stone, and that fall he undertook what would be the first real media profile of the Most Dangerous Man on Television. To get the story, he spent weeks riding shotgun in John's frenzied late-night world. Then, despite the considerable damage to his sleeping patterns, he pretty much stayed there. For reasons that can only be ascribed to basic human chemistry, Glazer was quickly adopted into a circle of company that only Danny, Judy and maybe a handful of others enjoyed.

But the sudden jolt of success was not without problems. John craved fame and success, but the actual acquisition of it was never easy for him. It was as if the sound of the applause started a feedback loop of doubt and uncertainty in his mind, invariably setting off a chain of events that seldom ended well. Also in that second year, the success and profile of the show itself were far greater than anyone had planned. It had become indispensable to NBC's advertisers. Hurried contract renegotiations took place, and the performers' salaries soared from $750 per week to $1,600 per week, leaving John face to face with what would become one of his mortal enemies: disposable cash. Things moved a little fast for John that fall, in part because, as he would later say to Glazer in the profile, "When in doubt, I floor it."

John and Danny cross America

MITCH GLAZER, *writer:*

New York and *Rolling Stone* and all the big magazines had all been focusing on Chevy. But for me the excitement whenever John came on-screen was jarring. Danger is the wrong word, although that's what we ended up using as the title of the piece: "The Most Dangerous Man on Television." It was just a comedy I hadn't seen before. I went to my editor at *Crawdaddy* and said I'd like to do a piece on him.

I called John directly; he didn't have any buffers back then. The negotiations were hysterical. While I was talking back and forth with John, he was talking back and forth with Jann Wenner, the editor of *Rolling Stone*, and Jann was telling him exactly what to ask for: cover shot, copy approval, everything. I'd never had anybody demand that stuff up front, and I'd never given it. But John was getting the best advice possible, so it was brutal. We finally agreed that he could read it and if there was anything particularly jarring we could talk about it, but he never had editorial control.

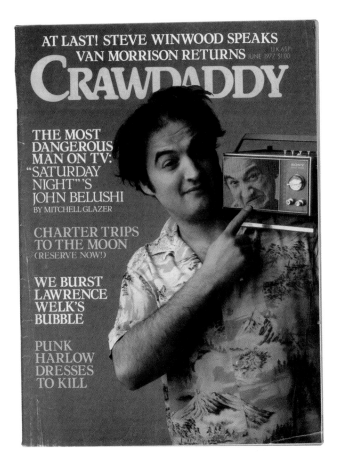

I went up to the Bleecker Street apartment. Laila and Judy answered the door, and I think they thought I was the delivery guy. I was young and I had really long hair. John came out, and then he took me to this bar in the Village. It was a real workingman's bar, a drinker's bar. This was around ten or eleven in the morning, and nothing is grimmer than a bar like that in the daytime, a bunch of winos and regulars drinking on their lunch shift. We talked for a while. I remember coming home to my girlfriend's house and having kind of a heavy feeling about him. He was going through a rough time. Even then—and this isn't hindsight—I was just a little anxious for him.

I was crazy about him, though. We bonded instantly. It was like family. I was there, hanging out in his dressing room, virtually every Saturday night from the minute I met him until the minute he left the show. It became a routine, and I got to see what his life on the show was like. There were times in that second year when it was everything he wanted: Chevy was gone and he was The Guy. But they were pushing him really hard. I had no concept of what live TV was like. It was an astounding, ripping energy and pressure that they put themselves through. O'Donoghue used to describe it as grabbing a live wire and taking a jolt. I was exhausted, and I was just watching. I would actually see him much calmer and stronger later on, but he was pretty whipped then. There was the inevitable high of having done the show and gotten through it, but then there was also a crash. You could see the effects that the rollercoaster was having.

HAROLD RAMIS:

When *SNL* was starting its second year, John asked me to come to New York and meet with Lorne, who asked me to work on the show. I turned it down. It just didn't feel good to me. I could tell that the work habits at *SNL* were not healthy, just not good at all. John was already starting to look exhausted, and not just physically.

CANDICE BERGEN, *host:*

The change was quite dramatic. Everyone had been affected by this incredible notoriety. Certain people had become household names and others hadn't, yet they were all on equal footing on the same show. John was obviously one of the ones

who'd caught on. They were under incredible pressure. People suddenly had money, and so anything they were inclined to pursue in terms of recreational drugs was no longer off-limits because of affordability.

LORNE MICHAELS:

Toward the end of the first season, John had figured out how things worked with the host's limousine. He'd somehow drop the host off at his hotel and then drive around for several hours with his hand on the automatic roof switch, just sort of enjoying New York from that perspective.

Each person in the cast got two tickets, and John was always overextending himself in offering them around. He was always taking them out of my desk or pleading for them or putting people on a list. He was proud of the show, and he was kind of puffed out about it. That part was always there, and as the season wore on that part started to get bigger.

He came back that fall and said, "People really love the Samurai…Maybe we should start doing more of those." And this was the one thing that he swore he wouldn't keep doing. But he was starting to get feedback about what the public wanted for the first time. We hadn't been out of New York, or even the office, in the better part of a year.

That summer I had hired John and Danny as writers on this Beach Boys special with Zweibel out in California. We spent a lot of time together, and that was probably the period when we were all closest. We were in the first glow of our triumph. The show had won three Emmys that June. That first intoxicating period of success is incredibly confusing. You get to meet everyone you ever thought you wanted to meet, and they want to meet you. It was a very heady time, and John started to lose his balance a little. He was testing all the boundaries at that point, with Judy, with everyone at the show. And with Chevy gone, the thing he'd most hoped for—to be the alpha male—had now happened, and it was scary. I think he ran from it.

MARILYN SUZANNE MILLER, *writer*:

That fall, we did several shows at studios out in Brooklyn because Studio 8H had been taken over to do election coverage for NBC. It was chaos. Our offices were still in midtown, and the studio was in the middle of nowhere. You had to take a car service back and forth through all hours of the night. Nobody knew where they were going or what they were doing. With all the confusion, it was impossible to keep track of the secretaries and the typists, let alone John. He fell off the grid a little bit.

BUCK HENRY:

"Samurai Deli" is of course my sentimental favorite, but "Samurai Stockbroker" is so memorable just because of what happened. It was really my fault. We never rehearsed that much. The blocking was never that secure, and the timing of the Samurai sketches was always kind of improvised to begin with. I was always fairly aware of the fact that I could get hurt from this swinging samurai sword, but that night I forgot. I moved in just a step too close, and John swung back and lodged the blade right in my forehead. Right after that I was supposed to jump out the window like a suicidal stock loser; however, in my disoriented state I took the wall with me, and that cut my leg up, too. So I made a complete mess of myself. My pants and my face were all bloody. It was really very exciting. We had a long commercial break right after it happened, and fortunately, that gave me a chance to recover.

I have heard since that after the accident John said to Lorne, "You know, if Buck can't finish the show, I can do most of his stuff." I don't know whether that's true or not, but I like the idea that, having embedded this sword in my bare head, he lobbied for my part. And then, to add peculiarity to injury, someone asked if there was a doctor in the house. There was. It was John's doctor! He just happened to be in Brooklyn seeing the show that night. So it was like some weird conspiracy with John's doctor being there.

For me that event was always the signature value of the show. Chevy put a bandage on his head for Update and led with a news piece about my getting hit. And then Jane put her arm in a sling, and finally by the end of the show the camera pulls back and half the guys working the cameras are on crutches. I was so proud of that show.

ANNE BEATTS:

It was a seesaw period in his life. There were a lot of eruptions going on at that point.

ALAN ZWEIBEL:

Judy, in an attempt to give John some regimen, started hiring limousines to take him out at night, sort of to make sure he made it from here to there and would be supervised along the way. And also to siphon off some of the cash so he couldn't use it for other things. She had her hands full trying to rein him in.

JUDITH BELUSHI PISANO:

It was rough. He was just spending too much time at the show, too many nights on the town and too much money on coke. I hit a wall and I snapped. In early November, I asked him to move out, and he did. We were separated for about a month.

MICHAEL KLENFNER, *Atlantic Records executive*:

I first met John around that time. I was doing promotion on an album from the first year of *SNL*. He was staying at the Essex House hotel in New York because, as I later learned, Judy had thrown him out. I went up, knocked on the door, no answer. I knew he was supposed to be there, ready to do some promotion with me in the New York City area. Something was just wrong, so I went to the maid on the floor and told her I was the guy's manager and I needed her to open up the room. She did, and I went in. There was John, passed out, with a lit cigarette lying on the bed.

DICK EBERSOL, *producer*:

In order to work things out with him and to make him feel appreciated, I flew him back to Los Angeles with me every Sunday and let him stay at my house until the following Wednesday. He'd sleep all day, stay up all night and just generally be John. Things seemed to be going well until I was walking down the hall one morning and noticed smoke coming out from under his bedroom door. I ran in and saw that he'd fallen asleep with a lit cigarette and his mattress was on fire. I woke him up and threw water on the bed to put it out. He just shrugged, moved over to the other bed and went back to sleep.

ALAN ZWEIBEL:

I, like everyone else, used to snoop around Lorne's desk after he'd gone home. One day I came across a message from Dick Ebersol on one of those "While You Were Out" pads. It read: "I have the Albanian. Everything is under control." It was around that same time that I started hearing the word *schvitz* more and more in the lexicon of the seventeenth floor.

MICHAEL KLENFNER:

I turned John on to the Tenth Street Baths. I figured he needed it. I thought it was a place that could help straighten him out and clean him up. The first time I took him he didn't even want to go in. Pretty soon he was going all the time. It's this old Russian bathhouse in the East Village where you could go for a steam bath, a *schvitz*, and relax and wind down. Back then it was men only. There were great things there. You'd go downstairs and have a steam, a shave, and then go upstairs in your bathrobe and sit in this old barber's chair and get a nice haircut. They had a barber there named Hollywood Joe who used to work for the movie studios back in the day. With the Yiddish accents, they used to call him "Hollyvood." John loved that. You'd come out of there like a new penny.

PENNY MARSHALL:

I was in New York for the Macy's Thanksgiving Day Parade, staying at the Sherry-Netherland hotel. John showed up on my doorstep looking like a lost orphan. I called Judy and said, "I got him."

"Keep him."

So he spent most of the Thanksgiving holidays crashed out on my hotel room sofa.

ROSIE SCHUSTER:

He'd been on the outs with Judy. I didn't have the whole backstory on what exactly had happened, but he just had this look, this vibe about him. You could see that he had nowhere to go for Christmas, and it was so sad. He looked like a boy who was saying, "Please take me in and make me be okay and let me feel at home again." So I sat down with my brother and wrote "Adopt Belushi for Christmas," about how he needed to be placed in a home. It ran on the

ADOPT BELUSHI FOR CHRISTMAS

©1976, Edie Baskin

Candice Bergen: Well, it's the last show before Christmas, and after it's over we'll probably all go out and celebrate before heading our separate ways for the holidays. Gilda's going home to Detroit, Danny up to Canada, Laraine to Los Angeles. Jane'll stay here with Patrick and, I guess, Garrett'll be going back to Africa. Yes, everybody's going home. Everybody...except for Belushi.

Now, we all want to help John, but then we've all helped him so much already: putting him up, talking over his problems with him, lending him money. So now it's your turn to help. And believe me, if you like good acting and you just plain get off on good vibes, then here's an offer you just can't refuse. *Saturday Night* proudly announces the Adopt Belushi for Christmas contest. Write in immediately and state your case in twenty words or less why you are the ideal family to adopt Belushi for Christmas. With his swarthy good looks, John will appear right at home in any family with a depressed European background. John's had all of his shots, he's an eager eater, plus he comes with his own attractive wardrobe, which includes a Kahoutek T-shirt. Let Belushi share his many stories and songs with the kiddies.

John Belushi: *Chestnuts roasting on an open fire... Jack Frost nipping at your nose...* Hi! I'm John Belushi! But you can call me "Beloosh," just like my close personal friend Chevy Chase does. You know, it's corny, but I love Christmas. I'd love to sit around the yule log and play with your daughter. Actually, I'm not doing much this Christmas. Anyway, how 'bout dinner? I'm not fussy. I'd like some candied yams, some plum pudding, a roast goose stuffed with drugs. A quadraphonic sound system would be real nice. And I could use a car, if you've got one, a nice, brand new car. If you've got a fifteen-year-old girl, of course, that'd be nice. Fourteen, I don't care. Sixteen. A nice girl.

Candice Bergen: So, if you think you're that special American family, why not write to: ADOPT BELUSHI FOR CHRISTMAS care of SATURDAY NIGHT, Box 409, New York 10019. Runners-up will receive a personal phone call from Don Pardo. Come on, what do you say?

Candice Bergen show just before the holidays, and in a strange way it captured something kind of perfect about him at the time.

JUDITH BELUSHI PISANO:

During that month I picked up some work at *National Lampoon* and tried to keep busy. John called a few times and asked how I was. I kept the conversations short. He left some money in the mailbox once or twice. Then in December he asked if he could leave some clothes at the apartment. The next thing I knew, he was back as well. He showed up in great shape, made a beautiful apology and plea for another chance and, obviously, won me over.

The show was going on break for a few weeks, and we decided to spend Christmas in Aspen with my brother Rob. On the third day there, I overheard John talking to Rob about a wedding. After a while, I realized he was talking about us. He said he wanted me to be taken care of in case anything happened to him. We had talked about getting married, but with all the difficulties we'd been through I'd assumed that plan was on hold. Apparently, John didn't. I thought, okay, do I still want to get married? And I decided, well, if we're going to live together again, we might as well. But now I had to explain some things to John. "I heard you tell my brother that we were going to get married," I said.

"Well, yeah, aren't we?"

"Well, sure, but you don't just *get married*. You need blood tests and a license. You have to plan, John."

"Oh."

It was about an hour drive to the county seat to do the formalities. We took the blood test and were told to come back in a week for the results; then we could take that paperwork to the courthouse for the license. I realized that day would be New Year's. "Will the courthouse be open that day?" I asked.

"Oh yeah, sure," the nurse responded. I always trust nurses.

Come New Year's Eve there's a terrible storm. This time it takes us about two hours to get to the hospital. We pick up the blood test results and go over to the courthouse. It's closed. But we try the doors anyway and find one open. There are two women behind the counter. The one with her hair in curlers tells us they're not open.

"You can't be closed," John insists. "We have to get our marriage license."

"Looks like you're out of luck."

"But both our families have flown in for this wedding. They're waiting for us, with the minister, in Aspen. They all have to leave tomorrow."

She looks at us disapprovingly, but asks to see our identification. I present my driver's license, and John, who of course doesn't have his, proceeds to unfold a newspaper clipping he's pulled from his pocket. "Well, ma'am, you see, I'm John Belushi, and this article tells you my name and my age. See, right here, I'm twenty-seven. And there's a photo. That's me." He gives her a winning smile.

Incredulous wouldn't even begin to describe her reaction. She throws up her hands in disbelief. "Well, there is no way you can get a marriage license without proof of who you are and when you were born. It is absolutely not possible."

"What do people do if they don't have identification?" I ask. "What if it's been lost, or you don't drive and don't have a passport? Are you saying that no one, *no one*, has ever gotten a marriage license without ID?!"

At this point, the other women speaks up. "Well, if you could get a judge's confirmation that would do." She gives us the names of three judges. We hurry to the hall pay phone. The first two attempts come up empty, no answer. Number three's the charm.

"Hello, Judge? I'm sorry to bother you at home but, you see, I have a problem… Are you familiar with a show called *Saturday Night Live*? …No? Well, my name is John Belushi…"

Somehow, miraculously, John convinces the judge to come in on New Year's Day and sign a formal affidavit. We get the license. Then we drive another two hours back to Aspen. Meanwhile, my brother's busy entertaining the minister, who had started to doubt that we would ever return. "No, no, stay. They'll be here. It's just the storm. Have some more wine," Rob told him.

By the time we got back, two bottles later, they were a little drunk—especially the minister, who had been fasting. But it was a sweet ceremony. We exchanged our vows and toasted with champagne. It certainly was a night to remember.

With the popularity of SNL *among college students, the performers and writers had begun to speak and perform on the university lecture circuit to earn a little extra money. That January, while speaking at a college in Rhode Island, John went flying off the stage in a spectacular samurai leap, took a very bad spill and blew out his knee. He spent a week in the hospital and went to work in a wheelchair (and a very bad mood) for several days after that. Otherwise, the rest of the winter and spring proceeded seemingly without incident.*

As part of his renewed commitment to Judy, John had agreed to start seeing a therapist for what they believed at the time to be largely a behavioral problem, merely a lack of self-control exacerbated by a few anger management issues. He went every week for the next four months, eased his foot off the accelerator and life moved forward. But if John's personal life had been going through rocky terrain, you'd never know it by tuning in to NBC Saturday nights at eleven thirty. John's rapport with the audience, as well as the other writers and performers, had only gotten better.

TOM DAVIS, *writer*:

The best thing I can say about John is that if you put him in your sketch he would make it work. He might muff a few lines, but he would make the audience laugh and make it a memorable sketch, whether it deserved to be or not.

ALAN ZWEIBEL:

John didn't need a script. Words were not John's friend. He was not a word-friendly guy. It's not that he couldn't

Mr. and Mrs. John Belushi, New Year's Day, 1977

deliver lines; he did and often wonderfully so. But what he needed was a road map, an arena to play in. We gave him arenas. Writing stuff for John was easy. All you had to do was get the script sort of halfway there, and he'd say, "Eh, this sucks but I'll make it work." And then he'd go out onstage and figure it out. I had never seen anything like it. Of course, I was the Jew who'd been writing for Catskill comedians, so anything was new and amazing to me in those days. That being said, I've never seen it since.

MICHAEL O'DONOGHUE:

John wasn't so good on complex dialogue. He could remember colors. He was very good with colors, and faces. And he could do shapes, you know, balls, triangles, that sort of thing. Actually, John did pretty good on my dialogue. He had some trouble in *1941*, clearly, where all he could

Recuperating at New York's Lenox Hill Hospital

remember was how to scream at certain intervals. But he wasn't bad. Dialogue isn't really the important thing. It's pulling it off. That is the important thing, really. John gave it his best shot. He was always in for the ride, and I really appreciated that. He went "balls out," as the bikers say.

TOM DAVIS:

John wasn't as good as Danny at reading cue cards. Danny could read them cold and you'd never even know. With John, you could tell he was reading them, and so Franken and I were always kind of irked that he didn't seem to learn his lines. But we were missing the point. For John, the whole point was getting out there on live TV and trying to do it *without* being prepared. That's what gave him his energy. That's why Lorne and Chevy started doing things like tying his shoelaces together while he was on camera.

MICHAEL O'DONOGHUE:

Fear was always John's greatest ally. It was for all of us, quite confidentially. If John got frightened enough he would do

amazing things. The *Honeymooners* bee sketch, for example, was one that he just loathed and despised. He thought it was going to make him look like a fool come airtime, and he didn't want to look like a fool. So he pulled it out.

DAN AYKROYD:

We would go and do these college lectures to make extra money. We were at one in Rhode Island, and John was doing the Samurai. He came across the stage in this magnificent *House of Crouching Dragon*-type leap. Unfortunately, there wasn't any stage where he landed. About three quarters of that leap was incredible. The last quarter was a little rough. It was about a ten-foot drop. He twisted the hell out of his knee, spent a week in the hospital, missed a show and went to work in a wheelchair for a few weeks after that. It impaired him for the rest of the season and bothered him a lot throughout his career. But you'd never know it seeing him dance.

JIM DOWNEY, *writer*:

John was never very verbal as a performer, and in the history of the show he's the only cast member who was ever able to get big laughs without speaking at all. I wrote a series of sketches loosely based on those little games kids play where they ask each other things like "What if God and Superman got in a fight?" They would always start off with a question written in from some eight-year-old kid in Iowa, and then there would be a serious dramatization, acted out as if it were actually researched by experts and so forth.

The one I wrote for John was "What if Napoleon had a B-52?" John was so excited about playing Napoleon. He kept wondering whether he should try and do Rod Steiger's Napoleon or this other guy's Napoleon.

We used the show's control room as CentComm and Danny played the sergeant at arms who walked John through the scene: "Emperor, I'd like to go over the armaments we'll be taking into battle today. Here we have the cluster bombs. We call 'em daisycutters..." And John followed him around dressed as Napoleon with the hand in the jacket and the Napoleon hat— and he never spoke. Not a word. All he did was nod, quietly inspecting the ordinance, and it was hysterical.

As Napoleon Bonaparte, with Laraine Newman and host Steve Martin

RICHARD BELZER:

The actors couldn't really "improvise," per se, because it's live TV and the cameras are all blocked and everything is timed down to the last second. So you had to do all your lines and stick to the cue cards. But what John could do, and was brilliant at, is that within those limitations he could always create something new, something extra to throw in that just took it to the next level. And he did it on live national television.

BERNIE BRILLSTEIN:

John had such concentration. I'd be watching the show behind the camera, and he'd just look at me in the middle of the scene and wink. He knew right where he was going next. John always knew.

ROBIN WILLIAMS:

When John was performing he was in total control. If he were going to fling himself across the stage, he had to know that he could do it and not hurt himself or others. I think he could do that easily. You could see how he worked. I think the center of his cyclone was always pretty calm.

BILL MURRAY:

In "Samurai Deli," he threw a tomato up and cut it in half in midair. That's not luck, you know.

JIM DOWNEY:

When Belushi was funny, it was always things that you couldn't write—a look, an eyebrow—and so you were always surprised. With Billy or Danny you remember long, complicated scenes or concepts. With Belushi you remember great moments, just little three-second bits.

ANNE BEATTS:

John could make people laugh by raising an eyebrow, but I think it would be less than giving him his due to suggest that's as far as his talent went. He also was really good at impersonations, and he struggled long and hard over them. If you spent half an hour with John, he could do an impression of you. He had an actor's craft, and he worked at it and made significant choices about what he did. He certainly made it all seem effortless, but then that's the trick, isn't it?

MARILYN SUZANNE MILLER:

I used to write these pieces for the show that were more dramatic. They were funny, but they were more "character pieces" than sketches. When Sissy Spacek came on to host, she'd just won the Oscar for *Carrie*. I wanted to write something for her that had a little weight to it. At that point, John was only known for these crazy characters like Joe Cocker and the Samurai, things that didn't involve a lot of complicated dialogue. But I just felt like John was strong enough to play opposite her.

MICHAEL O'DONOGHUE:

TV Guide came up to the *Saturday Night Live* offices and did a story on us. One of Lorne's favorite things to do at that time was to call you into his office and then make you wait while he made lots of phone calls to celebrities. John did a great imitation of this. He'd be Lorne on the phone saying, "Nicholson, can you hold just a second? I have Mike Nichols on the other line. Mike, can you hold for a second? I have Mick Jagger on the other line. Mick, I'll be with you in a second, I've got..." And so on.

So John did his imitation for this reporter, but before he did it he took all the photographs in the office—which at that time were mostly of Candy Bergen; Lorne had one of the largest collections of Candy Bergen photographs in existence—and tilted them sideways at about a thirty-degree angle to create some sort of *Cabinet of Dr. Caligari*, German Expressionist atmosphere. Then he got behind the desk and did this shtick. And then, very carefully, he went and put every photograph correct again.

Lorne went nuts when he read about this. He was so pissed. Not because John was parodying his upward mobility, but because the Bear Man had been pawing his photographs. The real genius of the stunt was not in imitating Lorne, but in knowing enough to fragment that reality while doing it.

He was up for the challenge, but to do it, to really act it, he couldn't just read it off the cue cards. It was an incredibly wordy sketch. Basically, the premise of it was that they were this young white-trash couple who'd just gotten married, and he was having some man problems in the bedroom because he thought she was attracted to somebody else. John struggled all week. I'd track him down like a schoolmarm yelling, "John! Get over here! Now!" and we worked on the character and the dialogue over and over and over again. He busted his ass to hold his own with this Oscar-winning actress, and it was tremendous. He was tremendous. I think it was the best acting he's ever done.

When we went to the Emmys that year, we had two shows up against each other for the award. One was the Elliot Gould show with O'Donoghue's famous "Star Trek" sketch, and the other was the Sissy Spacek show with my sketch. Michael was all set to get up and give his speech when Tim Conway announced that the winner was *Saturday Night Live* with Sissy Spacek. And it was because of John. Because he broke his ass in this piece to get it right. He would have been capable of so much more if anyone had ever paid him enough attention and he'd tried hard enough and had a good director—none of which was ever the point at *Saturday Night Live*. But it could have been the point if someone had given him the shot. Nobody in Hollywood gave a shit about what John could have been, but that's what John could have been. John could do anything.

ANNE BEATTS:

Our natural tendency was to write things for John because he was so great, but many things the women writers did he refused to be in. At a certain point, he made a regular practice of going to Lorne and asking for the girl writers to be fired. But I didn't take it personally.

TOM DAVIS:

There was a lot of testosterone in those days. The girls learned to fend for themselves when they came up against that.

ALAN ZWEIBEL:

Sometimes in the writing meetings, John would be particularly mean to the girl writers. He would be just nasty

John in Marilyn Suzanne Miller's "Romance" sketch

to them, and we'd all sit there like, *oh shit*... But then the next day I'd see him walking in with boxes of chocolate and bouquets of flowers to make up for the way he'd behaved the day before.

ANNE BEATTS:

I think it was more complicated than just pure and simple sexism. John would refuse to be in things we wrote and went on and on about how the girls weren't funny. But even in the most negative periods between John and myself, he would always come and do really sweet things like give me a back rub. He gave great back rubs. You felt that there was a certain goodwill underlying the somewhat monstrous behavior. It was like having a brother that you don't always get along with but are very close to nevertheless.

LORNE MICHAELS:

John would always get into a fight and then back down. He'd make a lot of noise, and then you'd be like, "What? That's it?"

GOIN' SOUTH

JUDITH BELUSHI PISANO:

The summer after the second year of *SNL*, John's manager got a call from Harry Gittes, the producer on a film called *Goin' South*. It was a western being directed by Jack Nicholson. John had played a Mexican sheriff in Michael O'Donoghue's "Minute Mystery" sketches; Nicholson had seen it and wanted him for the part of Hector, the deputy. It was a really small part; the producers were half expecting him to turn it down. But John felt it would be good to have movie experience before *Animal House,* and he was dying to work with Nicholson. The biggest reason John made the movie, though, was because of his father, Adam. Adam loved the old, classic TV cowboy shows like *Bonanza,* and John thought nothing would make him happier than to see his son riding a horse in a big Hollywood western.

JACK NICHOLSON, *director*:

When John showed up on location in Durango, I told one of the assistants to take him over to the dentist and get him fitted with a gold tooth for the part.

"A gold tooth?" he said. "What the hell do I need with a gold tooth?"

"Trust me," I said. "Go to the dentist."

Naturally he fell in love with that gold tooth and wore it everywhere.

On that first day, when he came back from the dentist, I asked him exactly why he had made the trip to Durango.

"Have you ever seen *Lawrence of Arabia*?" he asked.

"Yeah," I said, "I've seen it."

He grinned. "Well," he said, "I came for you, Lawrence."

We developed a pretty close relationship in Durango. John looked to people he liked for dedication, and he returned it in kind. Not many people would have come so far and been so enthusiastic about such a small role.

MARY STEENBURGEN, *co-star*:

John and Jack both really appreciated each other's creativity. They were both kind of wild. Most nights we'd all have dinner at Jack's house, and we'd all eat and play music and tell stories and sing. The people on that movie were important to me, because it was my first film and they were a bridge to this whole new world I was entering. John was one of those people. I was this young kid just trying to put one foot in front of another, and John really went out of his way to reach out to me and reassure and encourage me.

ED BEGLEY, JR., *co-star*:

For all the things that you hear about John, he was actually a very sobering influence in my life. My drinking in those days was pretty bad. For me, *Goin' South* was actually a big party with some occasional work. One day in particular, a day that was a culmination of weeks and weeks of my behavior, he literally came and pulled me out of the bar and said, "Come on, Ed. That's enough."

"That's enough? What do you mean?"

"Get out of the bar, put the drink—give me that! C'mon! Come out to the car. We're going to go for a ride. You haven't seen sunlight for weeks."

He gave me a big hand up, made me see there was more to Durango than the inside of a bar, and I've always been grateful for that. We had a great time riding around Mexico, but then the problems started because of the schedule. The producers had promised Lorne Michaels that John'd be done for the start of the third season. Sometimes he'd sit around for days on location and not even get to shoot anything, and then he'd have to fly this crazy commute back to New York.

It just got more and more difficult. All this came to a head one day when John went to go talk to Jack and the producer's told him he couldn't see him. Everybody's tempers flared and there was a huge screaming argument. It was pretty tense for the rest of the shoot.

JUDITH BELUSHI PISANO:

By the end of the shoot, John wanted desperately to be gone, and the producers wanted him gone, too. It was a huge headache for everyone.

Six months later they needed John to do some voice looping for the film in LA. When he asked for a per diem to cover his expenses, they paid him a hundred dollars, and just to be insulting, paid him with a bag of change, handed over by the limo driver. John was incredibly sensitive and that really hurt him.

As his first film experience, it was a major letdown. The only redeeming part was the friendships he forged with Jack and the other actors on location.

MARILYN SUZANNE MILLER:

It was largely for the benefit of his male friends. The show broke in very clean lines between the boys and the girls, and you have to take that into account. One on one, he never did that stuff with me. All that big male bravado he put on was just a show for the guys, and they're all so stupid because they all believed it. It's just ridiculous. It isn't true. And I especially know that because of the way he treated Judy.

RICHARD BELZER:

John had to be dragged kicking and screaming into the women's movement, and that was all Judy.

ANNE BEATTS:

John ended up having a lot of negativity toward me and Rosie Schuster on *SNL*. I think a lot of it was really because of *Titters*.

DEANNE STILLMAN, *writer*:

Anne Beatts and I had sold a book called *Titters: The World's First Collection of Humor by Women*. Judy was in the art department at the *Lampoon* and we asked her if she'd do the design for it. John's first contact with *Titters* was hundreds of small pieces of paper all over his living room and Judy frenetically cutting and pasting and working on the book. This started in 1974 and went on literally every day for a year. He was pretty tolerant about it for a while. And then he got pretty intolerant. We moved it out of their apartment and got an office, but that was a totally different problem because now Judy was gone all of the time. John and my boyfriend formed the Titters Widowers Association because we were gone so much. Later, when Anne and Judy and I sold the sequel to *Titters*, *Titters 101*, I called one day and John answered the phone. Before he put Judy on he said, "Listen, are you calling about *Titters*?"

"Yes, I am."

"I'll give you $50,000 to leave my wife alone."

ANNE BEATTS:

The idea of Judy having a career was difficult for John. If you'd have asked him, objectively and intellectually he'd

With Gilda Radner

have said, "Of course Judy should have a career. Of course Judy should work." But when you got right down to it, those old-world, Albanian instincts were pretty strong. He came from a family where the mother was pretty much in the kitchen, and I think that did affect the way he related to women who were out in the world. He was uncomfortable with it and didn't *really* want it to happen. He struggled with it.

MARILYN SUZANNE MILLER:

When we took the show down to New Orleans we were there for ten days, and I was so violently ill by the end of the taping that I had to get back to my hotel room or I was going to pass out. But I couldn't get anywhere, because the streets were full of drunks. John grabbed my hand and said, "I'm gonna get you home." He found two cops and got in front of me like a shield, and together they took me through the horrible, drunk-filled, vomit-filled streets of New Orleans back to my hotel. That's how John treated women.

LORNE MICHAELS:

John's was a very European personality type. He grew up in the sort of environment in which, when the father was home, everybody tiptoed around the house. So there were difficulties when there was a woman authority figure. But he also had a very strong sense of responsibility that came from

I felt cheated by his death, because I always wanted to go three rounds with him in a mud pit. Still, in spite of ourselves, we developed a warm relationship.

—Rosie Schuster

the same place. When you put John in charge of something, he never let you down. He was responsible for getting more people more jobs in film and television than you can imagine. You would walk into a studio or any kind of work environment and John seemed to know everybody, always, everybody's name and everybody's face. He always had that kind of interconnectedness with people.

LAILA NABULSI:

John was always making friends, and that was very important to him. And Judy had an amazing capacity in that she had to share John with so many people. Their house was always open; anybody could come over at any time. She was very understanding of who he was. She was unconditional when it came to sharing him with the rest of the world, and I don't think it was easy a lot of the time.

PENNY MARSHALL:

John would show up at your house and make spaghetti at three in the morning, leaving a trail of handprints all over the kitchen. But such behavior was tolerated because you knew you could always do the same to him. Any time of day, you could call or drop in, and if you had a problem you had his undivided attention. He was a great hugger, John. When he hugged you, you felt hugged.

And he liked to be the godfather, the wise man. He would play that role a lot with my daughter Tracy. He'd always talk to her about who she was seeing, how to act on a date, the importance of staying in school. And I wasn't necessarily allowed in on the conversation.

After Rob Reiner and I had separated, I was going out with Art Garfunkel, and John asked me, "Is he good to you?"

"Well, you know, medium," I said. So one night I was getting ready to go out. I'd told John to watch the phone, and Art called. John answered and proceeded to tell him that if he didn't treat me nice he'd beat the shit out of him.

When I got on the phone, Art was a little rattled. "John Belushi just threatened my life," he said. "He told me if I didn't treat you nice he would beat me up."

"Yeah," I said, "he will."

MICHAEL O'DONOGHUE:

A lot of people treat me like Dr. Mento the intellectual, not like a real human being. John didn't know enough to do that. He'd call me up and say, "Hey, Mike, you want to go see *The Howling* tonight?" Well, of course I want to go see *The Howling*. I'm a guy. John was very compassionate toward me. Few people are, quite frankly. The scorpion god that set up this world for some reason just likes people to screw me over. John, when I would get sick, would go and buy me orange juice and cranberry-and-turkey sandwiches, just to cheer me up. One time I was depressed—heavily depressed—and he went out and got a Nerf basketball and a little basketball hoop, came over and said, "Come on, Mike. Let's play basketball. Ooh, ooh, come on. Let's play basketball." And he forced me to play. Few people would do that. And it cheered me up. Nerf basketball, cheer anybody up.

ELLIOTT GOULD, *host*:

I never stayed very long at the after parties, as I wasn't too friendly with anyone there other than Gilda. But John would always come over to the bar, where I would usually be by myself, and just hang out with me, and we'd have a shot of tequila. He demonstrated a sort of silent goodwill toward me. Everyone was nice to me, but I was especially appreciative of John, because he seemed to me to be such a purist, and also because, no matter how much tumult and activity was going on around him, he always seemed to be in a very solitary place.

AL FRANKEN:

Mostly what I remember, to be honest, is the fun, just all of us laughing. What's really never been captured—either in the things that have been written about John or about *SNL* in general—is the fun that we had. We just laughed and laughed all the time.

MITCH GLAZER:

We laughed to the point of pain.

RICHARD BELZER:

We laughed so hard we'd fall down on the ground unable to breathe.

JUDITH BELUSHI PISANO:

Sometimes we laughed so long we couldn't remember why we were laughing.

MICHAEL O'DONOGHUE:

I am very anal retentive, and John used to come over to my apartment and just move things around. Drop a paper on the floor, miss an ashtray a little bit, until finally he could see me just tensing up. That was his idea of a fine joke. Another joke he used to do was to sit on me. Which, if you recall what he looked like toward the end, sort of like a refrigerator, you can imagine what it felt like. He would jump on me if I got a real good one in. That was like Noel Coward to him.

JIM DOWNEY:

Everyone got shanghaied and made to go on Belushi Adventures from time to time. They were always really impulsive excursions, like hitting a music store to buy a zillion audio cassettes at a time or sometimes just going and picking up his laundry. But it was always good fun. After a few hours you'd be like, "Uh, John, I really need to get back. I haven't started…"

"Pussy! C'mon!"

DAN AYKROYD:

There was far more affection than rivalry amongst everybody. Having the run of that building was amazing. Going out and having a cigarette on the roof garden overlooking St. Patrick's Cathedral, going up to the radio mast room at the top of the building. It was a close-knit community, like being in a college dorm.

LAILA NABULSI:

John loved to rent limos and go out all night. We'd head up to Catch a Rising Star and hang out with Richard Belzer in his little office downstairs and just laugh hysterically for hours. Then we'd take off and John would be like, "Let's go here! Let's go there!" and we'd run all over town hitting different clubs and seeing different people.

Eventually you developed this sixth sense of wondering, where's John? And then all of a sudden you'd look over and see him at the door with the eyebrow up that said, "C'mon, let's go."

He always had the next place lined up. You had no idea where you were headed. You'd just have to say, "Okay, bye!" to whomever you were talking to and jump up and run out. It was out of the question to say, "Oh, you go on without me." You were on the train.

MICHAEL O'DONOGHUE:

There are a lot of people that you can learn things from, but you couldn't learn much from John, because you couldn't hope to emulate it. He would go into a restaurant, usually the Odeon or someplace like that, and talk to all the different tables and go in the back and meet the chef and screw around with the busboys, and suddenly everybody in the restaurant would be focused on John. Well, I can't do that. If I tried to do that they'd arrest me.

TOM DAVIS:

John had a power over people. He was out by the elevator around eleven o'clock in the morning one day, and he was crying. It was something about his mother, or his family. So because he was crying, I started crying. And while I was getting all teary-eyed, the elevator came. John quietly got on and disappeared without saying a word. I was left there in the hallway weeping when somebody came along and said, "What's the matter with you, Davis?"

I just stood there for a moment. "I don't know." And I didn't. I had no idea. But that's the kind of emotional power John had.

Opposite: John and Mitch Glazer in **Crawdaddy** *photo session outtake*

MITCH GLAZER:

He was just mischievous. One week I'm staying with him at his rental house in Lambert's Cove on Martha's Vineyard. Judy's away. It's around one in the morning. I say goodnight. He says goodnight. And then a few minutes later I'm in my bedroom going to sleep listening to WBCN. They're broadcasting a live concert from some music club somewhere on the island, and all of a sudden the guy on the radio says, "Hey, we got John Belushi here!" John's on the radio with a full-blown party going on in the background. I walk over into his bedroom, and he's gone. He'd just kind of gone out the window.

AL FRANKEN:

John was impossible to resist if he wanted something. When Fran Tarkenton hosted the show, I wrote a piece in which Belushi played a coach. It was late Tuesday night, and Belushi said, "Come over to my house. I want to read you something from Dick Butkus's autobiography." John wanted to get his football philosophy—which was Butkus's philosophy—on the screen.

I needed a break from the office anyway, so we went down to Judy and John's apartment. He got out Butkus's autobiography and he read it to me. The entire thing. Cover to cover. I'm supposed to be at the office writing the show and I'm like, "John, I gotta…"

"No, no, wait, wait…"

I was there until at least six or seven in the morning, just listening and occasionally going, "John, it's really pretty late…"

"No, no, hold on…"

And he read me the whole thing. It did inform the sketch in a certain way. I like Dick Butkus, and I do love football. By the end it was just absurdly hilarious. Part of it was his insistence that I stay there, and part of it was just my fascination with: how long will he go?

MARILYN SUZANNE MILLER:

Whenever we left the office and were going someplace, John would just grab everyone in the vicinity and say, "Let's go!" And we'd go. John wanted everybody to be having a good time wherever he was. He himself was kind of a moveable feast of a good time. He wanted to be behind the bar, serving everyone drinks. Everything was always fun with John. Always. Who else would go to Lorne's house at three in the morning and say, "Okay, so *now* what are we doing?" How can you not love that guy? Lorne didn't know how to get rid of him.

LORNE MICHAELS:

The doorman would ring me around four thirty in the morning and explain that a "Mr. John" was downstairs. I'd get up and answer the door, and John would come in and

He would call me, always at the oddest, most ungodly hours. If the phone rang at three in the morning either someone's sick, someone's dead or it's Belushi.

—Alan Zweibel

we'd talk. For the longest time I actually thought there was a reason for it, that it was about something pressing or urgent, but it was just to hang out. He was making a gift of himself, which he did pretty well.

JANN WENNER:

Our doorman sort of knew who he was and would just let him up to our place. We never locked our door, because we were too lazy to carry around keys. John would just wander in and crash on the couch, and then you'd come home around midnight and find him asleep in your house. It was always pleasant, though. He was always fun to have around. John was just *there*. He was a fact of life.

MITCH GLAZER:

One evening, after the profile was finished, the phone rang in my living room at precisely the same moment when my live-in girlfriend of four-and-a-half years was throwing me out. I was pretty numb and confused when I picked it up. "Hey, what're ya doin'?" It was John.

"Well…uh…well, actually John… Oh, Gayle and I are, y'know…breaking up."

"Good. I'll be right over to get ya. You can stay in the back room. Hey, bring your Stones records. Mine are all fucked up. See ya in five minutes."

I didn't even have a second to get depressed about it, and I never looked back. John was completely irresistible. He wouldn't take no for an answer, and he wouldn't allow you to miss the fun. Some nights it was like there'd be a knock at your door, you'd cautiously open it just a crack, barely enough to see out, and suddenly all the forces of nature would blow into your apartment, use your phone and suck you out into the night. And it was always a spectacular ride. ∎

Chapter 8

AND WE'RE JUST THE GUYS TO DO IT

the worst house on campus

JOHN LANDIS:

When *Animal House* had one of its many anniversaries I got a call from a guy named Peter Biskind, who at the time was the editor of *Premiere* magazine. This is a story that exemplifies what movie-star journalism is mostly all about. He called me up and said, "We think *Animal House* is an important American movie and we'd like to do a big retrospective piece for the magazine. Who should I talk to?"

I gave him the cast and crew list and said, "Here, talk to all these people. They'll give you the story."

He came back to me about four months later and said, "I'm sorry, but we're not going to do the piece."

"Why not?"

"Well, there's no story."

"What do you mean there's no story?"

"Everyone we spoke to had a good time."

Above: With director John Landis (left) and Bruce McGill

When Ivan Reitman inked the deal to produce the National Lampoon Show, he did so with a very important provision: if he could get a movie made based on the show's material, he would get to direct and produce it. By the summer of 1975, most of the show's cast had been snapped up by SNL and the new Howard Cosell show. Fortunately, Harold Ramis was not one of them. Reitman called him in California and offered him $2,500 to write a movie treatment. Ramis came back with a story called Freshman Year that had very little to do with the Lampoon Show and a lot to do with his own experiences at college. According to Ramis, "It was too personal, too sentimental. No one really responded to it."

Wanting to be more in tune with the Lampoon style, he asked to be paired up with one of the magazine's editors. Enter Doug Kenney. Kenney was the magazine's resident high school and nostalgia expert. He'd been the driving force behind the 1964 Yearbook Parody, as well as the author of numerous classic stories like "First High" and "First Blowjob." Together they decided to take the treatment in a new direction, starting with the improbable premise: what was Charles Manson like in high school?

The result was a convoluted, somewhat confusing story entitled Laser Orgy Girls. It followed a young Manson as he seduced innocent coeds, brought them to the desert and forced them to worship flying saucers—only to then spirit away in one of the spacecraft with its time travel controls set to Dallas, November 22, 1963. "Doug had a Kennedy obsession," Ramis explains.

In Reitman's words, "It just didn't work." At his suggestion, the writers took the story back to college, this time enlisting the help of the magazine's resident college and fraternity expert, Chris Miller. Miller had written several seminal college stories for the Lampoon, among them "Pinto's First Lay" and "The Night of the Seven Fires." He was hoping to use them as the basis for a screenplay of his own, but when Kenney offered the opportunity to combine their efforts, he gladly accepted.

By January of 1976, the team was finally headed in a solid direction, plotting the classic story of the slobby, loveable Deltas rallying against the uptight Omegas and the Nixon-like Dean Wormer. Simmons and Reitman began shopping the concept to major studios in Hollywood while Ramis, Kenney and Miller sat down over eggs Benedict at a small restaurant in the West Village and began plotting what would be the most successful, highest-grossing film comedy of all time.

CHRIS MILLER:

Harold, Doug and I were having our very first meeting about writing the treatment for *Animal House*. We met on a Sunday for brunch at a place called Casey's in the Village, down near Sheridan Square. We wound up staying there for several hours coming up with the basic vision for the movie. Alone among the three of us, I had actually been in an "animal house" in college. So we were talking and I said, "Well, you know, one thing about animal houses is that at the center of every great animal house is a great animal." There was a pause. And then we all looked at each other and said, at the exact same moment, "Belushi."

HAROLD RAMIS:

We always saw John as Bluto. There was no question there. Chevy was supposed to be Otter, Aykroyd was going to be D-Day and Bill Murray was supposed to be Boon. As it turned out, John was the only one who wanted the gig.

CHRIS MILLER:

We were throwing around names for our great animal character, and I said, "Oh, I've got a name for you. This guy I knew at Dartmouth." They looked at me, and I said, "Bluto!" Doug Kenney laughed so hard he fell out of his chair. The name was instantly adopted.

IVAN REITMAN:

Doug Kenney would walk into my office all the time saying, "Hey Ivan, have you ever read a comedy script this funny? This is the funniest comedy script ever!" And in a strange way, he was right. The movies of our generation were quite serious, movies like *Five Easy Pieces*. Bob Hope and Phyllis Diller were still the comedic voices of mainstream entertainment. We worked on something like seventeen drafts of the screenplay, and the studio hated all of them, right till the very end.

CHRIS MILLER:

The whole time we were writing the movie we kept teasing John about it. "Hey John. We're writing a movie for you. You're gonna be the star! It's gonna be big!"

"What? What is it?! What's it about?"

"Oh, well, we can't tell you about it yet. We'll fill you in later." Drove him crazy.

JUDITH BELUSHI PISANO:

John really wanted to be involved in writing *Animal House*, but the deal was set, and he wasn't included. It probably wasn't realistic to think he could have worked on the script during the first year of *SNL* anyway, but that didn't stop him from thinking it was a good idea.

IVAN REITMAN:

I was still hoping at that point to direct it, and I was given the news that—having only directed the low-budget *Cannibal Girls* up to that point—they didn't think I was experienced enough. It was one of the great heartbreaks of my life. John Landis had just done *Kentucky Fried Movie*, which had actually done fairly well, so we met with him.

JUDITH BELUSHI PISANO:

When John first read the script, he liked it, he liked his character, but he was disappointed with how little screen time he had. Bluto was in perhaps a quarter of the film, with even less dialogue. John had been of the impression that his role was the lead. He wanted it beefed up. The biggest disappointment was that he was not in his favorite part of the story. He wanted to be with the guys on the road trip.

JOHN LANDIS:

Universal said that if I didn't get John Belushi for the part of Bluto, they were not going to make the movie. So with that threat hanging over my head, I got on a plane to New York. On the flight I read this article by Mitch Glazer that had sort of helped make the *myth* of Belushi. It was like, "Oh my God. I'm meeting Godzilla."

Our first meeting was at the Drake Hotel. John came up to my room and he made a hell of an entrance. He came in and started making all these insane demands about the script, the character, he had to be on the road trip, this and that. It was outrageous, and at the end of it I said, "No! No! Are you crazy?" It was clear that he was just testing me and was very nervous himself.

We talked about it at length, and while we were talking he picked up the phone and placed this outrageous order with room service—shrimp cocktails and margaritas and beer and all this stuff. We talked a while longer, and we agreed to meet the next day, and he left. And then of course ten minutes later: *knock, knock.* Trays just started arriving. It was like the Marx Brothers. Fortunately, Universal paid for it.

STEPHEN FURST, *"Flounder"*:

Animal House was my very first job as an actor, ever. I was very excited, but very nervous, too. We were brought up a week early for orientation and group bonding, and the very first night John Landis called us together for dinner at the hotel. When I got to the restaurant there were two empty seats left, one at the very end of the table and one right next to John Belushi.

I was very naïve, much like Flounder, and the last thing I was going to do was sit down next to the star of the movie. So I immediately headed for the seat way down at the end. And as I was headed that way, John got up, physically grabbed me and pulled me to come and sit next to him. He had this grumbly voice that he always used with me, and he said, "Hey, kid. What're you doin' sittin' all the way down there? Come an' sit with me." And that just immediately broke all the ice.

PETER RIEGERT, *"Boon"*:

At that first dinner everybody still had beards, moustaches and long hair. It was intense. It was like the gunfight at the OK Corral. Everybody was looking at everybody else thinking, I wanna kick your ass. No way you're gettin' by me. Because that's what you want. You want scene stealers. You don't want

to work with people who aren't going to try and do great work. I'll never forget that night. We were ready. They could've started shooting that night if they'd wanted. All we needed were the haircuts.

JAMES WIDDOES, *"Hoover"*:

For the rest of that orientation week, we just drove around, getting to know each other and looking at all the locations. We had a lot of dinners together and found very quickly that we were exactly who we were cast as.

STEPHEN FURST:

The smartest thing Landis did was bringing us up early for that week. The World Series was on, the Yankees against the Dodgers. We all got together to watch it in John's room. The New York actors were rooting against the LA actors, and it just created a great sense of camaraderie.

JUDITH BELUSHI PISANO:

John and I decided to have a party to watch the World Series. We were still in our motel room, so it was tight, but that was actually good because it literally and figuratively brought us closer together. It was all very relaxed and fun, but there was a certain electricity in the air. It was funny, but the Delta actors were already forming a bond that unintentionally excluded the Omegas.

MARK METCALF, *"Neidermeyer"*:

I got there and I went to the production office, and they gave me my per diem and said, "Landis wants to see you right away. He's in the restaurant across from the Roadway Inn."

So I went over and walked into the restaurant, and Landis was there with this group of guys at a big, round corner table. He waved at me, I started over and then he yelled, "That's him! That's Neidermeyer!" Then Belushi leapt up and started screaming and throwing food at me, and all the other Deltas joined in. That was my welcome to Oregon.

SEAN DANIEL, *Universal Studios executive*:

Just before they began shooting, I went up to Eugene to see how it was going, wish them well and check on the studio's investment. I was bearing a very important item: a recording of the Isley Brothers' "Shout." We had just recut a new cover for the movie, and I had the cassette. When I got out of the car Belushi didn't give me so much as a hello. It was, "Do you have the cassette?"

He grabbed it out of my hands and went immediately into his room, slammed it into the recorder, turned it on loud and listened to it very carefully. Then he came out and said, "Okay, it's all right." So that was that. The song had passed muster. Since I was the one who'd brought it, I guess I was all right as well.

JUDITH BELUSHI PISANO:

John was incredibly concerned about the music for *Animal House*. It had to be a party in its own right. He wanted to hear music from the movie on the radio. It's a little-known fact that he sings "Money," which kicks off the first big scene of the movie, the Delta recruit party.

JAMES WIDDOES:

The first weekend John had flown back to do *SNL* and the rest of us went to a party at the university's SAE fraternity. Everybody was led upstairs to the party except for me, because I was the last person to come in. While everybody else went upstairs, I was stuck in the hallway of this fraternity with about ten guys. They were circling me and giving me all sorts of shit. One of them said, "You Hollywood fags think you're gonna come up here and steal our women." I actually stood there thinking, wow, I may get the shit beat out of me, but that is such a great line.

Then, all of a sudden, the upstairs door opens, and it's our group coming back down. I've been hanging out for about ten minutes at this point and it's getting really tense. We finally all start to file out and I'm the last one, and the guy who's been giving me the most shit is standing at the door and he says, "Have a nice night, asshole." And I—in a tremendously stupid moment in my life—take my hand and pop his beer up in his face. Well, we all get the crap beat out of us. The entire SAE house empties out on our white asses, I mean, it was *big*. And of course, once we get back to the motel Tim's ear is ringing, Bruce has a black eye, Peter's got a ruptured something or

other and I'm going, "Oh my God. I'm so sorry, I'm so sorry."

But then, all of a sudden, Bruce decides, "No, wait a minute. This is perfect. We're bonded now. We *are* the Deltas."

PETER RIEGERT:

When John heard about the fight on Monday, he was so upset that he'd missed it. He was like, "We've gotta go back and get 'em!"

We said, "John, we were outnumbered twenty to one!"

"Well, we've got the teamsters! Come on, we'll kick the shit out of 'em! Let's go!"

BRUCE McGILL, *"D-Day"*:

Fortunately, cooler heads prevailed.

JAMES WIDDOES:

Right from the get-go, what I was so struck by with John was how desperately funny he could be a) with very little to say, and b) in an environment like a film set, where you're just not supposed to laugh. There was take after take where John would be doing something and everyone would be holding his breath—sometimes for as long as two minutes—waiting for Landis to yell cut. And then as soon as he did there'd be this explosive, and I mean huge, release of laughter the second the scene was over. The whole shoot was like that.

TIM MATHESON, *"Otter"*:

John had these little tests to see if you were full of shit or not. He'd say, "Gimme a hundred dollars."

You'd be like, "Uh...okay." And you'd give him a hundred dollars. But then there would never be any discussion about getting it back. I didn't have that much money in those days, so a week or two later I said, "John, you owe me a hundred bucks."

He was like, "Yeah, yeah, right."

"No, no," I said. "You owe me a hundred bucks. Now, gimme a hundred bucks." So I got it back from him, and I remember him looking at me in a different way after that. He would just test you to see if he could push you around, because people would let him get away with murder.

JUDITH BELUSHI PISANO:

John knew he had to make Bluto a great character. It wasn't *written* as a great role; the writers knew John's work and wrote a great structure for him to work within, but he had to fill in the blanks himself, and that was the intention. John made it look easy, but he knew that responsibility was on his shoulders.

BRUCE McGILL:

John was clearly the engine that drove this thing, in the structure of the script, and in the energy of his performance. John thought of himself as a physical god. He probably thought he could have been a ballet dancer if somebody asked him to. In the scene where he smashes Stephen Bishop's guitar, the guitar was supposed to break apart on the very first crack. The effects department had cut almost all the way through it in several places. Everybody, John included, was expecting it to explode the first time he hit it against the wall. When it didn't, John's physical prowess was impugned, and he was furious. But he kept it all within the character and within the context of the scene. What you see in the movie is really a scene gone wrong. John just wouldn't let go of the thing until it was in splinters.

STEPHEN FURST:

It was raining in Oregon the whole time we were shooting and so the footing was never very good. And as John was running into the dean's office, he slipped on the grass and fell down out of frame—complete accident. I busted out laughing. Most of the time, that would be the end of the shot, but Landis yelled, "Get up! Keep going!" I have no idea how he did it, but he just popped right back up, and that's when he did that little spontaneous hop. It was like a basketball move the way he was shifting his feet around. The little physical things like that were just hysterical.

BRUCE McGILL:

I learned a lot from John in terms of pacing. Once we're inside the dean's office, he and I are laughing about tricking Flounder with the blanks in the gun, and then we hear the gunshot and the thud of the horse hitting the ground. What Landis wanted us to do was come out of our own little world

With director John Landis

and then return face front, almost in a theatrical representation of our shocked realization. I got back to front way faster than John. Drawing out moments like he did, with that great face, enabled the audience to stay with him better. There was just a degree of mass appeal to the pace at which John let a series of facial gestures unfold. He'd let the audience get ahead of him. They knew where he was gonna go, so when he got there, it was even funnier.

JOHN LANDIS:

What Belushi had that was so great, and what he did so well in *Animal House*, is that you can actually watch his thought process. He had extraordinary physical and facial expressions. You can see the ideas seeping through his skull.

JAMES WIDDOES:

One of the things that was so spectacular to watch during the filming was the incredible connection that he and Landis had. During the scene on the cafeteria line, Landis was talking to Belushi all the way through it, and Belushi was just taking it one step further. What started out as Landis saying, "Okay,

now grab the sandwich," became, in John's hands, taking the sandwich, squeezing and bending it until it popped out of the cellophane, sucking it into his mouth, and then putting half the sandwich back. He would just go a little further each time.

TIM MATHESON:

He did the entire cafeteria line scene in one take. I just stood by the camera, mesmerized.

JUDITH BELUSHI PISANO:

John loved Landis. He liked *Kentucky Fried Movie* for its fast pace and laugh-out-loud humor, but also for the fresh look Landis put on-screen. And he liked the fact that Landis had worked his way up in the business. They became good friends during *Animal House*. John trusted Landis because he was smart, funny and a good storyteller, and that made all the difference in John's confidence on that movie.

KAREN ALLEN, *"Katy"*:

I was very enamored of the way that they worked together. Landis was very, very eager to just let John do his thing and

At the Delta House (from left): James Widdoes, John, Peter Riegert, man with beer, Tom Hulce (in sweater, facing away), Tim Matheson, man with mermaid

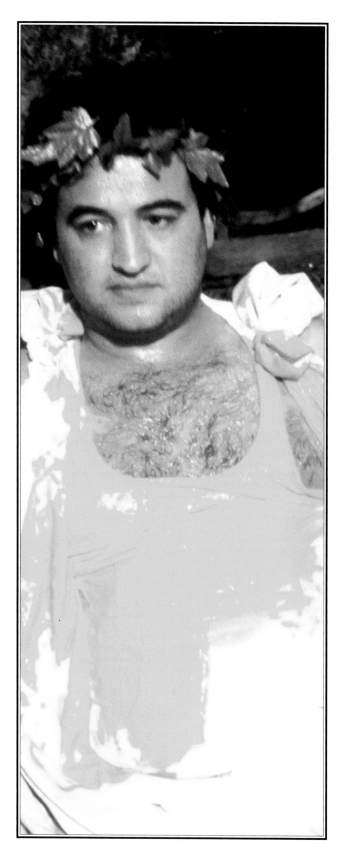

discover what he might do with this character. Sometimes he was directing John, sometimes they collaborated, and sometimes he'd just turn the camera on and say, "Do something."

That's what happened the night he decided to pick up that jar of mustard and pour it on his stomach.

JAMES WIDDOES:

There is a little teeny cutaway to John at the toga party. He's sitting in the chair, in his toga, and he looks over at a big jar of mustard. Now, in the film, all you see is that he looks over, picks up the jar and then empties it on his chest. What was actually shot was that, plus another minute of a sort of mustard ballet. John slowly started rubbing mustard all over himself, painting his body with it, playing mustard bongos on his chest and making little mustard shapes on his face.

Then he started to sing.

"I am the mustard man… I'm the goddamned mustard man…" It was really quite remarkable, but there clearly wasn't time for it in the movie so it had to stay in that little cutaway.

BRUCE McGILL:

With improv you always get a bunch of crap, but you also get one or two little bits of gold. And when John came up with gold, it was tremendous.

TIM MATHESON:

John was the only one Landis would let go off-script. He just turned the camera on and let Belushi do what he wanted to do, because he had a great sense of proportion and a great sense of truth.

I think *Animal House* was the best movie John Landis ever did. There couldn't have been a more perfect person to direct it. He had that sense of humor down. He understood that we were the heroes and couldn't be total jerks; we couldn't be mean to each other. He took out any jokes where we made fun of each other. I give him a tremendous amount of credit for the spirit on the set, the tone of the movie. He liked to keep us on our toes by throwing stuff at us all the time. Things would just go sailing through the scene; it was usually just plastic or paper or water.

Cheering up Flounder

BRUCE McGILL:

There's one great moment when John is bringing Pinto and Flounder through the front door at the rush party and a beer bottle comes flying in and, without even looking at it, John just catches it in mid air. That was completely spontaneous.

JOHN LANDIS:

What I think is so successful is that John's inner sweetness comes through. The character of Bluto is genuinely sweet. A lot of Bluto's best moments weren't scripted—it's just John. He had tremendous warmth. The scene where he's cheering up Flounder is really the closest you'll ever see to the real John in the movies.

STEPHEN FURST:

I've never laughed as hard in my life as I did on the set of *Animal House*. The very last day of filming we did the scene where Bluto is trying to cheer up Flounder because his car's been totaled. There was a great deal of familiarity and camaraderie on the set by that point, and the take you see is, I believe, take number eighteen. Normally we got everything done on that film in two or three takes, but for some reason, that day neither John nor I could get through that scene without laughing.

JUDITH BELUSHI PISANO:

For the scene with Flounder, Landis told John to try and imagine he was making a baby laugh. I don't think he could have given John a better direction.

BRUCE McGILL:

It's hard to separate John and Bluto. His very life suggested that character to the guys that wrote it, so they're inextricably bound. And I think because John's talent was so raw and so untechnical and unschooled, it was inevitable he'd bring a large part of himself to the performance. Bluto anchored and centered that film and became something that's still unique. Not many comedies do what that one did; it just wove its way into the popular culture.

With Judy at the toga party

MARK METCALF:

John was Bluto, but he was also much, much more.

JAMES WIDDOES:

When we got out there, John used to say to all of us, "You guys are all actors. All I do are these sketchy, funny comedy things." But, in fact, there was no finer actor than John.

TIM MATHESON:

At that time, there was a lot of snobbery between LA and New York. New York actors all thought LA actors had sold out, that we were just pretty boys and didn't have real talent.

John steered clear of that. Comics rarely laugh at other people, but John always gave you a laugh when you needed it.

PETER RIEGERT:

I never knew him as John Belushi the icon; I knew him as John Belushi the actor. And what I loved about John was that he was a generous actor. Your being good was as important to him as his being good. And that's a great player. He didn't need my oxygen; he didn't need for me to fail for him to succeed. Being great in a mediocrity is no achievement. Being great in something great, now that's special. And that takes everybody.

JOHN LANDIS:

It was a very communal set. We were all out there together in Oregon at the Roadway Inn, like neighbors under the high-tension lines. *Saturday Night Live* was an incredibly hot show. John would be on location with us for three days, and then everyone would get together on Saturday night and watch our boy on TV, and then the next day he'd be back. It was a good time. I was only twenty-seven. We were all young, and it was very exciting.

JUDITH BELUSHI PISANO:

We couldn't afford the plane tickets for me to travel with John to New York and back each week, so John had to do it all on his own. He was on the set Monday, Tuesday, Wednesday, and then he'd take a puddle jumper down to San Francisco and catch the red-eye to New York. They'd pick him up in New York and take him straight to his dressing room Thursday morning. He'd sleep a little, write, rehearse and do *Saturday Night Live*. Then, after wrapping the show around one thirty or so, he'd catch a 6 AM flight Sunday that got him to Eugene around one in the afternoon. It was slightly easier than the flights to Mexico during *Goin' South*, but only because he didn't have to go through customs. Those Sunday afternoons were pretty much John's only downtime all week.

BRUCE McGILL:

People always ask me what Belushi was like on *Animal House,* and I say, "Tired."

CHRIS MILLER:

I was very impressed that anybody could do what he was doing, but then John always had stamina to spare.

MARK METCALF:

My memory of John is very different than what you hear. Everybody always asks me what was it was like to work with John Belushi, expecting me to say he had a vial of cocaine slammed up his nose the whole time. It wasn't that way at all. He was always on time, always straight, always a good, hardworking actor. Pretty early on, he and Judy moved out of

"Mr. Blutarsky...zero point zero..."

the Roadway Inn to a house outside of town so he could get more privacy and rest.

BRUCE McGILL:

After the big rumble at the SAE house, we were stuck in the motel. We didn't go out. So Matheson and I went in together on a rental car so we could get to the liquor store and stock up on party supplies. Thanks to a little white lie to the night manager, we were able to borrow a piano from the lobby, and my room became party central.

John wasn't there for the big parties. He was really whipped and would crash hard on Sunday after we watched, as he would put it, the fabulous Walter Payton and the Chicago Bears. He'd usually make it back just in time for the game.

JAMES WIDDOES:

We were all working pretty hard and fast, and Sundays over at John and Judy's house were so nice and mellow. You couldn't go outside 'cause it rained all the time, so everybody would go over to John's and hang out and watch football. When I think of the softer, calm side of John, I think very often about those days over at their house.

KEVIN BACON, *"Chip Diller"*:

On *Animal House*, I was a little bit of an outcast. It was my first movie. I was eighteen. The Deltas tended to hang out together, and so I was touched that John went out of his way to invite me. He'd gotten lox and bagels, brought them all the way in from New York. I was just stunned by that, by the generosity. I couldn't afford lox on what I was making. It was expensive. And he just had piles and piles of it with champagne and mimosas that he'd bought for the whole cast.

MARK METCALF:

Those Sundays were great. John was a gracious host. One of the nice things, and I think one of the reasons that movie's as successful as it is, is that there were no movie stars the way there are movie stars now. Nobody had so much ego that they were separate from everybody else. It's different now, because if we made that movie today, John would be getting $25 million and the rest of us would be working for scale and then there would be a huge wall thrown up between us. But that wasn't true at the time.

PETER RIEGERT:

The great thing about being in a success like that is you're linked forever, to it and to the people who made it. It's a band of brothers kind of thing.

TIM MATHESON:

From the very moment we all sat down at the table that first night at the Roadway Inn, you could just look around and see that everybody was who they were playing, and it was like, "Wow, this is pretty fucking great." In that regard, we *were* fraternity brothers, and I think because of that we just sort of embraced and accepted each other for whomever and whatever we were, no questions asked. That was the way John always related to me, and I to him. When he didn't have to be, he was a dear friend.

STEPHEN FURST:

On the last day of shooting, John was giving out these publicity pictures to some of the fans near the set; he was always great with his fans. I was a fan, so I got one of the pictures, and

"Nothing is over until we decide it is!"

I asked him if he would sign it for me. He took the picture and he wrote, "To Frank," and then he crossed it out.

Then he wrote, " To Bob," and he crossed that out.

Then, "To Jimmy," and he crossed that out.

And finally, "To Steve, I hate you. Leave me alone you scumbag fuck face. Belushi."

And then he gave me the picture. I treasure it to this day. ∎

Chapter 9

I SEE THE LIGHT

getting the band back together

FRED KAZ, *musical director, Second City:*

About a year or two before the *Blues Brothers* movie, John was researching himself into a ball of energy about singing the blues. His complete immersion into that purpose was just a wonder. The man was not born the greatest musician of all time. In fact, if you want to know the truth, there was always something a little bit to be desired in his time even. But his ability to immerse himself into what he saw and wanted to reflect as an actor was such that he could come up with a totally acceptable facsimile through study. In music, we always say, "A person got it or he don't." John proved that's a cop-out judgment. He was a soul man. He *became* one through his own volition, which is just an amazing thing.

Despite the success of Saturday Night Live *and* Animal House, *and as much as John had achieved as an actor, his fantasy was to be a rock-and-roll star. Deep down, beneath all of John's layers, all of the media labels, all of the show business mythology, at heart he was just a metalhead from the suburbs, big on Led Zeppelin and Black Sabbath, with a rabid devotion to the Rolling Stones.*

Starting with their first meeting, Dan Aykroyd had been preaching to John about the blues, the roots music of black American culture. And John had acquired a casual interest in it, but nothing too serious. Then one night, during the location filming for Animal House, *John and Judy went to hear a blues band at the Eugene Hotel. John was taken with the band's young singer. Not only did he look like Danny, but he played blues harmonica like Danny too. The band was tight and the music reached out and grabbed John by the throat; he was mesmerized. After the show, he hung around. Somebody in the band recognized him and introduced him to the frontman, Curtis Salgado. At that moment, John was born again. He wanted to know the origins of the songs, wanted to know who the writers were—he wanted to know everything. By all accounts, he returned to New York a changed man.*

While John's third year at Saturday Night Live *produced some of his best work, from the short film "Don't Look Back in Anger" to the classic "Olympia Diner," the show increasingly became his day job, a backdrop against which he and Danny could pursue their love of music. In time, the show would also become a platform to launch the singing and dancing duo of Joliet Jake and Elwood Blues, a rather unlikely musical act whose legacy would reach far beyond what anyone could have possibly imagined.*

DAN AYKROYD:

John and I came up with the Blues Brothers at my speakeasy in Toronto, the 505 Club. This was when he was up recruiting talent from Second City for *The National Lampoon Radio Hour.* After the show, we went back to the bar and had a party and I started to play some old blues records. John said, "Who's this?"

"This is the Down Childs Blues Band. They're local. You're from Chicago. You should know about the blues."

"Nah, I'm into heavy metal," he said. "Grand Funk. Allman Brothers."

"Well, that's all blues."

Sometimes you'd think John had forgotten about you because you hadn't heard from him for a while. Then all of a sudden a bunch of blues tapes would arrive at your house with a note: "Listen to these. John."

—Penny Marshall

We started talking about putting a band together, and Howard Shore, who went on to become musical director of *SNL* and who was there that night, said, "Yeah, you could call yourselves the Blues Brothers."

And, eventually, that's what we did.

JOHN LANDIS:

The evolution of Jake and Elwood is very convoluted. It's like the Dead Sea Scrolls. So many people claim authorship. Ultimately, the whole thing came from John's love of black music. Danny was the first to turn John on to it. Then Curtis Salgado truly converted him and gave him more than just a passing interest. Until then, I think John had really just been humoring Danny. After that, with John it was like being a born-again Christian. He just went berserk.

JUDITH BELUSHI PISANO:

Curtis was really taken with John's enthusiasm and sincerity for music. They became instant friends. When John had any downtime, Curtis came over with armloads of recordings, and they would just disappear into the music. Over the remaining weeks of the shoot, Curtis relayed the Unabridged World History of the Blues, and John absorbed every last word. Somewhere along the way he picked up his first porkpie hat—which was dark brown, not black—donned the Ray-Bans and took to wearing the dark suit coat. That was the start of his metamorphosis into Jake Blues.

BRUCE McGILL:

I was there the first night he got up and sang. We'd gone to the Eugene Hotel to hear this jazz/swing band. They played a lot of standards. John talked to them and then came back to the table. "They said I could get up and sing a song, but I don't know if I should," he said. I told him to go for it so he got up and sang "Hey, Bartender." It was the first time he got up and, without making a joke of it, sang in public.

JUDITH BELUSHI PISANO:

From then on, John's pockets were always bulging with cassette tapes. He'd spend hours at different people's houses, insisting, "C'mon, listen. I've got to play you this song." And then he'd jam a cassette in their stereo and turn it up—loud. When he'd worn out his welcome, he'd just move on to the next person's place.

He did it to all of our visitors, too. Whenever anyone new would come by, he'd say, "Let me play you some music!" The regulars all knew what was coming and would say their goodnights, waving the newcomer on. "No no, go ahead. You'll have a great time." Then the house would start vibrating, and about an hour later the latest victim would stumble out in a daze, going, "What?! I can't hear you!"

BOB TISCHLER:

He threw himself into the blues like a hurricane. He'd come over to my house, pull every blues record in my collection out, play one cut on each of them and then leave them all in a heap on the floor.

ALAN RUBIN, *band member*:

He had this incredible shelf of 45s. He'd put something on for about four measures, say "Nah," pull it off and then snap it in half. Then he'd put another one on, "Nah," throw it on the floor and stomp on it. It was like Blutarsky from *Animal House*.

JUDITH BELUSHI PISANO:

It was a little too intense for most people, but there was a method to his madness. What he was doing was finding out which songs people responded to. All those frenzied late-night listening sessions evolved, over time, into the playlist that became the albums and the movie soundtrack. John saw what the Blues Brothers were going to be long before anyone took him seriously.

LITTLE CHOCOLATE DONUTS

TOM DAVIS:

We filmed it at some local high school on Long Island. John was having a good time. He was doing great the whole time we were filming. Then a crowd of locals started to form. Some kid said in a very loud voice, "I like the fat guy." It was a little hard to get John out of his trailer after that. He finally came out to do the high jump, and during the take he hurt his knee. The director had him bundled in a blanket, saying maybe we should take him to a hospital. I was just rolling my eyes. I didn't think he actually hurt his knee. I think he was just bummed out because this kid called him fat.

ANNE BEATTS:

He had to run and jump over hurdles all morning, and by the end of the day his leg was really in quite a lot of pain. Then we had to go down to the locker room of this sports arena and do the product shot with John eating the doughnuts. He had to keep doing it over and over, doughnut after doughnut after doughnut. By the end of it he was in the foulest mood. Every time the camera stopped rolling he would be absolutely obnoxious and horrible, and then as soon as the camera came on he would be smiling and cheerfully eating doughnuts. When you see him in the final piece, it certainly looks as though he's happy and not a person who's been using all sorts of obscenities that you can't say on TV and is in massive pain from a leg injury.

SEAN DANIEL:

We had a screening of *Animal House* in Atlanta before the movie was released. John and Judy were coming in and some of the suitcases were lost. John was crazed, extra crazed. All of Eastern Airlines was out searching every terminal for this luggage. Clothes were never something John really worried about, so none of us really saw what the big deal was. Finally, the suitcase arrived and he grabbed it, unzipped it and flung it open; it was his entire collection of blues cassettes.

JAMES WIDDOES:

One night, my girlfriend and I were literally in bed around eleven when I got up to answer the buzzer and heard, "Jamie, it's John! Comin' right up!" He came up with Judy and was like, "C'mon, c'mon. Let's go, let's go." Sure enough we got dressed and went downstairs and he took us right up the street to a blues club over on Columbus. The next thing we knew we were walking home down Seventy-second Street at three in the morning, wondering what the hell had happened. He was really tough to say no to.

DANNY KORTCHMAR, *musician*:

Late one night we leave his place down in the Village around one or two in the morning. We're walking down Bleecker, and it starts to rain, I mean a torrential downpour. But John and Danny don't want to go home. We keep wandering the streets of the Village and they start to sing all their favorite tunes, starting with "Flip, Flop & Fly." They just burst into song, snapping their fingers—and it's pouring. All of us are completely soaked to the bone, just dancing and singing in the rain in the middle of New York City. There's nobody else on the street. It was like something out of a movie.

LAILA NABULSI:

For a while after John got married, Danny wasn't around as much. His attitude seemed to be, "Well, he's married now…" And I think John used the Blues Brothers as a way to pull Danny back in, to keep him close and remind him that their partnership was just as strong as before.

MITCH GLAZER:

When I first met Danny he was a bit of a freak, and he wasn't faking it. Danny's blazingly funny, but truly very shy. He was hiding behind Elwood's shades. John really loved him and muscled him out into the world. In a way I think their friendship made Danny whole.

JUDITH BELUSHI PISANO:

After all these weeks of immersion and research, he started getting up onstage and playing with different bands around town, singing "Sweet Home Chicago" or "Hey, Bartender." Pretty early into his Jake Blues period, it became more than just an attitude; it turned into a full-blown alter ego.

DAN AYKROYD:

The Blues Brothers look came from a lot of things. One was an old John Lee Hooker album cover. He had the hat and the shades. We also had this philosophy that these characters were rebels. They were bad guys. They weren't morally evil or spiritually bad; they were just bad in terms of the law, and they had to play it straight, hence the whole Lenny Bruce thing of going onstage wearing a thin tie and looking like an FBI agent, just to present that conventional, legitimate look to the straight people out there. When John did the Shelley Bayliss character on *SNL*—that 1950s hipster comedian—that was when the suit and glasses first appeared. And technically, the first Blues Brothers number ever was the "King Bee" song done in the bee costumes.

JOHN LANDIS:

Ultimately, I think the hats and glasses and the outfits were just a socially acceptable way of doing a kind of blackface.

JAMES WIDDOES:

The first time the Blues Brothers ever really performed live was after one of the *SNL* after parties. Willie Nelson was the musical guest that night, and he and his band were playing a late set at the Lone Star. We were all up on the balcony above the stage, and all of a sudden John and Dan got up and started doing the Blues Brothers with Willie Nelson and his band. I just remember Willie Nelson looking at John and Dan like, "What the hell are you guys doing?"

DAN AYKROYD:

That first appearance we were pretty scared. I just played tiny, nothing little harp bits and danced around while John sang "Flip, Flop & Fly" and a couple of other songs. We were worried, but Willie Nelson backed us up. Doing easy material with a band like that behind us, we ended up coming off pretty good.

JUDITH BELUSHI PISANO:

One night we were at this club called Trax. Lorne Michaels was there. John got up with the band and sang a few songs, and Lorne said, "Why don't you warm up the show with the band on Saturday night?" So John and Dan started warming up the audience and did pretty well for a couple of weeks. Then Lorne asked them to perform on the show.

For that first *SNL* appearance, Jake and Elwood didn't have their own band yet, so they performed with some of the *Saturday Night* musicians. They were billed as the musical guests for the show, which was an important distinction. They fought for that position because, had they allowed the characters to be used in a skit, by contract they would have become the property of NBC. From both a legal and a personal standpoint, it was imperative for John and Danny to keep control of Jake and Elwood.

MORT COOPERMAN, *owner, Lone Star*:

John was one of the biggest blues fans I've ever met. His early lack of sophistication was natural and even charming. He'd been after me for some time to book John Lee Hooker into the club. When I did, John came by and asked me to introduce him. Hooker was standing there, dressed in black, a woman on each arm, wearing dark shades. I said, "John Lee Hooker, this is John Belushi."

"Hi," Hooker said blankly, shaking John's hand.

"You know," John said, "John Belushi. I'm on TV."

Another blank stare from Hooker. Then he peers closer through his shades and smiles, "Oh yeah, you're one of them Muppets, ain't ya?"

John loved it. A year later, Hooker was signed for the *Blues Brothers* movie.

The Blues Brothers during their **Saturday Night Live** *debut*

On April 22, 1978, the Blues Brothers debuted on Saturday Night Live, *opening the show with Floyd Dickson's "Hey, Bartender" and returning later in the evening with Willie Mabon's "I Don't Know," two songs that would become staples of their act. Hosted by Steve Martin, the episode also featured Martin's "King Tut," the swinging Festrunk brothers and the medieval barber Theodoric of York. Even today it's considered by the cast to be one of the best and most satisfying shows of* SNL*'s first five years, making it arguably one of the best ever. Nobody really understood exactly what the Blues Brothers were, and the act was not nearly as polished as they would eventually make it, but it was the first seismic rumblings of things to come.*

We all wondered why they were dressed up like Hasidim. That seemed odd. But it sure worked, didn't it?

—Tom Davis

TOM DAVIS:

The Steve Martin/Blues Brothers show was the only time I remember the show being good from beginning to end. Everyone was happy after that show. But that's how rare that was. It's the only one I can remember.

JIM DOWNEY:

John always took the music much more seriously than Danny. Danny knew that it was at least a little bit of a comedy-slash-music thing, but John, who had always been a little loose and casual about the comedy, was deadly serious about it. The first time it was on, we were all like, "Okay, Danny knows this is a bit of a joke, but John has no idea."

TOM DAVIS:

Everyone at *SNL* was pretty skeptical of the Blues Brothers when they started. It just didn't occur to us that they could

At the contract signing with Atlantic Records (from left): Jerry Greenberg, Michael Klenfner, Danny, John and Bernie Brillstein

pull it off. They did the first couple of things on the show, and we were like, "Okay, that was fun." But we still didn't realize that the millions of people who were watching really went for it in a big way. We were the last ones to figure it out.

MICHAEL KLENFNER:

The idea for *Briefcase Full of Blues* was born in a house John had rented on Martha's Vineyard. We were up late talking about how great the *SNL* performance had been and how we should do a record. I took it to Jerry Greenberg, the president of Atlantic. He just stared at me with a look of complete and utter disinterest. I said to him, "Jerry, this is gonna be fucking huge."

So finally me, John, Danny and Jerry get a meeting with Ahmet Ertegun, the company founder and chairman. This is at a time, mind you, when Atlantic Records was heavily into "Le Freak" by Chic. We get into this meeting, we sit down,

Jerry turns to John and Danny and he says, "You know what you guys oughtta do? You guys oughtta cut a disco cover of 'Stairway to Heaven.'"

I practically choke. I look over at Danny and I can tell exactly what he's thinking. He says, "Mike! May I *speak* to you for a moment?" Then we step out of the office and they say, "What the fuck are you doing to us?"

I say, "They don't know what the fuck they're talking about. He's just making comments because he wasn't the one to bring it in." So we go back in and I say to Jerry, "That's not gonna fly. They've got to cut a typical blues album—and they want to do it live."

JUDITH BELUSHI PISANO:

When the offer for the album came up, John and Dan decided it would be good to work some clubs. They could polish the act and check out other musicians at the same time.

MORT COOPERMAN:

John spent a lot of time at the Lone Star because it was near his house and because so many of the acts we booked—Delbert McClinton, Bo Diddley, Kinky Friedman—coincided with his musical tastes. He came by one afternoon and said he wanted to do a "Blues Monday" at the club, similar to what Woody Allen does with jazz at Michael's Pub uptown. I put him together with Doc Pomus, who put him in touch with Roomful of Blues, a great blues band that had been struggling along for some time. They worked things out, made some preparations and did a show at the club. The audience response to John and Danny was enormous. Musically, it was obvious that neither of them was in a league with Roomful of Blues, but the crowd loved their good humor and spirit.

After the show, Belushi went up to one of the band members, who was a little drunk, and asked, almost like a little boy, "How did I do?"

Above: At the Lone Star with Roomful of Blues

The fella replied, in so many words, "You *sucked*. You were total shit and should never have gone onstage."

John just caved. "But they *liked* me," he said. The band pissed on him because of an ego crunch; the crowd was more interested in the fun John and Danny had whipped up than the band's technical expertise, and the band resented it. To make matters worse, the band then did an interview with the *SoHo Weekly News* in which they ragged and ridiculed John and Danny for not being fucking blues archivists. Ironically, John had privately asked me to give all the money from this and any future gigs to the band.

MITCH GLAZER:

There were two ways of looking at the Blues Brothers. One was as just dilettantish celebrity slumming, which is how Roomful of Blues saw it; the other was as guys who loved the music and cherished it and respected it, and were having a blast, which is how Cropper and Dunn and all those other guys saw it. The critics were split. The audiences weren't.

MICHAEL KLENFNER:

After a few gigs, John and Danny realized things weren't moving as smoothly as they'd hoped. We decided to ask Paul Shaffer to help put a band together. Shaffer came to my office to meet with me, John and Danny, and told us he didn't think he could do it because he was in the middle of producing "It's Raining Men" for the Weather Girls. We told him this would give him a lot more credibility outside of the *Saturday Night Live* band than "It's Raining Men," which was really more of a novelty. Paul, who's real smart, came back and said, "You're right." That's when things started to fly.

PAUL SHAFFER, *bandleader*:

We set aside some time for John, Danny and me to put a band together. Unfortunately *Animal House* had just been released, and it was such a huge deal, the opening of that movie, we didn't really get much done. John was becoming a movie star that very week. I'd go to his apartment every day, and he'd have to keep taking calls and giving interviews. Not much got accomplished.

One of the few things we got done was to hire Steve Jordan. He was playing drums for *Saturday Night*, and we agreed we couldn't do any better. We originally planned to go with just two horns, a trombone and a tenor sax for a more bluesy sound. Lou Marini and Tom Malone were both top studio musicians also playing with the *SNL* band. John had liked the way they sounded when they backed them up on the first show, so they were hired. Alan Rubin and Tom Scott wouldn't join until later.

After that it was very important to John to get a hot lead guitar player. He was anxious to fill that position right away. We auditioned a few people and he was prepared to make an offer, but I asked him to wait. That night, about eleven o'clock he said, "We gotta go ask Doc Pomus."

We went down to Kenny's Castaways, found Doc and told him what we wanted. He said, "I know just the guy: Matt Murphy. He played for James Cotton, Little Walter. He's the real deal." I didn't know who he was, but we pretty much decided to hire him sight unseen.

MATT "GUITAR" MURPHY, *band member*:

I was swapping licks with Johnny Winter at a club one night. These guys came up and one of them said, "Hi, I'm John and

OLYMPIA DINER

DON NOVELLO, *writer*:

Originally, the name of the restaurant in the "cheeseburger, cheeseburger" sketch was the Pyreaus Café, but John's father had owned a restaurant named the Olympia, and he asked me if we could change the name to that. So I did.

The sketch is based on the Billy Goat Tavern, under Michigan Avenue in Chicago. I don't know if John had ever been there, but Billy Murray knew it. The owner was this old Greek guy who would hit you in the head with a cane when you walked in and yell, "Get a haircut!" He had all his cousins working for him; he'd brought them over from Greece one at a time. John's character was the heart of the sketch. He really understood the working-class immigrant mentality.

JIM BELUSHI:

One character of John's that definitely came from our family is Pete, the "cheeseburger, cheeseburger" guy. When I saw him do that character, I went, "My God, he's doing Uncle Paul." And then I kept watching it and John was doing that thing where he breathes in and out like he's really frustrated. That's what my dad would do anytime you asked him to borrow the car. It would just make you shake. So that character was definitely my uncle and my dad. I think he kind of rolled them both up in one. And the Elizabeth Taylor sketch, that one was definitely my sister and my mom put together, although I probably shouldn't say that.

this is Danny. We're making an album. Would you like to help us make it?"

"I would be glad to help you," I said. After we talked a bit and I'd agreed to do it, we were negotiating and John said, "Well, the pay is $650."

"Oh, well, I think maybe it should be a little more than that," I said.

"Oh, no, no, I'm sorry. Did I say $650? I meant $6,500."

I almost fell off my chair.

PAUL SHAFFER:

Before we hired Matt Murphy, I got John to promise that we'd find a rhythm guitar player, too. Blues guitarists aren't always good rhythm players.

At that point, Tom Malone said, "I've been playing in this band with Levon Helm. Steve Cropper and Duck Dunn play with us, and they're both available." I knew of Cropper and Dunn from Stax Records and Booker T and the MG's. They were perfect, ideal. I said we should hire them both right away.

JUDITH BELUSHI PISANO:

John and I didn't know Cropper and Dunn by name, but we knew their work. It so happened I still had an old MG's album, and, sure enough, there they were on the cover. When we found out that Steve Cropper was *the* Steve of "Play it, Steve!" from Sam & Dave's *Soul Man*, we thought that was the coolest thing. John wanted to do *Soul Man* just so he could say it, too. We later learned that Steve and Duck had been on tour with Otis Redding when his plane crashed in December of 1967, John's senior year in high school. They were supposed to be on that very flight, but changed plans at the last minute.

MITCH GLAZER:

At that point, getting Cropper and Dunn would have been, to me, like getting Lennon and McCartney. I couldn't even conceive of it. But for John, it was just a matter of picking up the phone.

STEVE "THE COLONEL" CROPPER, *band member*:

Usually when people call me in the middle of mixing or overdubbing or something like that, I'll have somebody say I'm busy and can't come to the phone. Well, this buddy and I had a thing where he would call and pretend to be somebody famous like, "This is President Nixon" or "This is Stevie Wonder" or whatever. So I get this call one day in the studio, and they say, "John Belushi's on the phone."

So I'm like, "Yeah, whatever," and I pick up the phone and say, "Hey, Alan, what's goin' on?"

"Who?"

"This isn't Alan?"

"No, this is John Belushi."

DONALD "DUCK" DUNN, *band member*:

The night John asked me to join the Blues Brothers band, he phoned around three in the morning and woke me out of a sound sleep. He said he was John Belushi and he was gonna make me rich and famous if I'd come to New York and rehearse for a show that would be recorded live for an album. I thought he was a buddy of mine who was just pulling some shit on me, and I hung up on him.

A few minutes later he calls back, convinces me it's really him and talks me into the whole damned thing. Then he asks me, "Would you shave off your beard?"

"What for?"

"Oh, nothing. Never mind. You can keep it."

DON'T LOOK BACK IN ANGER

TOM SCHILLER:

The title "Don't Look Back in Anger" was a combination of the Bob Dylan documentary *Don't Look Back* and a British New Wave film from the sixties called *Look Back in Anger*. John was just starting to peak on the show, and I wanted to do something good with him. So I came up with the idea for a short film of John visiting the other cast members' graves, because I have this fascination with what people will look like when they're older. And because we really did think of him as indestructible. No one thought he would be the first to die.

The morning of the shoot we met at a place called the Bonbonniere in the West Village at seven in the morning.

He was sitting there having a tomato juice with Worcestershire sauce and an egg yolk because he was totally hungover. We took him to my place, put on the old man makeup and then drove out to the cemetery in this van. John went to sleep in the back, and even though we were bouncing along at fifty, sixty miles an hour, he stayed perfectly sound asleep the whole way, like a big medicine ball rolling around in the back of the van.

We got to the cemetery. I wanted to get at least one master shot right at the beginning before we messed up the snow so I said to John, "First just do it once all the way through." He hit his marks at each headstone perfectly and nailed the entire thing in one take.

Never did figure out why he wanted the beard to go, but he sure did help my damned career.

DAN AYKROYD:

Duck and Steve were legendary R&B bass and rhythm guitar players, real men of soul. They legitimized what we were up to and gave us a purpose and a depth beyond just being some kind of comedy act. We respected their talent, their abilities. They recognized that although we weren't the greatest vocalists, we were good front men; we provided an

energy and sort of a package to reintroduce the world to the music they made great.

JUDITH BELUSHI PISANO:

At that point we were really flying by the seat of our pants. There was a lot of research involved, but it was also instinct. Dan and John knew that pretty much everything was riding on how they played this hand. And they were really smart. This was not a fluke or a lark, but a moment they had worked toward for a long time. We were busy getting everything together, hiring

LAILA NABULSI:

John was really good about looking out for everyone else in the band. I remember one night I was hanging out with John and Keith Richards late into the night, and Keith said, "There's this great blues guitar player you should check out."

John said, "Well, we have Matt 'Guitar' Murphy."

"Well, you know," Keith said, "you never know. You might need somebody, and you should check this guy out."

And John got really stubborn about it. "Listen," he said, "*this* is the band, and *we* stick together. Once you're in the band, *that's* it, *that's* the band."

"Yes, John, but *sometimes things happen...*"

And then John and I both realized he was talking about Brian Jones. John looked like he'd been jolted in the head with a cattle prod. "Oh...yeah. Okay, yeah, I guess you're right."

But John had this very idealistic philosophy about the band being a family.

OLD BOYFRIENDS

JOAN TEWKESBURY, *director*:

Paul Schraeder had written this movie, and it was originally called *Old Girlfriends*. It was at the moment in time when everyone decided to do women's movies. So it got changed over to *Old Boyfriends*. And when Paul Schraeder handed it over to me, he said, "I want John Belushi to play the high-school boyfriend."

I said, "Absolutely perfect." John hadn't yet played any kind of regular role where he was just a normal person, but certainly the potential was there.

I went up to Eugene, Oregon, to meet with him while he was doing *Animal House*. The test as to whether or not he would do the movie was pinball. He took me to this local college bar and said, "C'mon, we're gonna go play pinball and we'll see who wins." By some stroke of absolute and total luck, I won every single game, and he said he would do the part.

The premise of the movie was that Talia Shire was on a trip, revisiting all of the men in her life who had wronged her and finding closure. John played the high-school boyfriend who'd told everyone he'd slept with her even though he hadn't. Talia's character comes back to town planning to seduce him and then leave him hanging.

When she finds him, it turns out that he never really grew up and still plays with his high-school band at hotel bars and so forth. The band was all John. I told him, "This is what you know. This is what's important to you, and so you choose it." My only contribution there was to make sure the scenes were shot properly. He picked the songs. He picked the musicians. As I recall they were actually his pals from a band in Chicago that he'd played with.

I only had John for about six days. He had no time to rehearse, because he was doing *SNL* in the interim, but the thing that was really great about John was that when he was there he was always focused and ready to work. He was nervous and a little frightened about playing this straight character in a dramatic film and not being able to hide behind his bag of tricks, but he was ready to give it a go. He would always say to me, "Aren't I supposed to be doing something here?"

And I'd say, "You are. Just by being, you're doing it." His talent was that natural. It's hard for a lot of actors to get into their heads that just being still and listening is half the battle. There's a lot of energy that goes into that. John was very physical. If he wasn't jumping around or being silly, he felt like he wasn't doing anything. But he was. I'd always tell him he was the next Harpo Marx. I would have loved to have done a completely silent role with him. But in spite of his insecurities, he was a consummate professional. As long as you gave him a framework and let him know that he was safe and he was cared for, he was fine.

As soon as *Animal House* came out, though, I got really nervous. I knew that everyone would be coming to our movie expecting to see Bluto, and John just wasn't Bluto in this movie at all. The first night that our movie opened in Westwood, a lot of people had come to see John, and a lot of people were very angry. It was an awful feeling. I loved what John had done in the film. He was beginning to trust himself enough to show all these different facets of his talent, but the phenomenon of *Animal House* just killed any chance the audience had of appreciating it. There was a screening in New York for the *Saturday Night Live* people, and they were not very helpful, either. They were expecting a comedy and didn't react to it the way that he wanted, which in turn validated all of his fears.

It's the ultimate trap for someone who breaks through with such a powerful identity. It's hell to pay to try and shift that around. It's scary. What I got to see, hanging out with him that first day in Eugene, was this really vulnerable side of him. To me it was like he never really left Wheaton, Illinois. All of the other stuff in his life felt to me like it was superimposed, like someone trying to catch up to his own self-image. Personally, I found him to be one of the most lovely and silly people I'd ever met. He was charming. There's just no other word for it.

people, booking studio time, but meanwhile something went screwy with the record deal. Atlantic didn't want to put out the money up front for the nine nights of live recording. John was pushing for the cash and getting really worked up over it. We had all these commitments we had to meet.

Coincidentally, about this same time John got his bonus from Universal for *Animal House*, $250,000, the first real money we'd ever had. I knew how much John wanted this to happen, so I suggested we front the money to get it done. We were looking at spending between $150,000 and $200,000 in the space of a month, which was more than John had made from two years of *SNL*, *Goin' South* and *Animal House* combined. I never thought we wouldn't make it back, but that was a pretty naïve assumption on my part. Rule number one for actors is Never Use Your Own Money. It wasn't the first rule that we broke, and it was the best investment we ever made.

MITCH GLAZER:

They booked studio space for a solid week of rehearsals. That was the first time they all played together. John and Danny had played with the remnants of the *SNL* band, but this was the first time Murphy, Cropper and Dunn had showed up. Everyone was very nervous about being good. These were the best session guys in the business. They all wanted to hang out with John and Danny, but they were all professionals, too. Nobody wanted to be embarrassed. The second they got together, though, it was so exciting and so powerful that it blew me away.

LAILA NABULSI:

The first day of rehearsal, they sounded like they'd been playing together for twenty years.

DAN AYKROYD:

At the beginning it was mainly John's burden and John's bag to carry, because he had the bulk of the vocals. Once he started working with the band, I began to see places where I could apply myself, specifically on the harp, backup vocals, dancing and the choice of material.

John and I had a good meeting of minds on the music. The album couldn't be all blues shuffles; that's just too monotonous.

It was the beginning of the end of their being on the show.

—Anne Beatts

We had to mix it up some. So we went with "Messin' With the Kid," but we also selected Delbert McClinton's "B-Movie Boxcar Blues," because it was not a traditionally structured blues number.

JUDITH BELUSHI PISANO:

Creating the "legend" of Jake and Elwood was the most fun. We had this band, all successful and well-known musicians in their own right, and we made everybody take on these make-believe personas and fictional backstories to fit into the world of the Blues Brothers. It was a little bit of method acting brought to the musical stage.

Laila and I did a lot of the grunt work: booking studio time, renting equipment, making reservations and transportation arrangements. By night, Danny, John, Mitch, Laila and I threw ideas around, listened to blues records until our ears bled, and then scoured the city for even more inspiration.

I designed a logo for the band and ordered T-shirts, buttons and everything a band should have. A day or so before the first show, somebody called and told me it had all been delivered. I drove over to the amphitheater. By the time I got there, every last bit of it had already been stolen—liberated would actually be the better term. I had to place an entire second order on rush, just so we'd have something to hand out to the crowd opening night.

BOB TISCHLER:

By the time he'd found and rehearsed the band, John had learned so much more about running a show like that than anyone thought he could. Onstage, he did a great acting job in terms of punctuating the show with some good performing techniques, like the cartwheels and all that. On that first record, you can really hear Danny's biker mentality and John's friendly antagonism mesh as they discovered each other and really forged that bond. It was after that concert that they really started referring to each other as "brothers."

DANNY KORTCHMAR:

After the Universal Amphitheater show, everyone was caught up in the blues. It was a huge cultural phenomenon. Everyone started wearing skinny ties, black suits and porkpie hats. People started getting Blues Brothers bands together. Everybody was talking about it. Some felt that it was just crass commercialization. I mean, this is Hollywood. But John and Danny did it with such reverence, and had so much fun doing it, that it was impossible to see one of their shows and not be caught up in the fun—which to me is what rock and roll is all about. Everyone's got to have a ball. Today, people are still interested in the blues because of the resurgence they created.

PAUL SHAFFER:

I didn't realize at the time how good it was, and how good John and Dan were at doing it. Partly as a result of having seen so many imitators and tribute bands, I see now how difficult it is to pull off the whole package. Since those years, I've worked with Solomon Burke, Wilson Pickett, James Cotton, and even in the light of all that, I can still say it was a damn good act.

DAN AYKROYD:

The Blues Brothers went from hobby to obsession to national phenomenon in less than a year. Two months later, when Carrie Fisher hosted the show in November, we made our encore appearance on *SNL*. We opened with a cover of Sam & Dave's R&B classic "Soul Man" and came back for a double performance of "(I Got Everything I Need) Almost" by the Down Childs Blues Band and "B-Movie Box Car Blues." Essentially, Lorne Michaels gave us a free advertisement for our album. We put "Soul Man" out there as a single, and then *Briefcase Full of Blues* went on sale the first week of December. It went platinum within a week and sold almost three million by the time it was all over. Disco was on its way out. That's what you have to remember. Disco was dying and New Wave hadn't started yet. There was nothing on the radio, and that's why we were able to slot right in there. We had two more albums, the movie, T-shirts, action figures. I think there was a pinball machine at some point. We were on top of the world. ■

Chapter 10

(I GOT EVERYTHING I NEED)
ALMOST

the American Dream

TONY HENDRA, *director*, Lemmings:

What I would say about John, if I had more to drink, is that he was a very American life force, in terms of comedy. As another kind of immigrant, I felt that what made you laugh about John was peculiarly American, that the raw energy of this country was summed up in the way he hit the stage. But at the same time, I've also always felt that there is an enormous void at the center of America, a void that has to do with promise and disappointment and impossible expectations. Behind all this energy comes what? When you finally get where you're going, what then?

J ohn was like a gangster in that he knew how to spend money
lavishly for the right reasons," observes fellow Second City alum
Joe Flaherty. And in that first year after his TV, film and music
trifecta, there can be little doubt that John Belushi enjoyed the
material trappings of success. He moved from his Bleecker Street walk-
up to a two-story, parlor-floor brownstone apartment around the corner
on Morton. Rented limousines became his standard mode of
transportation. He ate well, as did all of his friends. He took private
jets to the coast, built an insulated, soundproof vault to blast his very
loud music collection, and since there was no need for a second wife, he
bought his first one a Mercedes.

But as anyone who's been there can tell you, beneath all the toys
and gadgets there is another side of success, a simpler, more private
side, and that is the gut-level satisfaction of Having Done It. And few
things reflect the gut-level satisfaction of Having Done It quite like
buying your parents a house. Or better yet, a ranch with horses. Adam
Belushi had grown up on a farm high in the mountains of Albania.
One of the few things father and son had shared growing up were rare
evenings around the television watching the great TV westerns like

Maverick and Bonanza. Adam's only recreation outside of his days
and nights of endless work were two horses he kept stabled near the
family's home in Wheaton. The horses had been lost along with his
restaurants.

And so, as one might easily have guessed, one of the first things
John did with his money was buy his parents a ten-acre ranch just
outside San Diego in the Cuyamaca mountain range of southern
California. Since leaving Chicago in 1972, John had had little or
nothing to do with his family, keeping them at arm's length for fear
that their needs would burden and drag him down. But now there
were considerable means to meet those considerable needs. College
tuitions were paid. Relatives and in-laws were put on the company
payroll. Interest-free loans found their way across the Atlantic and
into the hands of distant Albanian cousins he had never even met.
Like any son, John took great pride in the fact that his familial
obligations, along with a good measure of guilt, had seemingly been
put to rest.

But beneath all of that, beneath all the cars and jets and wives and
limos and ranches and restaurants and horses there is still yet another
side of success, and that is the side that nobody likes to talk about
because it just might spoil all the fun.

Above: With his father Adam

JOHN LANDIS:

When we were making *Animal House*, John could still go to a restaurant and be "that guy on TV." Even though *SNL* was a media darling and all the kids on the campuses loved it, it wasn't what you would call a household name. Then out of this movie he became this instant star, and that's terrifying. You can't go to a restaurant. You can't go to the store. You're not allowed to be in a bad mood. And John was truly gregarious; he genuinely loved people. But it alters your life.

On top of that, Bluto and the Samurai and a lot of the characters he played were so big that people expected him to be big. It was like if Belushi didn't do something outrageous, they'd be disappointed. And John, he didn't want to disappoint anybody.

CARRIE FISHER, *actress/writer*:

One time he wanted to go to Disneyland. I said, "We can't go to Disneyland, John. *You're* the Matterhorn. It would make too much of a scene." He was just a big event wherever he'd go. He got a kick out of things, at least at the beginning. I think he enjoyed it for a while. Then he started to feel hunted by it.

JEAN JACKLIN, *mother-in-law*:

I remember John getting very upset one time. We were in a shop and some nut walked up, punched him in the ribs and said, "Hiya, Bluto!" John made a fist. I think he was planning to use it, but he didn't.

MICHAEL McKEAN, *actor*:

John was on his best behavior during the Universal Amphitheater shows, and after that he wanted to cut loose and party a little bit. We all went out to a club called the Starwood to see this vocalist friend of Bette Midler's. Just as we walked in, some crazy *Animal House* fan came charging up to John with a hamburger and tried to stuff it into his mouth. John just popped him one. It was one of the few times I've ever seen someone take a clean, movie-style punch. It was pretty great, I gotta say. John was worried that he was going to get sued, but we all said, "No, no, you did the right thing. This guy basically attacked you with a piece of food."

JUDITH BELUSHI PISANO:

After John and I got married, we moved from Bleecker Street to a bigger apartment in the Village on Morton. Danny started calling it the Reich Palace because the living room and dining room were on a grand old parlor floor of a brownstone. It had sixteen-foot ceilings with beautiful chandeliers and two big marble fireplaces. The first day I took John to see it, he just he walked through real fast and said, "If my mother knew I lived in a place like this..." And walked out. I thought, well, I guess he doesn't like it. And then a couple of days later he said, "Let's get that apartment." So we moved into the Reich Palace.

LARAINE NEWMAN, *performer*, SNL:

We decided to go see *Alien* one day. We were really excited, but once we got to the theater, John saw that there was a really big crowd, and he got scared. He ditched the whole situation and wouldn't go in because he was afraid of getting mobbed.

MICHAEL KLENFNER:

The real bottom line is that John was a good, simple guy. And I don't mean simple*ton*, but simple, basic and down to earth. He just felt he had to live up to that persona that he—*he*—had painted himself into.

JANN WENNER:

He became a victim of it. He'd always have to come over and be the professional crazy guy, the dope guy, much like Hunter S. Thompson. If Hunter showed up, people wanted the Hunter S. Thompson Experience, and it was the same with John: let's get the drugs and party. And John was torn about it. He was trying to figure out where it was good for him and where it was bad for him. It was an easy entrée, an easy way to make friends, but he also felt it was a little cheap and a little bogus.

KAREN ALLEN, *co-star*, Animal House:

One night, John and I had gone to see a blues group and we ended up sitting and talking for a couple of hours. He was trying—in a protective, big brotherly way—to share with me

his experience of what it was like to become famous, and just how disappointing it was. How, as a performer, you've yearned for the attention, you've yearned for the spotlight, you've yearned for people to like what you do, and then at some point everything that you've ever longed for turns into this thing that's very difficult. It was the most real conversation I ever had with him.

MARY STEENBURGEN, *co-star*, Goin' South:

Dealing with success is very, very hard. And you can't talk about it, with anyone, because nobody wants to hear it. It can be confusing when tons of people want something from you. People "yes" you to death where the week before nobody treated you any differently than anybody else. Suddenly your jokes are a little funnier, the things you say are a little more clever—and the thing is, *you know* what it was like just a week ago. You still know that, and so it's incredibly lonely and confusing. And if you put drugs on top of it, you're in big trouble.

HAROLD RAMIS:

Some time after *Animal House* had come out, Doug Kenney and I went to go to some publicity photo shoot for the movie. When we got to the studio, I said, "Where's John?"

Someone said, "John is on the floor of his dressing room and says he won't get up until someone brings him some cocaine." That's when I realized something had really been torn inside him.

JUDITH BELUSHI PISANO:

Later, John would say what a difficult time that was. He was confused and scared. I think he couldn't help but wonder, once you're on top of three completely different entertainment industries, where do you have to go but down?

MICHAEL PALIN, *host*, SNL:

To be in America at that time and to be on top of the music scene and the television scene and the movie scene all at once, it makes you sort of an outcast. You can't go anywhere without people wanting a bit of you. And even if you're staying at home, there are people who'll come by and just want to bask in the reflected glory. He was so popular, and so much was being demanded of him in such a short time, that I'm surprised he was able to deal with it.

JUDITH BELUSHI PISANO:

With John's life as constrained as it was, it was becoming impossible for him just to move about and hang out with his friends. The Blues Bar came about really as a way to find that freedom again.

DAN AYKROYD:

My assistant and I had just bought a couple of Harleys, and we were looking for a place to store them. We were down at Dominick and Hudson, down by the entrance to the Holland Tunnel, and we saw this bar for rent. It was only $400 a month. So we originally leased the place as a motorcycle barn. Then it only took us about a week to realize, "Hey, this would be a great place for a party."

MITCH GLAZER:

It was mostly Danny's energy that got the Blues Bar going. He had done those illegal booze cans, as he called them, up in Canada. The first time John and I went there, he was all excited to show me the place, but Danny hadn't given him the key—either that or he'd forgotten it, which was much more likely. He called Mark Lipsky, his accountant, for a copy. Supposedly someone was on the way, but it was taking too long for John, so he just sheared the doorknob off with a cinderblock, and we went in.

It was such a shithole that it took my breath away, literally. It was tiny, the floors were all ripped-up linoleum and it stunk. It just smelled old and weird. I said, "Nobody is ever going to set foot in here." I don't think the bathrooms even had toilets when we first got there. There was just a pipe with a hole in it. On opening night, Danny put a red plastic rose in the women's room, you know, "for the ladies," but I honestly don't know if any woman ever actually went in there. They were the most terrifying bathrooms I'd ever seen in my life.

LARAINE NEWMAN:

It was like they had taken over a building that wasn't really working. I don't know how they got a permit, or if they even had one. It seemed like they had no running water or electricity. It was just foul.

JUDITH BELUSHI PISANO:

We opened the bar in November of '78, just a week before John and Danny did the Blues Brothers on *SNL* for the second time. The Grateful Dead were the musical guests that night, and they came down to check it out. Keith Richards and Francis Ford Coppola tended bar. From that very first night it was *the* place, but as celebrity hangouts go, it was a few steps below lowbrow. It really felt more like the Wheaton Youth Center, a basement where we used to hear bands and dance in high school.

JIM DOWNEY:

Every Saturday after the show we'd always go to some fancy restaurant for the after party, but we would never stay there long. Those parties got worse as Lorne got more into the social aspect of things; they'd be packed with agents and publicists. After that we'd head down to the Blues Bar, which was off in an old, deserted part of town. The show was obviously much hotter and hipper then than it is today, but somehow we'd give all those hangers-on the slip. The Blues Bar was for us. It was like a clubhouse. I never remember getting home before dawn.

KAREN KRENITSKY, *secretary*:

John, Danny and Judy opened the offices of Phantom Enterprises and Black Rhino Productions in November of 1978, and they hired me to run them. Judy interviewed me at the office of Mark Lipsky, their accountant. We just chatted, really, and then she took me down to the apartment in the Village to meet John. I was so nervous. The first thing John said to me was, "Hey! You're smoking my brand of cigarettes!" That was the end of the interview; I was hired.

Every day John was in town he'd storm into the office barking, "Get me the Jenkins file! *Please!!*" Then he'd burst out laughing and put on a punk or R&B record, loud. Besides being John and Danny's official business headquarters, it was also kind of a clubhouse where their friends could drop by and a museum where they could display all their memorabilia.

The work part was a little crazy. You were never sure where to locate John. You were never sure John was going to make a plane when you booked it. You were never sure he'd make it to his hotel room when the plane landed. You were never sure about much, except that, at Christmas time, he always played Frank Sinatra's Christmas album all day long.

The Blues Bar was possibly the single coolest thing around. Whatever is in that building today, there ought to be a commemorative plaque.

—Jim Downey

TOM DAVIS:

Danny did security. He had a camera on the door, and you had to knock and know somebody to get in. If somebody made it in and was obnoxious, they got the bum's rush. I was really grateful to John and Danny for caring enough about their friends to host us there every week, because we needed a place like that. There was no going home and going to bed after the show was over. We were too wound up. I must have gone dozens of times.

MITCH GLAZER:

It had the most spectacular jukebox you ever heard. John and I went to Bleecker Bob's and just bought singles, everything from obscure, weird reggae to the R&B stuff you'd expect.

LARAINE NEWMAN:

The music was amazing. All sorts of people would drop in: David Bowie, James Taylor, ZZ Top.

JUDITH BELUSHI PISANO:

Occasionally the police would come by and take Danny and John outside and talk to them about the noise or something. But there was never any heavy pressure. The New York police loved them.

JIM DOWNEY:

John and Danny didn't mind the cops. Actually, they wanted them to come in. That way they had more security. They had nothing to hide there. I mean, John could walk into Fort Knox and they'd just open the doors and say, "Look around. You want anything? Take a couple of bars."

MITCH GLAZER:

The Blues Bar was all organic and amateur and unspoiled, even for people who were completely jaded. I mean, who could be more decadent and jaded than Keith Richards? He's

certainly seen it all. But he loved the vibe in there. The drinks were free. There was no money changing hands. It was authentic. However long a run they had of it, it was a small miracle. The press knew about it, but somehow it remained this weird secret. I don't remember ever even seeing a single photographer there.

MICHAEL PALIN:

You always had such a buzz after the show, however good or bad it had been. It was just the fact that it *had been*, had happened. You'd just done ninety minutes live on American television, completely in the danger zone, where you had nothing to hide behind. I felt it was about the coolest place you could possibly be at that time, much better than Studio 54 and all those places the stars usually went. It was all very relaxed. It was only when I staggered out of there at dawn that I realized what a sort of bleak, industrial part of Manhattan it was. There was something very special about that place, and it was a place that Dan and John really related to. They'd had enough of the hangers-on and the limousines, and this was their way to sort of put the trappings of stardom in proportion and distance themselves from it, which was a very difficult thing for someone like John to do.

ANNE BEATTS:

It was really quite the scene. I think John was really in his element there, because he just enjoyed having people around, people who also didn't want the party to end.

MITCH GLAZER:

The windows were blacked out so it could go until daylight Sunday morning. I lived on St. Luke's Place, so I could just walk up Hudson to my apartment. I'd be passing dads and their kids going to the park, which is always a horrible feeling after you've been up all night. It was just a fun, rock-and-roll vibe. It never got sleazy or decadent or evil. The whole idea

Sergeant Tree and Captain Wild Bill Kelso

was to push the night back as far as we could. The interesting thing, looking back, is that some people could do that and not get hurt. But for others it's not enough. It doesn't stay innocent. The need for it shifts into another thing. It stops being fun and becomes something darker.

That fall, John began production on Steven Spielberg's 1941, *an epic, slapstick farce about a Japanese attack on the coast of California at the outbreak of World War II. It was the first film of John's three-picture deal with Universal, and he was to play Wild Bill Kelso, a gonzo fighter pilot hunting for Japs in the streets and skies of Los Angeles. The cast included Ned Beatty, Robert Stack, Treat Williams and old Delta frat brother Tim Matheson. As he had done with* The National Lampoon Radio Hour, *John used his newfound clout on behalf of his friends. He refused to take the part unless Dan Aykroyd was cast as Sergeant Tree. As the start of filming approached, he also lobbied the producers and won parts for Joe Flaherty and John Candy,*

stars of the new Second City television show SCTV. *It was a massive production, and one that was soon massively out of control.*

Though he had only a small supporting part, for the next four months John found himself back on the same transcontinental commute he had endured during Animal House. *Only this time, instead of the warm, familial atmosphere of Eugene, Oregon, he was stepping off the plane into the heart of the Los Angeles drug scene. In the late 1970s, cocaine was swiftly replacing freeway traffic as the dominant cultural touchstone of southern California. On many film productions it was delivered to the set as formally as Monday morning's bagels and orange juice. In other words, this was the last place on Earth you would ever send a drug addict with a per diem.*

As disorienting as his ten-year overnight success had been, what John needed was to slow down, relax and take it easy—which is exactly what didn't happen. It would never have occurred to the son of Humboldt Park, Chicago, to turn down a good opportunity, and at that point his opportunities seemed pretty much endless. With 1941

underway, John was the single biggest star in Universal's single biggest film production of 1978. At the same time, he was developing a Blues Brothers movie with Danny that would be Universal's single biggest film production of 1979. He was also, inconveniently, still the lead singer of one of the most popular musical acts in the country. Atlantic Records had him fulfilling promotional duties at every opportunity. The band itself was mounting full-scale, one-night blowouts at New York's Carnegie Hall, San Francisco's Winterland Ballroom, and at the Century Plaza Hotel in Los Angeles for the Radio & Records convention, the music industry's largest. And through all the jet-lagged days and sleepless nights, he never stopped performing ninety minutes of television, live, every week, from Studio 8H in Rockefeller Plaza.

John's stamina and personal fortitude had long been a source of astonishment to everyone. One of Aykroyd's many nicknames for his friend was "the Albanian Oak." John Landis used to say jokingly of his tireless young star, "Strong like tractor, smart like bull." Then there was also that time on Bedford Street when he got hit by a truck. But every man has limits.

JUDITH BELUSHI PISANO:

1941 was a hard time. It was a weird time.

BERNIE BRILLSTEIN:

I read the script and told John to pass. I just didn't get it. I told him, "If it's not funny, it'll be a disaster." But Spielberg was an icon. He'd just made Jaws and Close Encounters of the Third Kind. Everyone wanted to work with him.

TREAT WILLIAMS, co-star:

Working with Spielberg was an interesting situation. Danny and John were in awe of Steven. I think they were surprised—maybe even somewhat disappointed—to learn that he was just as in awe of them as they were of him. They were looking for a father figure, and Steven was this kid who comes in like, "Gee, you guys are great! Boy, it's great to work with you in this thing!"

JUDITH BELUSHI PISANO:

Thinking this was his first big Hollywood movie, John prepared for it very seriously. His uncle had been a World War II pilot, a hero who'd died in the Pacific the last month of the war. John

invited his uncle's widow and son to the Vineyard just to see all their photos and hear their stories. By the time filming was about to start, he'd worked up this great character with a John Wayne-type attitude and a streak of madness like Jack Ripper, the crazy general in Dr. Strangelove. Then we got to California and realized the movie was just a bunch of chaotic slapstick with no real story. All they wanted was Bluto in a fighter cockpit.

MARK METCALF:

Basically, Spielberg was trying to make Animal House Part II, but he didn't know what he was doing.

JOE FLAHERTY:

Spielberg had no idea how to do comedy. One day he called me into his trailer, showed me a take of the scene we'd just shot and asked, "Was that funny? Did you think that was funny?" I just stared at the screen and thought, oh jeez, we're in trouble.

TIM MATHESON:

It was my first opportunity to see a movie that literally ran unchecked. If you were supposed to do such and such work on this day, there was never a guarantee that's what you'd do. You'd never get it all done, or get anywhere near it. You'd sit in your trailer for six or eight hours, all night long, and never get out on the set. We would do stuff over and over again. The scene where John crashes his plane into Hollywood Boulevard was this enormous stunt. They did it three different times, and to no great distinction. At one point Aykroyd said, "These guys are playing bumper cars with Ferraris." They had all these incredibly talented people, and they didn't know what to do with them. They pissed money away on that film, just pissed it away.

ROBIN WILLIAMS:

I went to visit the set the night that they were dropping the P-40 War Hawk on Hollywood Boulevard They kept doing it over and over again. It was pretty insane. At that point they were kind of like, "This _will_ be funny!"

I think John was kind of gassed to be playing with the big toys. More than anything, he was like, "Wow! Look at what I'm doing." He was in shock that he was in the middle of all this chaos. It's intoxicating. One minute you're doing this little television show, and then the next thing you know you're in the midst of burning wreckage, jumping out of a World War II fighter plane. You've gotta go, "Whoa. Things are different." I think that kind of hit him.

JUDITH BELUSHI PISANO:

In the beginning, the sheer scale of it was exciting. Steven couldn't have been nicer, and he was very upbeat and even-tempered. And John got to meet Toshiro Mifune, his samurai hero, who was also in the movie. But the longer he sat around on location doing nothing, the more he began to worry. He kept thinking, but it's Spielberg! He wanted to believe in it, but they kept asking him to do things like scratch his crotch in the cockpit, as if that were funny somehow. John refused to do it. Then when we saw the movie, they'd shot a body double scratching his crotch and cut it together with John making these crazy expressions. By the end everyone felt it was a lost cause. John just kind of shut down and gave up.

TIM MATHESON:

When I saw him again during *1941*, he was pretty much out of control. I was concerned. Usually when I saw John, Judy would have him on a short leash, and we would just socialize and have fun. But it was supposedly a time when drugs weren't bad for you. We were very naïve about it, and John wound up in a faster lane than most everybody else.

We were shooting out at Indian Dunes near Magic Mountain, and he wasn't really prepared. He was a little messed up and he fell off the wing of the plane and they had to take him to the hospital. I didn't see the real actor. I didn't see a guy who gave a shit or cared much about making this a really good movie, like he did in *Animal House*. I did see a difference, and I was a little troubled and saddened by it.

BOB WEISS, *producer, Blues Brothers:*

I, like many others, was not fully aware of how many lives he actually led. Most of us went to sleep every night. There were times that I would go out with John and it was hard to keep up, and I have a pretty strong constitution. Toward the middle of the second day I'd be saying to myself, "How the

fuck does he do it? Then John introduced me to the Pico Burnside baths in LA. The clientele was old Jewish guys, young gay guys and us. We didn't quite fit in to either group. We had been on some insane fear and loathing tour with Ron Wood—this was back before *Blues Brothers* started—and John said, "Let's go see Seymour!" Seymour was the guy at the baths who did what's called *platze*, which is where they dip eucalyptus branches into warm soap water and lightly flagellate you. It's very therapeutic. You go from steam to sauna to pool and back again; it's fantastic.

I finally realized what was going on there was that he wasn't turning in or winding down. He was recharging his battery to head out again. So we went through this whole thing, the *schvitz* and the sauna and everything else, and John said, "Okay, let's get something to eat!" So we went down to this cafeteria and he polished off about ten pounds of meatloaf. Then we went to sleep for a couple of hours and he was up and back at it. But I had to get off the bus.

LORNE MICHAELS:

John lived his life in three eight-hour shifts. If you were with him for eight hours you'd think, oh, he must be exhausted, and you'd go home and go to bed. But then there was a whole different group of people he'd hang out with.

DAVE THOMAS, *writer/performer, SCTV:*

By that point John was overdoing it with drugs. Eugene Levy and I were writing a script for Columbia, and we were on the same lot as *1941*. We were walking to lunch and we went by the set to see how Candy and Aykroyd and all those guys were doing. When we got there, they were all just standing around. I asked Spielberg what was going on. "Danny's gone to look for John," he said. "We've been waiting here since seven thirty." This was at noon, and so there were just tons of extras standing around, burning thousands of dollars per minute. Danny had gone to try and retrace John's steps from the night before.

JOHN LANDIS:

He was commuting between LA and New York so much that he was getting really worn down. He got a very serious ear infection. The doctor would not let him fly, and all the guys back in New York of course were furious. They didn't believe him. They thought he was out partying on the coast, but it was actually true that he had this infection. John asked me if we could shoot something to send in. He wrote this little sketch. We shot it up at Steven Spielberg's pool. It was John lounging with all these Playmates in bikinis, eating sushi out in the gorgeous sunshine, holding up his doctor's note saying, "I'd *really* like to be there for the show, but..." Meanwhile, it was freezing in New York. I think it pissed them off even more. They never used it.

LORNE MICHAELS:

We played it at dress. It didn't get any laughs, and so we didn't play it on air. Plus, everyone on the show had a feeling like, "Hey, you can't do this. What we're doing here is important, and now you're saying that it isn't." That was the conflict. No performer likes leaving *Saturday Night Live*, because nothing is as satisfying. The adrenaline of being in complete control of this live broadcast is exhilarating. But being a movie star is irresistible. Nobody turns it down. People make noises like they do, but they don't really. John wasn't sure if he wanted it, but he wanted it enough to make sure it was his choice whether to take it or not.

In John's heart of hearts, he was the number-one cheerleader for the importance of the show and the work we were doing. He was a loyalist. After Chevy left, he was the driving force saying all for one and one for all. And I don't think he ever reconciled leaving it behind for the things that everyone else says are important. I think he did everything he could to hang on that year, but by the middle of the season it was apparent that it just wasn't going to work.

RICHARD BELZER:

During that last year, he really didn't want to be on *Saturday Night Live* anymore. He kind of resented being in New York. He was getting huge, and he'd rather have stayed out in LA being a Hollywood star. It was the only time, in all the years I knew him, that he and I had an argument. He'd missed one show because of the thing with his ear. I made a joke about it, and he just snapped at me. I was shocked. He seemed to be different and, not humorless, but certainly less fun-loving.

THE THING THAT WOULDN'T LEAVE

ANNE BEATTS:

Rosie Schuster, Jim Downey and I had written a series of parody horror films. One was "The Island of Lost Luggage." The other was "The Thing That Wouldn't Leave." And the Thing That Wouldn't Leave was John. He'd eat all your food, make long distance calls and so on.

We had these claws that we wanted John to wear to play "the thing," but he wouldn't put them on; he wanted to play it just as himself. Nothing was ever easy with John. He had his own vision of who he was and how he wanted to present himself. At the time it was just annoying, but in hindsight it was really John exercising his artistic right to make good choices.

LARAINE NEWMAN:

John *was* the Thing That Wouldn't Leave, the guy who wouldn't take the hint that it was time to go to bed. Late one night he and Mitch Glazer showed up, unannounced, at my apartment on Riverside Drive. They were drinking out of brown paper bags. Eventually, Mitch left and John passed out on my bed. So I called Judy just to let her know that I had him in possession. It was only in the morning after he left that I went over and looked in the brown paper bag. It was a carton of milk.

Backstage at SNL *with the Rolling Stones (from left): Mick Jagger, Keith Richards, Ron Wood, Bill Murray and John*

ALAN ZWEIBEL:

John was naughty. He needed someone to say, "No, don't do that," so that he could then try and get away with it. But he had gotten to a point where he was so famous that nobody said "don't do that" anymore. It's fun to be naughty, but at that point, who are you defying? Once people started bowing down to him, what rules was he going to break?

LARAINE NEWMAN:

It was that fourth year when things changed for John, when it slipped past being fun and became a serious problem.

LORNE MICHAELS:

When Kate Jackson hosted that season, we had built the whole show around John. He was playing NBC President Fred Silverman. He'd been out with the Rolling Stones all night and he was a mess. He looked terrible and he felt terrible and he didn't know his lines. We were stuck; there was no way of cutting it because it was a running bit the whole way through

the show. Someone came up to my room as we were doing the running order and told me that the doctor said John was too sick to go on. I went down to the dressing room. John was lying on his couch with a cold compress on his forehead. The doctor said, "His lungs are filling with fluid."

"I understand," I said. "But it's only another hour and a half, and then he can rest."

"No," the doctor said. "He can't do it."

John was just lying there with his eyes closed. I was furious. I had very little sympathy, almost none. "Well, what happens if he does it?" I said.

"He might die."

"What are the odds of that?"

He said—being dramatic, I think—"Fifty-fifty."

"I can live with those odds."

The eyebrow popped up. John looked at me with as close to a smile as he could muster, because he knew that I was trying to make at least a little bit of a joke out of the situation myself. I left the room, and he made it out for the show. He limped

America is a huge culture. And to be on top of that culture, even for a week, it just turns your head around. Being given too much attention and being paid too much money can be really tough. Most people don't escape it.

—Peter Riegert

through it, and it must have destroyed him knowing that it was a bad performance.

JIM DOWNEY:

The Kate Jackson show was the one and only time I ever remember John being messed up at airtime; it wasn't typical.

ANNE BEATTS:

There were drug problems and difficulties while John was on the show, but it was a protective environment in which he was able to survive. We took care of each other. I do remember that the phrase "where's John?" was said as frequently in rehearsals as "Live from New York, it's *Saturday Night*." But that was really in rehearsal. He would be late. He would be erratic, but at eleven thirty he was on, no matter what.

LORNE MICHAELS:

The peer pressure was too strong. There was no way you could fuck up and let everyone down. John knew the rules. He was one of the show's creators. He owned its success, and he was responsible if it wasn't good.

TOM DAVIS:

He'd always pull it off on the air, and so we never realized it was a problem. He'd take the host out and party really hard on Friday. Then the next day the host would show up not looking so good, and John, of course, would breeze in and be ready to go and just blow everybody away. He was miserable at dress and hard to work with during blocking and late to the studio, but he'd always get the huge laughs. Nobody could top that. And as long as he could pull that off, nobody was going to try and change him.

It was nobody's business what you did on your own time or in your own office. When it came to that, Lorne stayed out of it. I know he had great affection for John. He was worried about John. He just had a helpless feeling about it.

AL FRANKEN:

Years later, when Chris Farley was having the same problems as John, Lorne would say, "You're fired unless you go to rehab." He did the right thing by Farley. But he didn't do that to John in the fourth year, which he probably should have. He'd just get John a doctor who would make sure he could function for the show, and that was as far as it went.

John was partly a casualty of the ignorance of that period. There have been times through American history when drug use surges and becomes "new" again, and coke became kind of new again in the middle to late seventies. People had forgotten or didn't realize what it could do. That was the case with all of us. We were ignorant. We didn't realize that it could kill you.

ALAN ZWEIBEL:

We worked on a different curve back then. We all felt invincible. By today's standards, none of us should be alive.

JUDITH BELUSHI PISANO:

Everyone was using drugs, doing coke, including me. I didn't even like it. I didn't like the effects of it. But it's still a very seductive drug. You think, well, everyone's doing it, so a little will be okay. I finally resolved to quit. While things were running amok with *1941*, John and I actually began to get into some good personal discussions. He knew the drugs were a problem and it wasn't all fun and games anymore. I knew he'd need help, so I quit doing it completely and started lobbying our friends to back off too. At that point, we were still in the "I can cut back and control it" phase.

MICHAEL PALIN:

It was rare to get John to yourself, even for ten or fifteen minutes. But on one occasion he came by my dressing room and sat down, and we had quite a nice chat. He was a very sort of earthy character. He would scratch himself a bit and grunt. He was always sort of groaning for some reason, though I think it may have just been the way he exhaled. He was kind of a noisy person, even when he was still. His presence was like a simmering pot always about to boil over.

He seemed to be quite interested in how it all worked, how I coped with the expectations that came with Monty Python's success. We had just released *Life of Brian*, which had done quite well in America, but I didn't have anything else I was doing at the moment. I was in sort of an intermediate state, and I think he quite liked the opportunity to talk to someone who had been in a series that became really well known, like Python, and had finished that and was moving on. It sounded as though he was getting a little tired by that time. I felt like he found it quite hard to deal with, and there didn't seem to be anyone he could really share it with. It was like he was saying, "Look, there's a lot of bullshit around here, and it's nice to have an English guy who's not associated with all of it to talk to." With the speed at which he was working and the things he was expected to do, it was all a bit much.

JUDITH BELUSHI PISANO:

Things were up and down, but by the end of the fourth year John was much more resolved and confident. He knew that trying to do movies and *SNL* was too much. One time he looked at me and said, "I don't know if I'm coming or going. Sometimes I can't even remember what day of the week it is." There was just no way he was going to go back to being pulled in so many different directions. Leaving the show wasn't a decision he had to struggle with that much.

DAN AYKROYD:

We just looked at each other and decided that we'd really explored that form fully, that three-minute television sketch. He wanted to do films, and we were full on into *Blues Brothers*, which we knew would change our lives in one way or another.

LORNE MICHAELS:

When John left, Danny was supposed to be staying, but John saw what happened to Chevy when he left and so he took Danny with him. John was smart.

JIM DOWNEY:

We knew John was leaving, but the real shock was Danny. We didn't find out until the last minute that he was going, and people were a little angry with Belushi for luring him away. Billy especially, because he felt like he was really left out there to fend for himself. John had been away so much that we'd gotten used to it, and he was never the utility guy that Danny was, but we were just bereft without Aykroyd.

BUCK HENRY:

I was with Lorne out in the country when John and Danny quit. I said, "Did you try to talk them out of it?"

"No."

"Weren't you shocked?"

"No."

"Are you going to miss them?"

"Probably."

He was very even-tempered in a way that I didn't quite understand, and still don't. Not in terms of the professional, but more in terms of the personal. These guys made the show what it is, but Lorne put them in a place to make them world famous, rich and successful. I never knew Lorne to complain about anybody walking away from him. I think I took it harder than he did. But then, Lorne is Canadian. ■

Chapter 11

HOW MUCH FOR THE LITTLE GIRL?

a mission from God

JAMES BROWN, *R&B legend*:

When John and Danny invited me to be a part of the *Blues Brothers* film, they helped me get myself going again. I was going through a bad period at the time, having trouble getting my records released. They opened the door. John flew in to watch me cut my stuff for the soundtrack. He knew I was having problems, and he said to me, "How can I help?" He was *there* for me, understand?

RAY CHARLES, *R&B legend*:

John was a caring person, a gentleman from the get-go and a class-A cat who was into the music. I know for a fact that the *Blues Brothers* movie and soundtrack helped people like Aretha Franklin and myself reach the young kids who might not have known we existed. As far as commercial interest in R&B is concerned, John helped get the ball rolling again. Man, we owe him.

Above: Jake and Elwood, filming on Maxwell Street in Chicago

I n the summer of 1978, while John Belushi and Dan Aykroyd were still rehearsing for their upcoming shows at the Universal Amphitheater, John called Sean Daniel at Universal Studios. Then he reached over and put Elwood on the phone. (It wasn't Danny; it was Elwood.) And Daniel was told the legend of the Blues Brothers: two young orphans, one just out of prison, on a mission from God to raise $5,000 to save the Catholic orphanage where they grew up. "Sounds like a movie to me," he replied.

With Animal House *rolling along the way it was, the contract for the* Blues Brothers *movie didn't even require a handshake. Bernie Brillstein got on the line and finished the deal on the phone. When* Briefcase Full of Blues *went double platinum, the movie was rushed into production without a finished script or a finished budget, only a release date that director John Landis had agreed to meet—a rather ambitious proposition for a massive film production that included huge song and dance routines with thousands of extras, not to mention hundreds of stunt cars being wrecked, flipped, rolled and dropped from helicopters.*

Regardless, in early July of 1979, Blues Brothers *began principal photography in Chicago. For John, it was certainly the best and worst of times. He was returning to his hometown in grand style: Local Boy* Makes Good *on a mind-boggling scale. By day, he was in the recording studio with his musical heroes. By night, he was out on the loose and the whole of the city was his personal playground. But no matter the time or place, he still found himself wrestling with a crippling drug addiction, one that, as everyone was now painfully aware, posed a serious threat not just to his livelihood, but also to his life.*

DAN AYKROYD:

Over the fourth year of *SNL*, Judy and John and I sat down and came up with the backstory and the concept of the Blues Brothers, who they were and where they came from. I had taken a lot of sociology and criminology classes growing up and had always been fascinated with that stuff. So I sat down and used it in creating the profile of these two guys who start out as orphans, basically homeless, and end up in a life of crime because they never really had a family.

JOHN LANDIS:

All that stuff about going to prison was so foreign to John, really. Jake Blues was a very romanticized idea that John had of himself. He would have liked to have been that much of a hard-ass, you know, which he wasn't.

We wanted Aretha Franklin, John Lee Hooker, James Brown, Ray Charles and Cab Calloway. Fortunately for us, but unfortunately for them, except for Ray Charles most of these people weren't working that much. It was easy to get them. You called up and said, "Hey, you want a job?" That was not the hard part.

—John Landis

JUDITH BELUSHI PISANO:

Everything to do with the Blues Brothers evolved sort of naturally and organically. John was wearing the blues clothes more and more, and we were all adopting a bit of a pose. We were just saturated in it. We bought this old Dodge Polara because it seemed to have the right kind of blues attitude. Naturally, we decided to have it painted black. After a few days I got a call that the car was ready. I just turned to John and Danny and said, "Okay, I'm gonna go pick up the Bluesmobile." And none of us had ever called it that. It just came out. But they just looked at each other, smiled and hissed, *"The Bluuuuuesmobile."*

DAN AYKROYD:

I really didn't know how to write movies. I don't think I'd ever even seen a screenplay. I was told that most screenplays were 120 to 150 pages long, but when I sat down to write *Blues Brothers*, there were so many descriptive passages in there, just paragraphs and paragraphs of shots and concepts and ideas. Eventually it kind of ballooned up.

BOB WEISS:

Aykroyd had written a 324-page script. It actually had a story for recruiting each member of the band individually. It was delivered to me wrapped in the cover of the San Fernando Valley Yellow pages because it was as big as a phone book. Dan had tried to take a little of the sting out with a bit of humor.

JOHN LANDIS:

I essentially ended up becoming a co-writer because Danny's script, while fascinating and wonderful, was unfilmable.

JUDITH BELUSHI PISANO:

John and I thought Danny's first draft was fabulous. However, that script would have meant replacing the band members with actors, because they had loads of dialogue, and John felt strongly that the band members should play themselves. That would be a cool factor and a historic note. So they sat down with Landis to make the script work using the actual band.

BOB WEISS:

Universal had no idea what kind of movie we were going to make. I think Sean Daniel knew, but none of the other guys had a fucking clue. They just saw the money that *Animal House* did and gave the green light without any idea what we were going to turn in.

DAN AYKROYD:

John was my technical advisor for anything I needed verified on the Chicago side. A lot of people say that the city of Chicago itself was a character in the film, and that's all John. He brought the city alive. Although I did the physical scratching of the words on paper, John, and Judy as well, were really instrumental in creating the world of these two characters.

JUDITH BELUSHI PISANO:

Chicago, for many decades, had not been terribly accommodating to movie productions. It would have been tough to get a film like *Blues Brothers* made had it not been for the fact that John was a favorite son. Once they got in the door, Landis and Weiss put the right cards on the table to convince them we could pull it off. It was quite a feat on their part.

BOB WEISS:

This movie really took John back home. We were hooking into Chicago politics and the mayor's office; it was a big deal. Just before shooting began we were in Mayor Jane Byrne's office, and she said, "So what is this movie about?"

"Well, it's about these two characters, Jake and Elwood, and they've got about ten thousand traffic tickets." She offered to

take care of them for us. We laughed and told her we appreciated the offer.

Then she said, "Is there anything else I can help you with?"

"Well, we'd kind of like to drive a car through the Daley building."

She looked around the room for a moment, shrugged. "I don't see any problem with that."

JUDITH BELUSHI PISANO:

Before we left for Chicago, John called a meeting of the band and made his "farewell address," as he called it. Essentially, he told them things would be different in Chicago, that he was no longer the boss. They had to look to Landis and Weiss now so he could focus on his work in the film. We decided that Danny, John and I would stay at a different hotel than the band, to give us a little distance and, hopefully, some privacy. John felt he'd been living the Jake Blues thing long enough; he wanted to concentrate on making Jake a character, not just an alter ego. He had every intention of scaling back and buckling

down like he'd done for *Animal House*. But unfortunately, he being John and this being Chicago, that didn't happen.

STEVE BESHEKAS, *friend*:

When John and Danny brought that movie to town it blew Chicago apart.

ROSIE SCHUSTER, *writer*, SNL:

The weekend before *Blues Brothers* started production, John, Judy, Danny and I went to a resort in Wisconsin where Judy used to spend summers when she was younger. The trip was supposed to be a chance to relax, with the four of us sharing this tiny cabin, but a bunch of fans somehow found out about it and descended on the place.

Luckily Danny had parked a getaway car in the back—because that's how Danny is. We had to jump out the back window into these thorn bushes and beat a hasty retreat to a drive-in movie, which John watched with his head down.

TIM KAZURINSKY, *actor*:

When John was doing the *Blues Brothers* movie, I was in the cast at Second City. One night he came backstage and sort of hauled me aside and said, "I really like your work. You're gonna do well." I was blown away.

Everybody who's anybody who comes to Chicago stops by Second City, from Albert Brooks to Robin Williams. The audience loves to see them come onstage and say hi, and there's always a huge hand when they do. But John wouldn't do it. He said he didn't want to. I sort of hounded him for a while, and finally he broke down and said he would come out and wave to the audience.

So, one night he came by. All he did was walk out on the stage and stand there—and the place went nuts. It just blew up. I had never seen anything like it in my life. People jumped up out of their seats, knocked over tables, sent drinks flying. It was like somebody put jumper cables on their chairs. It was big, and it was frightening.

John went backstage—he just walked offstage real fast. And he had trouble talking because he had a lump in his throat.

He didn't perform that night. He couldn't. He was just all jelly in the knees.

BOB WEISS:

He was loved as a god in that town. There were times when I had the de facto role of bodyguard, because he'd get mobbed and I'd have to get him through and save him from autograph seekers. There were times when fans would just materialize out of thin air. In New York John and Danny had homes to go to, so it was different. But on location it was impossible. That was why they had to have the Sneak Joint.

DAN AYKROYD:

John Candy put us onto the Sneak Joint, right across the street from Second City. We'd all known about it before, but

---

Storming Chicago (clockwise from top left, opposite): John with Mayor Jane Byrne and nun; with Carrie Fisher; with Ray Charles; with Danny, shirtless; performing at ChicagoFest; with Judy; at drums; rehearsing; with Steve Cropper and Lou Marini at the Chicago Blues Bar.

it had been closed. And so we rented it and opened it back up. It became the second Blues Bar.

JUDITH BELUSHI PISANO:

It was a palace compared to the dive in New York.

STEVE BESHEKAS:

John called me up and said, "You want to work for us? We're turning the old Sneak Joint into a private club where we can hang out, and we want you to run it for us." I was working for my dad at the time, so it sounded pretty great. I immediately said yes.

JUDITH BELUSHI PISANO:

At first, the Blues Bar was low key, not the big party place like New York. It was an extended living room most of the time. People just hung out, listened to music, played pool. But it was inevitable that that would change. John and I had so much history in Chicago; it seemed there was another face from the past around every corner. Part of it was good, but it was also overpowering.

DEL CLOSE, *director, Second City*:

I lived about thirty feet from the old Blues Bar in Chicago. When even that became less of an escape because of all the public attention, he would come to my apartment, often knocking down the door.

FRED KAZ, *musical director, Second City*:

He was desperately searching for someone that saw his eyes, not his fame. I think to a large degree he found it at Second City. The first couple of times I ran into him, I could tell he was like, "Well, here's Fred, he's gonna be changed about me." And then I wasn't, and so from then he was the old John. I've found that in a lot of people I've known before and after the acquisition of fame. It's not that they've changed. It's that they've been put into a corner by those who want to change them.

GUS DIMAS, *cousin*:

John and I had another cousin named Chris Samaras. Chris and John went way back. But while John was off getting famous

on *Saturday Night Live*, Chris got into a pretty bad automobile accident. His face got very disfigured. They did all this cosmetic surgery on him, but after it was all done he never really looked the same.

So one night Chris says let's go down and see John at the Blues Bar. I had seen John intermittently over the years, but Chris hadn't. We get to the bar and John gives me a hug and says come on in. We're playing some pool and hanging out, but something about it is just wrong. It just isn't comfortable. Then after a while John leans over—and Chris is standing right there—and he whispers to me, "Who is that guy?"

This is a guy that he grew up with, who was over at his house all the time. I say, "John, that's Chris."

"That's *Chris?*"

Of course, Chris hears him and just blows up. "What? You don't even know who I am? You're such a fucking big shot you don't even remember your own family?"

John should've recognized him. I guess I can understand why he didn't. He really did look different. But after that I'm like, "Hey, you know what? Maybe we should just go. Chris, forget it. Let's go."

We walk around the pool table to head out. As we're going, John puts his foot up against the wall blocking our path and goes, "Hold on. Just wait. You have to—you gotta give me some time. You have to let me get used to this again. You don't have any idea how hard this is for me."

BERNIE BRILLSTEIN:

One weekend I was in Chicago with John. He said, "I can't go out. It's too crazy even just to be anywhere in public anymore." So we made him a disguise. I can't remember what it was. A hat and glasses, maybe. And we went to a bar. After about fifteen minutes he couldn't stand that no one recognized him. So he dropped the disguise, jumped up and yelled, "Hey! Drinks for everybody!" Then he turned to me and said, "Hey Bernie, you got a hundred bucks?"

DAN AYKROYD:

John was the underground mayor of Chicago. We had a permanent table set aside for us at the Pump Room in the Ambassador Hotel. We used to hail police cars late at night to

John, Danny, Steve Cropper and "Duck" Dunn jamming with local blues musicians

take us home. They were our own personal taxi service. We were right in the midst of the Chicago blues scene, and we were out seeing all of the major artists of the day, Perry Bell, Billy Branch, Sugar Blue, Little Joe Berson, Junior Wells. And they welcomed us. They knew what we were up to and they embraced it. Any of them that were available, we threw them in the movie. Walter Horton was still alive and we put him in. We were going to Maxwell Street every night and really living what we were making the movie about. We just had a lot of fun twenty-four/seven on that movie. We owned the town. Of course the next day it takes its toll. You're late. You fuck up a couple lines. But Judy was there all the time. She was very stabilizing.

BOB WEISS:

We were under tremendous pressure. This was a huge production. Our hands were so full it was hard to track where everybody was. We hired a rock-and-roll roadie, an old cowboy from Texas named Morris Lyda, to handle John. He had a time with that job. Tracking down John, the best you could hope for was to get a general idea of his last known whereabouts. We were all so busy it was hard enough just making sure that everyone was going to show up the next morning, and too often John was showing up after having gone all night.

JUDITH BELUSHI PISANO:

It's hard to imagine what it's like to have so much energy directed at you all the time. Every day there were more demands on John than he could possibly fill. You'd have to be very centered for it not to take its toll, and John wasn't.

BOB WEISS:

The makeup guy is the first guy you hit in the morning and the last guy you see before you go on set. We had this crazy, crusty, wonderful character named Shotgun Britton. In Elwood's flophouse in the movie there's that guy who yells out, "Boy, you got my Cheez Whiz?" That's Shotgun. He'd done makeup on movies all the way back to *Gunga Din* and *Citizen Kane*, and we figured he'd be the only one strong enough to handle John and Danny, get them set and going in the morning. So we basically hauled him out of retirement.

People always say to me, "Oh, John Belushi. He must have been really wild." But not really. Not the way you'd think. Truth be told, the one who has the potential to be truly crazy is Danny. I always expected to get a phone call from some fucking police department that they had Danny under arrest for some crazy thing. I never thought that would happen with John.

—Bob Weiss

He used to call John "Fat Boy," and he called Danny "The Other One." He even called them that to their faces. I remember John came in once and he was really hung over. He's sitting there, and Shotgun's working on him and rattling on. "Jesus Christ, kid. You know, once I had to stand Robert Mitchum up against the wall and paint eyes on his eyelids, he was so fucked up."

He was trying, in an almost paternal way, to shame John into shaping up.

DAN AYKROYD:

One night nobody could find John. We needed him for a shot, and someone said, "Well, I saw him walking that way.

Above: John and Danny with Shotgun Britton

He crossed the street and went into that neighborhood over there." So we started looking for him. We went house to house in the neighborhood sort of looking for telltale signs of him. Finally, somebody said, "Oh yeah yeah, he went into that house there."

We knocked and this guy came to the door and said, "Yes, Mr. Belushi is in. He's asleep on the couch." And this guy's a perfect stranger. Turned out John had walked off the set, gone to somebody's house, knocked on his door and said, "You know who I am? John Belushi. I'm tired and I'm hungry." He walked in, went over to the guy's fridge, opened it up, stood there making himself a sandwich, had a glass of milk, and then said, "Can I crash out on your couch?" John really was America's Guest; that really crystallized it.

JOHN LANDIS:

My wife Deborah was the costume designer on the film. She called John "the Black Hole," because he would flirt with girls and give away his sunglasses as presents, which was a problem because Ray-Ban didn't make that particular model of Wayfarers anymore, hadn't made them in years. When we contacted Ray-Ban they didn't want to know from us, and so Deborah had to go to a lot of old five-and-dime stores in black neighborhoods where they still had the glasses on the racks and buy them. I think we had about forty-five pairs, including the ones for all the stunt men. So they were valuable items, but John would just give them away to girls.

BOB TISCHLER:

John was going full throttle in terms of his partying, and everybody else was doing coke at the time too. So a lot of it was just trying to keep substances away from him so that he could keep it together. It was incredibly difficult because he was doing the soundtrack at the studio and shooting the movie at the same time. He was all over the place. He had to be in both places, back and forth, a lot of times on the same day.

JOHN LANDIS:

Most of *Blues Brothers* was a good experience; let me make that clear. Most of the days were good. On a six-month shoot we only lost four or five days because of drugs, which is a lot, but not nearly what people imagine. A lot of what people have heard has become mythology over the years. John was thrilled to be working with Aretha Franklin and Ray Charles. Whenever we were working with any of the guest stars, John and Danny were like little kids, and John was on his best behavior. He was totally charming and funny and sweet and nice. The crew loved him.

That said, John's coke problem had gotten very bad. He was difficult, and bad things did happen. At one point, I had to go into his trailer to get him, and he was not in a good way. It was like that scene from *Scarface* where Tony Montana just has mountains of cocaine around him on his desk. So I took the coke and I flushed it down the toilet. John was furious, and he went for me. We tussled a little bit, and then he just broke down and started sobbing. It

CARRIE FISHER:

I met John when I started hanging around the *SNL* people shortly after *Star Wars* came out. He just showed up at someone's apartment one night. Everyone was completely loaded in those days, but at that point it was really fun and no one was really scared about it yet. John wanted me to date Danny so that we could hang out more. I was about twenty-one and dating Paul Simon at the time, and Danny was living with Rosie Schuster. But John thought that we would be a good couple and we could all have fun together. So he invited me down to his house in the Village, and then he invited Danny over to join us, and then he passed out. That was his version of a blind date.

So Danny and I went out to some bar and had a beer and then we started having this clandestine affair where we would meet in parking lots and make out. That was John's favorite thing ever. In getting Danny and me to have the affair he got to be a part of it. They wrote a part for me in *Blues Brothers* and we all went to Chicago.

I really don't like cocaine. I can't stand it. But instead of being able to stop John, he got me started. Danny was trying to get me to eat because I'd been doing too much coke and one night I started choking to death on a Brussels sprout. Danny did the Heimlich and he saved my life. Then he proposed to me. I thought, shit, I'd better marry him in case that happens again. Danny was a fantastic person to have take care of you.

One night later on, Danny said to me while he was brushing his teeth, "You better get used to this, because you're going to be looking at it for the rest of your life."

And I just thought, ugh, oh my God.

But Danny and I had gotten *engaged* and a huge part had to do with John assembling what *he* wanted. John's perfect double date concept was me and Danny and him and Judy. He was in love with Danny and I being in love, and his influence was such that he could make it happen. But the problem was that now Danny had two people to take care of, which was a lot for Danny to do.

On the set in LA: John and Danny with Aretha Franklin

was a terrible moment. We were hugging and crying, and it was very, very hard.

My concerns were essentially for his survival. The whole idea was to keep John away from drugs, and also to keep drugs away from John. He was such a celebrity at that point that total strangers would walk up and give drugs to him.

BOB WEISS:

Blow was everywhere in those days. It was like a blizzard.

CARRIE FISHER:

John Landis came up to me and said, "If John does any more coke he's going to have a heart attack. If you catch him doing it you have to stop him, and don't do any drugs with him."

John came up to me one night at the Blues Bar and said, "Do you want some blow?"

I said, "John, should you really be doing that?"

He just screamed, *"Do you want some blow or not?!"*

And I just thought, how are we going to stop John from doing this? From doing anything? John was a life force. There was no stopping him from doing anything that he wanted. He was a sweet guy underneath it all, but he was a sweet man who was completely overrun by his appetites.

MITCH GLAZER:

It was pretty bad by that point. Judy was living through more of the downside of it that we couldn't see. There were

hills and valleys and she was just neck deep in it. It would break your heart, but as a friend you could always leave and figure that John was strong enough to handle it. You could always go back to your life, but that was her life.

JUDITH BELUSHI PISANO:

Looking back, it's glaringly obvious that we'd all been in pretty serious denial, but of course you don't know that at the time. The biggest obstacle to getting John help was that I honestly didn't think of him as an addict. I was totally ignorant of those things. I thought an addict was someone who was constantly and physically dependent. With John, there'd be days, weeks, sometimes months of nothing but the good old loveable John. Then he'd spin out, and the problem would rear its ugly head again. And so I thought it was something he could control, or was failing to control. The "Chicago plan" was just to keep drugs away from John. At first, it seemed that's what John wanted. I tried to be the policeman, confronting all the crew members and band members to make sure everyone was helping. Danny and Landis and a lot of friends, we all tried that tactic, but it couldn't work, because it was a bad plan. John still wanted the drugs and he would find them.

On October 27, 1979, location filming for the movie finally came to an end. Cast and crew packed up and headed to Los Angeles for three additional months of interior work to complete the film. While the orphan Dan bunked up at his office on the Universal lot, Judy and John rented a secluded house, deep in Coldwater Canyon, from actress Candice Bergen. Pam Jacklin, Billy Belushi and Peter Aykroyd, the blues siblings, came for an extended visit. Life resumed some semblance of domestic routine.

In order to start work on Blues Brothers: Private, *a companion book to the movie, Judy took an office near John's, allowing them to work together daily on the lot. With the help of the surrounding stability, John moderated his drug use, began to live a bit more healthily, and, as he had done so many times in the past, convinced both his loved ones and himself that the problem was at least under control. His renewed efforts yielded some of the film's best moments, including the standout musical scenes with Aretha Franklin, Ray Charles and James Brown.*

For the first time since the Animal House *premiere eighteen months before, John wasn't being pulled in a million directions at once, and for the next several weeks of that bright and balmy Los Angeles winter, only one true disaster appeared on the horizon. On December 14, 1979, John, Judy, Dan and Penny Marshall attended the premiere of Steven Spielberg's* 1941.

PENNY MARSHALL:

John was very excited about *1941.* It was his first big Hollywood premiere. I was shooting *Laverne and Shirley,* and so I had the wardrobe people at Paramount get me and Judy these 1940s dresses, and the guys got tuxes. They picked me up at the lot because I was in rehearsals all day, pulling up in this vintage 1941 automobile.

John and Danny were like little kids. They practiced all this little business they were going to do with the car at the theater, opening the hood and so on. We drove up to the theater, as nervous as we could be. Then we finally got inside for this big gala premiere…and it was the most hostile audience I've ever seen in my life. The whole movie, nothing. Silence.

Well, anxiety attacks all around like you wouldn't believe. You can't walk out in the middle of it. You just have to hold on. Then you have to walk out through the press—and the press hated it. We had to keep these happy faces on to make it through the lobby and into the car, but once we made it there we got in and screamed, "Oh my God, was that horrible?! Was that horrible or am I just crazy?"

The 1941 *premiere: Danny and Penny Marshall; John and Judy*

Then we were all supposed to go to this party afterward at the Hollywood Palladium. Judy and I said, "Well, do we go to the party or do we not?"

And they said, "No, we go." And so we went. It was a little depressing, but both John and Danny were very honorable. They stuck by the film. There are rules. You don't want to abandon Steven, so you just make it your job.

TIM MATHESON:

Everyone was looking for Spielberg to make a fall; it was his comeuppance.

JOE FLAHERTY:

John didn't even get a chance to shine in it, and he took the brunt of its failure.

JUDITH BELUSHI PISANO:

John felt really bad that the film didn't work, like he'd done something wrong. The movie was so expensive to make, and John felt as if people blamed him for it, like he'd gone and set the money on fire himself.

PENNY MARSHALL:

The next month Judy had a big birthday party for John the same night as the Golden Globes. Spielberg was my date for the Globes, and I said, "Well we have to go to John's birthday party." Steven was quite depressed about *1941*, needless to say. So here we are, all dressed up; we head up to John's house and everyone is wearing buttons that Michael O'Donoghue had made that read: "John Belushi: Born 1949, Died *1941*."

BOB WEISS:

When that movie bombed, it was not good for *Blues Brothers*. For a while they called us *1942*.

JOHN LANDIS:

What happened was that within a period of two years there were five films made by Hollywood studios that cost more than $24 million: *Star Trek*, *1941*, *Apocalypse Now*, *Heaven's Gate* and *Blues Brothers*. The reason that $24 million is important is because it's the amount that *Cleopatra* cost, and that's the movie that bankrupted Fox and forced them to sell off their back lot.

So if you look back at the contemporary reports, all of them are like, "Hollywood Out of Control!" But in fact it had a lot to do with the realities of the economics of moviemaking. They were all gigantic movies with big stars and big production values. They were all bloated to begin with, but the studios tended to blame the directors and the stars because it made for a better story. The bottom line is that most of those movies wound up making money.

You hear a lot of numbers thrown around, but the fact is that *Blues Brothers* cost twenty-seven million bucks, which was

"Jesus H. Tapdancing Christ! I see the light!"; Jake Blues gets religion

a shitload of money in 1979. But John was the star of the biggest movie in the world, *Animal House*, and their album had gone double platinum. So all of a sudden this development project that they had on the back burner turned into something they wanted right away.

DAN AYKROYD:

John loved hanging around with the people who were running the business, Wasserman and Sheinberg and those studio executives. He really made all of them close friends and he was very, very good at all of it, very diplomatic, charmed them all to death. That way the sting of the budget on *Blues Brothers* didn't hurt so bad. They didn't like it, but they had too much respect for John to really come down on him.

SEAN DANIEL:

Universal liked the fact that John was in movies that audiences embraced and lined up to see. John was this wonderful force to have on the lot, to have in your life. John had his home here. He was trouble. He was not easy to live with or have as a citizen, but everybody loved him.

BOB WEISS:

When we were back shooting on the lot at Universal, John found out that one of the soundstages we were using was where *Phantom of the Opera* had been shot. So he went wandering around and exploring. A few days later one of the crew came up to me and said, "I think Belushi was crawling around down under the stage. I found his signature." So I went to look and found that he'd signed his name on the wall with a caulking gun. It had hardened up and there it was, as if marking his place in Universal's history in a weird kind of way.

DAN AYKROYD:

We really had the run of the place. We had one of the strongest franchise offices on the lot. The possibilities of what

"How much for the little girl? The women, how much for the women? The little girl, your daughters...sell them to me."

JOHN LANDIS:

The real tragedy is not how over-budget the movie was. It's how much better John's performance could have been without the drugs. You can see it. There are some scenes where he's all there and some when he's clearly not. The best thing that ever happened to the Blues Brothers were those dark glasses. The idea of the sunglasses was just us being perverted. What's the most important part of an actor's face? The eyes. So we said, "Let's cover them." But it did help a lot in disguising John's condition.

For his scene with Carrie, where he finally had to take off his glasses, I told him, "John, you have to take off your glasses in six days. I don't want you eating, smoking or drinking anything that will fuck with your eyes." And he did it. If you watch the movie he looked great and he's really funny in that scene.

we could do then were unlimited. We had a fabulous bungalow right across from the *Phantom of the Opera* stage. I actually lived there on the lot. John had the house. We'd get in our golf cart and roam all over. We'd go up to the Frankenstein castle and crack open a couple of beers.

One of the things I did take advantage of at Universal was the motor pool. I'd drive anything I wanted, like old police cars or pickups. One day I went back and found a vintage Mercedes World War II German Army half-track personnel carrier with a straight-12 diesel engine. Eight- or ten-speed transmission. When I showed John that thing he was like, "Wow!" We were in the midst of planning this big soiree, and I said, "Wouldn't this be a great centerpiece for the party we're having Friday night?"

There was a gentleman with us at the time named Big Louie. Big Louie wasn't big, but his reputation was. He claimed to be a professional smuggler. So at the end of shooting Friday night, Big Louie and John and I went out there and I was like, "Uh, I think I can drive it, but I don't know if I can even get it into third."

And Louie, who'd been a heavy equipment operator, said, "I know how to drive this thing." He got in and sure enough fired it right up. John sat next to him. I followed in the old Dodge 440 police car. We pulled up to the front gate at Universal. The guard looked up, saw John sitting there in this half-track diesel troop carrier with a cigarette in his hand and his feet up on the dash, and just waved 'em on through. And off we went through the streets of Hollywood. It looked magnificent at the party.

SEAN DANIEL:

I always wondered just how terrified that security guard must have been when that troop carrier didn't show up on Monday morning. I know the teamster we sent to pick it up thought it was hysterical.

JOHN LANDIS:

Things got worse again toward the end of the movie, in part because John injured his knee. He was in real pain when we shot the big concert sequence at the Palace Hotel where they sing and dance to "Sweet Home Chicago" and "Everybody Needs Somebody to Love." I wanted to use a stunt double for some of the things and he wouldn't hear of it.

BOB WEISS:

I got the call that John had hurt his knee falling off a skateboard. I thought it was a joke. I couldn't think of a worse thing to do than try to learn how to ride a skateboard the day before your climactic singing and dancing number.

John was out at some guy's place in the Valley. I went out there, and when I walked in the door everybody was limping around, trying to make a joke to cover up what was not such a good thing.

I don't know what the fuck the doctor did to him. He pulled the worst-looking shit out of his knee, put some other shit back in, and somehow John pulled it off. He was great. This was one of the biggest scenes in the movie, thousands of extras, singing and dancing and jumping around, and John fucking did it. He was a trooper. The show goes on, and he got that. He learned it doing *SNL*.

I never sat down with John and discussed mortality versus immortality, but I do know for sure there was a part of him that deep down thought he couldn't get hurt, that he could do anything. And when you start to buy that shit, that's the worst time.

JOHN LANDIS:

John and I were walking along outside the Universal lot having a screaming argument. There was a guy who had showed up on the set. I knew he was giving John drugs and I'd had him banned him from the lot. I just lost it and I took John outside and told him, "You let that guy on the set one more time…"

"You can't tell me who my friends are."

"I don't give a fuck who your friends are and believe me this guy's not your friend."

He was pissed off at me because I'd embarrassed him. He told me to go fuck myself. Then he stepped out onto Lankershim Boulevard and stuck out his thumb. Some perfect stranger, this long-haired dude in a convertible heading in the opposite direction, whipped his car around, did a complete 180, and screeched to a halt next to John. "Hey, Belushi!" he yelled. "Hop in, buddy!"

John, in full Jake Blues regalia, hopped over the door into the front seat and said, "Take me to the Chateau Marmont!" And they went roaring off. The world was at the man's disposal, so to speak.

John Landis wrapped principal photography on Blues Brothers *on February 1, 1980. That same week John disappeared, presumably lost in the Los Angeles underground. Friends and family sat by the phone desperately waiting for a call. Three days later he resurfaced, acting as if nothing were wrong. Finally everyone realized that all of the attempts to moderate John's drug use had failed. For the first time, the idea of checking him into a treatment facility was openly discussed, but to little avail. Attempts by Judy and Bernie Brillstein to confront John resulted only in screaming arguments, belligerent denials and angry threats. There was little point in talking about a treatment program for John until he decided it was something he needed to do for himself. And for John to accept the need to get better, things would have to get worse.*

Six weeks later they got worse. The first week of April, John's grandmother Nena suffered several consecutive heart attacks. John was in Chicago to see his younger brother Jimmy debut in a new play when they received word. Weakened and frail, Nena was now bedridden in a San Diego hospital, near the family's new ranch. Jim flew immediately to California to visit, secretly sharing with her the news that his girlfriend

was pregnant and that they hoped to have a baby boy on the way. Nena held on for several days, drifting in and out of consciousness, asking again and again to see John. But John, drowning his denial and grief in any way he could, refused to go.

JIM BELUSHI:

I had just come back from San Diego, and I found John walking out of the Chicago Blues Bar. We were standing there in the alley, and I said, "I just saw Nena. You've got to go see her, you know. She's waiting for you."

"I know she's waiting," he said. "That's why I'm not going. The longer I stay here, the longer she'll be alive."

"John, you've got to go see her now. She's going to die." I started to cry.

John said, "Stop it. Stop crying right now."

"John, I can't. It's Nena."

"Okay, okay. Go ahead and cry." So I cried for minute, and then John said, "Fine, that's enough. We need to be strong for the women in this family. They're going to fall apart, so we can't. We're the men. So no more crying." I said okay. And I stopped.

JUDITH BELUSHI PISANO:

I called John from New York and he was still refusing to leave, so I got on a plane and went to Chicago. When I found him, it was obvious he'd been on a really bad binge. I told him I was going to California the next day, with or without him. He finally gave in.

When we got to the hospital, Nena looked so weak and frail my heart just ached. But she lit up when she saw John. He dropped his sorrow and turned up the charm. He was cracking jokes, putting on a little show. Pretty soon he had Nena and the aunts and uncles in the room laughing and smiling. After a little of that, she fell asleep. John, sitting in a chair next to the bed, rested his head on her pillow and fell asleep, too.

After the past week in Chicago, John didn't look so good himself. Billy grabbed one of the doctors and asked him if he'd look John over. John told the doctor what he'd been doing that week and for the past several months. The doctor told him, point blank, "You're killing yourself, and you've got to stop."

The next morning, while John was still asleep, I got the call from his Uncle Chris at the hospital. I went in and woke him up. I couldn't really speak, but I didn't need to. He looked at me and he knew. He immediately sat up, grabbed the phone and started making calls. He told his parents he would take care of everything. He called our secretary in New York and started making the funeral arrangements. He was a flurry of activity and then, suddenly, he hung up the phone and was silent. "I'm not going to cry," he said flatly.

John flew the entire family and all the relatives and in-laws back to Chicago. We paid for everything, the hotels, the cars, the flowers. John insisted that everything be done first class. The funeral was at the St. Nicholas Albanian Orthodox Church. It was all very magical. Incense and smoke swirled in the light shining through the Byzantine stained-glass windows in this old church. I couldn't understand the service, and so my mind drifted, thinking how odd it was to step back into this foreign world John had come from, and just how far away we'd traveled from it.

JIM BELUSHI:

It was a lovely service. John took care of everything that day. Nena was the heart, soul and conscience of our family, and so it was like we had lost a mother. On the way to the funeral, John spilled something on his shirt. We were going to stop at a little mall to get him a new one, but he said, "No, leave it. It looks vulnerable." We all laughed. Throughout the whole service John was stoic, his jaw set. And so was I. I was there for the women and the family like John had told me to be.

Afterwards we went to a banquet hall for a reception. I was standing to the side, talking to a couple of women, when all of the sudden the whole crowd shifted and looked to the center of the room, like someone had fallen or had a heart attack. I couldn't see, so I stood up on a chair to get a better look. There was John in the middle of the banquet hall, one arm around the bishop and the other around the priest, sobbing like a baby. ■

John and Nena at the family ranch

Chapter 12

FROM THE BOTTOM

the Smokemeister General

HAROLD RAMIS:

When the Blues Brothers opened for Steve Martin at the Universal Amphitheater, they had the best blues band ever assembled by a white man, *Saturday Night Live* was the biggest comedy show on television and *Animal House* was on its way to becoming the number-one comedy of all time. I looked out at John onstage that night in front of 7,000 screaming fans, and I actually consciously thought: he might not survive this.

Above: The Smokemeister General (right)

That April, the week after Nena's funeral, John admitted that his problems with cocaine had spiraled beyond his control and agreed to get help. But it would be done on his terms. Help came in the form of one Richard "Smokey" Wendell, the Smokester, the Smokemeister General, so named for the striking bear tattoos on both of his forearms. A seven-year veteran of the Secret Service, Smokey had recently entered the profession of freelance private security and was currently in the employ of Joe Walsh, guitarist for the Eagles.

Walsh, like John, had run into problems staying in control of his new fame and rock-and-roll lifestyle. He'd hired Smokey to handle all of his private security, protecting him from zealous fans and also from himself. While John would not consent to being committed to a treatment program, he felt he could beat the problem on his own with the right help, and this seemed to be the solution he needed.

Also, come June, the Blues Brothers were launching an all-out national tour to support the release of the movie and soundtrack album. Work had always been John's incentive for cleaning up in the past, and this time he knew the stakes were too high for him to slip. He approached Walsh. An introduction was made, and a deal was struck. Smokey would be paid $1,000 per week, plus expenses, for which he would live, travel, eat and all but sleep with John, shadowing his every move and keeping him out of harm's way. On April 16, 1980, he left his home in the suburbs of Washington and flew to New York City.

SMOKEY, *bodyguard*:

The Eagles were in Chicago at the Drake Hotel for the last show of their tour. John was there, and he and Joe started talking. "Everything's going great," John said. "I had this hit TV show, this hit movie and the Blues Brothers are really taking off, but at the rate I'm going I'm gonna need someone to help me."

"What are you talking about?" Joe said.

"The way things are moving, if I don't take care of myself and keep things together, I could wind up dead in a couple of years. This is just all way too fast for me."

"I got just the guy for you," Joe said.

"You mean that shadowy guy who always disappears and then when you turn around he's right next to you?"

"Yep. That's him. If you're looking for someone to help you get yourself together, he'll do it. But you won't like it one bit."

Pretty soon after that we were back in New York. John was in the studio doing the final touches on the *Blues Brothers* soundtrack, and there was a song that he wanted Joe's help with. Joe and I went over there, and John, traditionally, was tardy. In John's world he had a watch that only had one hand; whatever time it was, he seemed to think it was close enough.

Finally he showed up. The session went okay, but we were working against the clock, and there were just too many people in the studio. In my experience you can always spot the people who really have no reason to be there: straphangers, entourage people. John and Joe were working, and in the interim these "friends" were disappearing frequently into the bathroom. When they came out of the bathroom, I'd just go in and confiscate what they'd left behind. There's always a basic pattern to how they do this stuff; these guys aren't that creative.

So when John excused himself and went to the bathroom, I just waited. Then he came out and went over to the guest. They started whispering to each other. You could read the whole conversation in their faces: "Whaddya mean it wasn't there?" "It's not there." "But I put it there." And so on. So the guy went back to the bathroom. Then I went back to the bathroom. Then John went back to the bathroom. It was like a dog chasing its tail all night long. Finally, when John was on one of his trips to the bathroom, I went up next to this person, poured myself a cup of coffee, looked at him and said, "Look, we can do this all night long if you like, but it's going to be a lot more expensive for you than it is for me." Then I took one of the packets of cocaine out of my pocket. "Now, if this were just Sweet 'N Low..." And I dumped it into the coffee. Guy almost had a heart attack. That was a lot of money he wasn't going to see because it didn't cross the palm.

So he and John had another one of these conversations, and John went over to a table where there were two packs of cigarettes. One was the brand John smoked, and the other belonged to this other guy, and John proceeded to pick up the wrong pack. I went over and said to him, "I thought you smoked Merits."

"Oh, I smoke these too," he said.

I asked him to give me the pack. He wouldn't. I grabbed it. He jerked around and wouldn't let go. We started tussling and wrestled each other to the ground. I finally got it away from him, and, of course, it contained what had not made it past the bathroom. That's when John realized this was it—the game had started, and he'd lost round one. He turned to Joe and smiled. "You're right. I'm not going to like him."

Joe left; we stayed for a couple of hours and then went to the Blues Bar downtown. Judy, Danny, Mitch and a whole bunch of people were there. I sat and talked with Judy, watching the room from the corner. John tried to lose me several times that first night, unsuccessfully. Then when it came time to go, it was just John and me. Judy had left with Danny earlier. There was a car waiting for us out front. John got in curbside. As I was walking around, I heard the doors lock, and he drove away. Then he had the driver stop and I ran up and he pulled away again. And then he did it again. And again. And then, finally, he stopped the car and opened the door. I caught up and got in and he was laughing. And I thought it was funny. I got the joke: I'd fucked up. But it was also very telling. That was the first clue to me. If he'd wanted to take off, he could have just disappeared and left me standing there. But he didn't.

When we sat down at his house on Morton Street that first night, he wanted to get everything out on the table, lay it all out so we both knew where we stood. "I know what you're here for," he said. "I know what you're gonna do, but one thing I want you to keep utmost in mind is that regardless of what you do for me, it's even more important that you take care of Judy. Whatever she wants or needs, you make sure she has it. If she has somewhere to go, make sure she gets there. Now that Nena is no longer with me, my whole world is Judy. She's my whole world. Everything else is second."

He took his grandmother's death very hard. That was part of the problem of overextending himself lately. Over the following months, I found that it was something that he was very careful about who he opened the door for, as he was with a lot of things.

"Okay," he said, "let's get this over with. Ask away."

So I asked the first question I always ask, "Why are you in this situation? Why do you do the Candyland?"

"It's the pressure," he said. "The demands, the hours. You need drugs to deal with everything this business puts on you. It's hard to be on for everyone all the time. And it makes me feel good."

"But it's temporary, isn't it? You take enough to hit that plateau, and the next time you take the same amount and nothing happens, and so you constantly have to go further and further. From the looks of it, you're already there."

"What do you mean?"

"I'm sure you're now at a point where your intake is steadily increasing, and look at how much it's costing you."

We got into this conversation about pros and cons. Since I'm a person who doesn't do drugs at all, he didn't want to hear it. You're dealing with a situation where they know you're right, but they can't bring themselves to admit you're right. I said, "Well, are you okay with me being here?"

"Sure, I know you're up for the ride."

"No, no, that's the thing you have to understand. I'm not Judy. I'm not your manager. I'm not your accountant. I'm not your priest. I'm not your doctor. And I'm not your friend."

"Sure, but in time you will be."

"You don't know that. I represent everything that you don't want. I'm the grim reaper with sunglasses instead of a sickle."

He laughed at that. "So I'm going to hate you?" he asked.

"Well, how did you feel when we had the little incident in the studio?"

"Oh, I hated you. I hated you big time."

"Why?"

"Well, I guess for all the reasons you just said…Is this really the way it's gonna be?"

"Every day'll be a new adventure."

We were playing a game, and I understood that. I knew I was looking at a good actor. You can't trust actors. John was self-aware enough to go to Joe Walsh and say he needed help, yet here he was arguing with the guy he'd hired to help him. It's a diversion; you're lying to yourself.

The thing about it is that he was immediately comfortable with me. He did his usual thing with the fidgeting in the seat, the chain-smoking, the drinking lots of diet soda, but he stayed right there at the table and he kept talking. That was the second clue for me. The first was stopping the car, and that was the

second. He could protest and argue all he wanted. As long as he stayed at that table with me, I knew that he knew exactly what was going on and that he was up for it.

Finally he said, "Look, I'm still gonna try and do it. You're gonna try and stop me, and maybe you will and maybe you won't. I'll still have a good time being an actor, comedian and performer—all the things that this world wants out of me."

"But then you're resolving nothing," I said, "and the more you do this, the more you're taking away from the person and actor you want to be. It's going to take its toll on you. How are you going to deal with that when it stops working?"

"That'll never happen to me."

"Should we talk about all the people who've said the same thing who aren't here today?"

"Well, they just weren't careful."

"There's no such thing as careful. You'll keep going and going, and you'll keep doing and doing, and what happens then?"

"What do you mean?"

"What happens when you can't catch that buzz anymore? What happens when you've tried every drug there is and you can't reach that plateau you need to reach?"

He thought about that one for a second.

"I don't know," he said. "I guess you'd just go crazy."

★ ★ ★

On June 27, 1980, Blues Brothers *opened in theaters. Chicago* Sun-Times *critic Roger Ebert applauded the film; David Denby of* New York *magazine called it "hectic and stupid," and his sentiments were widely echoed. As a movie,* Blues Brothers *met with a great deal of unexpected resistance. But while it was a movie in the sense of being a narrative story shot on celluloid and then projected onto a screen in order to drive popcorn sales, for John and Danny it was always much more. It was a celebration of a time and a place in American music, a way to revitalize a lost part of our culture, a big, raucous party that happened to take place in movie form. And on that level, there can be no argument that it was a great success.*

Despite its lukewarm critical reception, Blues Brothers *would go on to make a spectacular amount of money. This was due in large part to the efforts of John and Danny, who were determined to spread the*

Once Blues Brothers *went out and became a hit movie, NBC got very serious about hanging onto their properties. After that we couldn't go near any of John's inventions for movie material, at least in terms of anything that he was doing on* Saturday Night Live. *The network was not happy; John took some pleasure in that.*

—Sean Daniel

film's message far and wide. The same night that the movie opened, the show band of Joliet Jake and Elwood Blues hit the stage at the Poplar Creek Theater in Chicago for the start of a national tour to promote both the movie and the unsung masters of American music.

Starting in Chicago and moving through New York, Washington and Dallas, the tour included twenty gigs in sixteen cities over six weeks, ultimately wrapping up back at the Universal Amphitheater in Los Angeles to record another live album. For John, the live shows meant two hours a night of singing, jumping, dancing, somersaulting and cartwheeling, sometimes for three nights in a row. Such an endeavor would be a challenge for anyone, in any kind of state, let alone someone fifty pounds overweight white-knuckling his way out of a five-year cocaine problem. But then John never did make things easy on himself.

JOHN LANDIS:

When *Blues Brothers* came out, we faced some unforeseen obstacles. This was before Reagan's deregulation policies took effect, and at that time theater owners, exhibitors, had a lot of clout. If they decided for whatever reason that they didn't want to book your movie, that was it. You were fucked. And in LA the theater you wanted to be in was in Westwood Village. That was the place for both prestige and big box office.

Well, one day Lew Wasserman at Universal called me into his office and introduced me to Ted Mann, the exhibitor who owned the Westwood theaters at that time. So we all said hello, and Lew went, "Tell him what you said to me, Ted."

Ted said, "Mr. Landis, I apologize, but we're not booking your picture."

"And why is that?"

"Because I don't want blacks in Westwood Village."

"…Excuse me?"

I was just shocked. As it turned out, theater owners across the country thought that no white people would go see *Blues Brothers*. I think we opened in less than six-hundred theaters,

and in most places we didn't open in prestige theaters, and this was when John was one of the biggest stars in the country.

Weirder still, MCA Records, which was a big label, didn't want the soundtrack. So it was made with Atlantic, which supposedly is a "black" label, but even Atlantic refused to put John Lee Hooker on the album because he was *too* black, and

too old. When John Lee Hooker was all of a sudden selling platinum albums again about fifteen years later, I was very gratified. But it just goes to show how interesting and out there John and Danny's vision was. And it worked. It made over eighty million bucks, and that's when you paid two dollars to see a movie. *Blues Brothers* was profitable from its first American run. It's also the first American movie ever to gross more foreign than domestic.

SEAN DANIEL:

The critics trounced it, and so people always thought it was a failure, even though everyone was going to see it. It was a big hit financially. It was a huge hit all over the world, yet it never really got its recognition. That drove us all crazy. John was always kind of angered that the movie just took shot after shot and didn't get a fair shake. A lot of people thought it was racist, that John and Danny were exploiting black music just to make money, and so John was hurt that his intentions had been misunderstood. In fact, as opposed to *Animal House*, where he liked to go to the theaters and hear about the sellouts and the ticket lines, he didn't stay as close to this movie.

JOHN LANDIS:

I was the one who put the whole "mission from God" angle into the script because the movie itself really was a mission. Danny had a passion and a vision for bringing the blues and R&B back into mainstream culture. His desire was to exploit his fame, and John's, to focus attention on these unacknowledged masters of American music—and we were completely successful.

DOC POMUS, *musician*:

When John and Danny recorded Joe Turner's "Flip, Flop & Fly" on *Briefcase Full of Blues*, the royalties that Joe and his wife got from the album financially resurrected their lives and his career. Same thing with Sam Moore and "Soul Man." It gave him back his performing status and his livelihood.

On my fifty-fourth birthday, John sent over two cases of champagne. He called later that night and we got to talking. He wanted to know if there were any other blues musicians I knew of that needed his help.

BERNIE BRILLSTEIN:

When John had power, he used it for his friends. If he wanted someone for a particular job, he'd call me and say, "Bernie, get on Universal. I want ten thousand dollars for so-and-so." On the Blues Brothers tour, the guys didn't make a nickel; they insisted on paying the band all the money, and they ended up losing a boatload themselves. They wanted the band to have a big payday because they thought they deserved it. I argued with them, but they said, "That's the way we want it."

DAN AYKROYD:

We lost about forty grand on that tour. John and I took a complete wash and bath on that. But we put together what I like to call the third greatest R&B revue in the world, the first being James Brown and the second being Tina Turner. Our band was as good as any band touring at that point in time—and much better than most. There's no doubt about that. The only weakness was the front men, but John and I knew our limitations.

MURPHY DUNNE, *band member*:

John and I were on the way to a show one night, and he said, "You know, a lot of people say I can't sing the blues." Then he smiled for a second. "Well, maybe so, but I sure can sell 'em."

I used to get more people saying, "What's the deal with John Belushi? He can't really sing, can he?" I think I'm a fairly well-qualified musician. I've been a producer for many years, and I think he sings a lot better than some of the other artists out there.

—Steve Cropper

SMOKEY:

It really was John's initiative to clean up for the tour. It was rough at first, but he was really, really good about it. We had to explain my presence to the band, because they didn't know jack squat about me. Judy did that. At that point, all the band members knew what John went through on the movie, and they knew that behavior would ruin the tour. So everybody was receptive to the idea.

DAN AYKROYD:

I liked Smokey a lot. John and I talked all the time about his problem, and it never seemed that he really wanted to help himself until that point. It doesn't start with anyone else. It starts with yourself, and that's when we knew he was serious. And so Smokey and I became instant allies. I said, "Look, I'm your friend in this. Let's work together." If John was gonna try and pull something off, I would get it to Smokey on a back channel and the buy or the deal wouldn't go down. He kept the scumballs and the sleazebags away from John, all those people who loved John and thought they were doing him a favor. He kept them away and enabled us to get through the tour without any impairment of John's talent or ability to perform. He was indispensable, and with his help we were able to keep John pretty much straight. We could not have done the tour and accomplished what we did without him.

SMOKEY:

The tour was really all work. He was very much into the job of singing, performing, keeping his voice right. Once we'd established the fact that the Candyland was over and it was time to work, he was fine. It was hard in the beginning. It took a bit of doing to divert his attention from being uncomfortable, to get him to exercise and keep his mind busy.

BILL WALLACE, *trainer*:

I had met John at his New Year's Eve party. He said, "Hey, I know you. I've watched you fight on television." I was the World Kickboxing Champion, Middleweight Division, at the time. So we talked for about twenty minutes, and then he said, "Hey! We're gonna do a Blues Brothers tour starting in June. You want to go with us?"

"Sounds fun to me," I said, figuring it was another one of those LA deals where somebody pitches you something and then you never hear from them again. But on June 16, I retired from kickboxing and went to work for John. My job was basically to work out with him and Danny and the band to keep them in good shape.

MURPHY DUNNE:

John was probably in the best shape of anyone on that tour.

JUDITH BELUSHI PISANO:

There were a few nights when, after the concert, I went out with friends while John stayed in. That was different.

SMOKEY:

He was very adamant about doing well. That was a big motivation for him. He'd say, "These people paid good money to be here, and I gotta keep it together for them. I can't let them down." His performances were very athletic, flipping and jumping, and with as much weight as he was carrying around it was exhausting for him. They would do three shows in a row, and, for the life of me, I have no idea how. A lot of his energy would be taken out on show days. When he was active he was a different person. The downtime, when nothing was going on, that's when he could get into trouble.

John was always well aware that the temptation was there. There were times when I was going somewhere, some errand, without him, and he'd be like, "Oh, wait. I'll go with you." He would consciously take himself out of any situation where he was alone. I never questioned and I never asked, but I knew why. He was not trusting of himself.

Once you're an addict, you're an addict. John wasn't holding and he wasn't using, but the temptation was always there. The hardest part is outliving the nightmares. Sometimes just getting through the night can be like death. Because I was there, I was the crutch that he'd use. He'd come and wake me up at four, five in the morning, for no other reason than he was feeling that void, that emptiness. "Get up, get up," he'd say. "Let's go. Let's talk. Let's go for a walk."

We'd have conversations that lasted for hours and went absolutely nowhere. Not that they were rambling and incoherent, but the substance of what we were talking about was irrelevant. We'd talk about the Three Stooges, Mr. Rogers, different TV shows. Most of the conversations were about comedy, now that I think about it. He'd try jokes and skits out on me. He told me once, "You're the hardest guy to make laugh." Other people laughed at his stuff all the time, but I didn't always go for it. He'd do some bit, and if I didn't laugh he'd turn to me kind of like a hurt little kid and go, "That was funny."

Above and left: Training with Bill Wallace (not bald)

"Not really. You're not always funny, you know."

"What do you mean I'm not always funny? I'm a funny guy."

"I'm sure that you are, but that wasn't funny."

"That wasn't funny?"

"That wasn't funny."

"Well, what do you think is funny?"

"What do I think is funny? I think it's funny that we're sitting here at five in the morning in our underwear having this conversation. That's what I think is funny."

We were like an Abbot and Costello routine a lot of the time. I think that was the reason we got along so well. We just had fun together. We never talked about anything serious. The whole idea was to keep the conversation light. Just the simple act of talking was a way of keeping himself occupied until the tide went back out, until the temptations subsided and the demons went away.

DAN AYKROYD:

John had tremendous respect for Smokey. And if John didn't respect you he wouldn't listen to you—at all. But he respected Smokey because he was tough and he was firm. Smokey let John know that even though he liked him, there was a line drawn in the sand, and if John crossed it he would quit. And John didn't want him to quit. Not only was he John's

protection, but he had great stories. Smokey was an ex-New York state trooper, an ex-Louisiana state trooper and Richard Nixon's primary Secret Service bodyguard from the time of his visit to China until the end of his presidency. He saw Nixon on his knees, praying with Kissinger. This was a guy who saw it all. Smokey was a great guy and a genuinely fascinating and stimulating person to have around. He was always pleasant. When John slipped up or was wrestling with those demons, those withdrawals, he was capable of the worst kind of verbal abuse. Smokey took it all, and he took it with a smile.

JUDITH BELUSHI PISANO:

We more or less hobbled into LA for the last leg of the tour. John had a lot of problems with his voice on the road. I guess people thought it was drugs, but it wasn't. And even though he was working out, he was gaining weight. His spirits were good, but he was exhausted.

DAN AYKROYD:

The touring was rough, no question about it. It was very hard. The stories of the road have been told over and over again by people in this industry, and there's nothing that changes. The road is the road.

It was pretty grueling. We didn't have time to party. When the shows were over, usually we were heading to the next town.

JOHN LANDIS:

    I don't think he was ever captured on film as brilliant as he was in real life. The people who were lucky with John were the people who saw him live, either at Second City or during the Blues Brothers concerts. He was just an amazing live presence.

The horn section (from left): Tom Scott, Tom Malone, Alan Rubin and Lou Marini

We were dancing every night so we were getting a great workout, sweating out all the toxins. John loved the live touring, loved the audiences. It was long and hard and every town seemed a blur, but it was a lot of fun. He probably lost his voice a gig or two before LA, and we finessed through it. But it was important in LA, because that's where we were cutting the next live record. A lot of that had to be redone in the studio.

SMOKEY:

The tour ended with a final stand at the Universal Amphitheater. We went to this function that Atlantic put on, and since we were in LA suddenly all the "friends" were back. It was like flashing back to that very first night in the recording studio.

It was a question of constantly watching hands. John would wear this tweed sportscoat with open pockets; they didn't have flaps. When he would work the room, it was like a reception line. "Oh, Johnny, you were great. What a show!" they'd say. And they were either palming packets into his hand or bumping up close and slipping them into these pockets. I must have confiscated eight or nine grams over the course of the party.

When this one person came up to shake hands with John, I slipped up and slid my hand between theirs and just shook his hand like I was saying hello. This guy looked at me like his parents had walked in on him doing something he shouldn't. John argued with me a bit. He said he'd been good and the

tour was over and he deserved a break. I told him, sorry, I was still on the clock.

Then I took all this cocaine and went back to the bathroom. Jimmy was with me, and I was flushing it all down the toilet. He couldn't believe it. He was like, "Does my brother know you're doing this?"

"Yeah," I laughed, "and it's killing him."

"I'm sure there's a lot of people out there who wouldn't be too happy if they saw this."

"I really don't care." And I didn't. I had finally gotten John in a good place.

He laughed. "Smokey, you're good in my book."

When the tour ended, Smokey was rewarded for his efforts with a two-week vacation, and John and Judy embarked on one as well, their first trip to Europe. They began with a week in Scotland, during which John mostly slept, slept and then slept some more. Next was London and then on to the south of France to share a chateau with Michael O'Donoghue and his girlfriend, writer Carol Caldwell.

From there it was on to Venice with more plans to see Germany, but the trip was brought up short by the arrival of devastating news. Doug Kenney, John's friend and one of the principal writers of Animal House, *had died. Just as it had for John,* Animal House's *success had brought Kenney golden opportunities in Hollywood as well as severe problems with drugs and alcohol. That summer Kenney*

John and Judy in Europe

and his fiancée Kathryn Walker had gone to Hawaii to help him get away, slow down and clean out. One afternoon, he was walking alone along the top of a cliff and—depending on what one chooses to believe—fell, jumped or was pushed to his death on the rocks below. He was thirty-three years old.

JUDITH BELUSHI PISANO:

After we left France, John and I went to Venice and spent the last week of August there. One afternoon, just as I was getting into the shower, John got a call from Bernie Brillstein. When I came out of the bathroom, John was just sitting there. "Doug Kenney's dead," he said. I burst into tears, and John held me. It hit us really hard.

KATHRYN WALKER, *actress*:

Doug and John were both family guys. They took care of people; they weren't self-obsessed or career obsessed. Hollywood success was hard for them because it was, of course, on Hollywood's terms, which they didn't like and I think wore them down. That kind of huge instant celebrity is like being electrocuted, you're more or less frozen in your tracks. You can't go back, and I don't think they liked where they were headed. They were antic and insubordinate, and they distrusted, to say the least, the opportunistic, devious, rather murderous atmosphere created by people they didn't really

find all that smart. So they were both burned. I don't think they knew what to do next, since they'd already defined the new thing. I'm sure there were differences between the ways they responded, but they seem moot. They both died, Doug mysteriously and John in more shocking circumstances.

CHRIS MILLER, *writer*, Animal House:

John and Doug both had a problem with not thinking as well of themselves as everybody else did. They didn't quite know how to deal with their fame and the high opinions that people had of them, because they, in fact, did not really have high opinions of themselves.

MITCH GLAZER:

I had gone to see John, and he said he had to say goodbye to a friend. Doug lived somewhere nearby in the West Village. When John and I got there, Doug was actually loading his suitcases into a waiting cab. He was moving to LA. John wouldn't help him. Wouldn't lift a finger. He kept teasing Doug: "I'm not gonna be a part of this." Then it turned harsher: "You can't go to LA. It's the worst, man. It's not for us." Stuff like that. And then, I remember the last thing John said to him—and it was heavy even at the time—he looked at him and he said, "You'll never come back." I never saw Doug again, and I'm not sure John ever did either. ■

Chapter 13

SEE IF YOU CAN GUESS
WHAT I AM NOW

crossing a great divide

BLAIR BROWN, *co-star*:

Just recently I was doing an event for WNYC's eightieth anniversary up at Symphony Space on the Upper West Side. This guy comes up to me and says, "Do you know what movie of yours I really liked? That one with you and—"

"*Continental Divide?*" I say.

"Yeah, yeah. That's it."

People of a certain age always sidle up to me and go, "You know, there was this movie…" And I always know which one they're talking about. It was such a surprising movie for people who saw it with fresh eyes and weren't expecting to see John play some sort of repulsive adolescent.

Above: With co-star Blair Brown

While it often seems that movie stars lead lives of endless freedom and indulgence, in reality their choices are actually quite limited, at least in terms of the roles they're offered to play. The major movie studios only want what they can sell, and they think they can only sell that which is tried and true and thoroughly unoriginal. Hollywood seduces actors on the casting couch, but it screws them on the typecasting couch. The sad thing is that most of them stay on it their entire careers. John was determined not to. After Animal House *and* 1941, *virtually every script John received was juvenile, disgusting or worse. He was stuck in the rut of the loud, obnoxious party guy, and it was a reputation he needed to lose, both on-screen and in real life.*

Continental Divide *was a movie that everyone wanted to make, a classic romantic comedy about a tough, streetwise Chicago reporter who falls for a reclusive, independent bird-watcher living high in the Rockies. The screenwriter, Lawrence Kasdan, was one of the most promising talents in Hollywood, just about to make his directorial debut with* The Big Chill. *Steven Spielberg was in line to direct and ended up as producer. Robert Redford, Richard Dreyfuss, Robert*

DeNiro and Al Pacino had all been considered at one time or another for the lead.

Bernie Brillstein fought hard to get the part for John. He saw it as his personal mission to soften up John's image by remolding him as a gruff-yet-loveable Spencer Tracy, a character actor with a heart of gold. This looked like the role to do it. Romantic comedy may have been an odd choice for John, but at the time, it felt like the right one.

BRUCE McGILL:

John always introduced me like, "This is my friend Bruce. He's a great actor."

After a while I said, "John, why do you make that distinction? You're an actor. I'm an actor. What's the deal?"

He said, "Aw, no I'm just a sketch player." He always felt, early on anyway, that he did something different. I always felt he was so talented, that what he did came so naturally and without any apparent effort on his part, that he kept thinking somebody was going to find out he wasn't really *doing* anything. That's not an unusual state of mind for really talented people. I think that's one of the things that drove John and frustrated him so.

He had the chops to be a great actor. You could see it in the brilliant impressions he did of great actors, like in his Brando. He did great characters. People mostly remember the broadest of his comedy, but there were a lot of facets to him. Even when he was just being himself there was something compelling about it.

—Richard Belzer

HAROLD RAMIS:

It's called the imposter syndrome, and everybody has it.

CHRISTOPHER GUEST:

For every comedian it's just a parlor trick. Basically, it's like someone who can run fast or throw a ball far. You can walk into a room and make people laugh. The fear, very simply, is that there's something that doesn't really connect, because, "I haven't worked for this." I've been working in this business for my whole life, and I've never met a person who doesn't deep down have a feeling that something isn't quite right.

BRUCE McGILL:

I felt he should let go of that vision of himself as a sketch player. I told him that the only difference between long-form feature films and sketches is that you don't reach a climax in every single cut. You make little pearls, and you pick a pearl that's your biggest pearl, and you string them on a necklace. We had a really interesting discussion about that one night, and soon after he went off and did exactly that in *Continental Divide.*

JUDITH BELUSHI PISANO:

John really wanted to find a role that would broaden his on-screen persona. He was also thinking of the big picture, finding a role that would make it easier for him to stay clean and stay healthy. One good script did come his way: *Arthur.* It was a well-defined character, a happy drunk with no ambition, and John would have made it funny. But it had the potential of becoming a wealthy, private-schooled Bluto, and after his experience with *1941,* he didn't want to take that chance. *Continental Divide,* on the other hand, had a theme and character that really hit home. It was loosely based on a beat reporter in Chicago, Mike Royko, whom John idolized.

MICHAEL APTED, *director:*

John was attached before I was. That was one of the attractions for doing it. I just thought he was a kind of meteor. I had seen his work on *Saturday Night Live* and in *Animal House,* and I just thought he had a lot of talent and potential range. From our conversations together, I felt he was serious about having a career as an actor rather than as a comedian as such, or as a personality as such. And the fact that he wanted to do this led me to believe that he had a strong interest in taking a different tack with a part of his career. That's really why I wanted to work with him.

When it came to casting Blair's part, I needed someone who wasn't flaky. I needed someone who could be supportive of John, because it was going to be John's movie, and it was going to be quite a difficult journey for him. I felt he needed to be surrounded by people who were on his side. And it was a difficult film to make as well; we had a lot of sitting on mountains and all that. I didn't want someone who would be very high maintenance, narcissistic or destructive. I needed someone who was very experienced and very accomplished and who knew what to do. Blair had a huge amount of experience in the theater and television and films, and I liked her a lot.

JUDITH BELUSHI PISANO:

Once John accepted the deal, he was nervous about it. His first reaction to working with Blair was not really good. He would have felt more comfortable with Carrie Fisher or Teri Garr, someone he knew. The first time he met with Blair, he didn't go with an open mind. Afterwards he felt better, because he liked her.

BLAIR BROWN:

John and I were such different people. We met in someone's office at Universal, and we could not have been coming from more different worlds. I'd been doing Portia in *The Merchant of*

Venice, and John was coming off of *Animal House* and *Blues Brothers*. He was very wary of me at first. Sort of like, "Who is this person?" Which of course was what Apted was after, because it was the same vibe he wanted for these characters.

BILL WALLACE:

After the Blues Brothers tour, John asked me to do *Continental Divide* with him. I stayed with him and Judy on Martha's Vineyard when we started training. I'm a freak when it comes to working out. If we're gonna work out, we're gonna work out now. So I'd always have to yell at him, scream at him, grab him and say, "Come on!" Didn't matter if he'd been out late or if he was hungry for breakfast. I'd get up and say, "Come on. You promised to work out at nine o'clock. We're gonna go work out at nine o'clock."

"I don't wanna."

And then I'd stand there and yell and scream at him. He was a wrestler in high school and played football, and so he was very good as far as agility and hand-eye coordination. He picked up martial arts very, very fast. He could do the boxing techniques pretty good, too. To get in shape for the movie we'd run a mile, do three sets of bench presses, three sets of curls, three sets of military presses, three sets of tricep extensions and three sets of full, incline sit-ups every day. Plus the martial arts and the boxing. He went from 242 pounds down to 198 by the end of the film. He was in great shape. Still chubby, because that's just the way John was. He was one of those guys that looked like a bowling ball, but he was in great condition.

JUDITH BELUSHI PISANO:

I think that with all the physical exhaustion on the Blues Brothers tour, John finally began to accept that he was actually mortal, that all the partying was going to catch up with him in the long run. By the time we were on the Vineyard getting ready, he had a totally new mind-set. It was kind of like he just took a big breath of fresh air and relaxed into it. It was a phenomenal change.

BILL MURRAY:

When John was doing *Continental Divide*, he was on a conditioning program, and he was real boring during that time.

He'd come over to my house and ask for Diet 7-Up and popcorn with no salt. And he'd be riding on a ten-speed bicycle, which was just really ridiculous. I mean, it's an image you can sort of figure out for yourself.

He asked me if I wanted to take karate with him from Bill Wallace. Then he said, "Lemme show you a side kick." He backed up about six feet and said, "Just stay right there. Now turn sideways." So I turned sideways. He took four hopping steps and kicked me right in the femur as hard as he could. I don't know how he didn't break my leg. No one's ever hit me that hard that I didn't hit back with a frying pan. He was really proud of it. He was like, "See? Hurts, doesn't it? I really got it down." He was like a kid in that way.

TOM DAVIS, *writer, SNL*:

Once he got the trainer, you'd go over to his house and instead of saying, "Hey, let's smoke a joint!" it was, "Hey, let's get on the exercise bike! Now let's do some push-ups and pull-ups!" If you went over to his house, that's what you got.

CARRIE FISHER:

John was in great shape when he got to LA to start rehearsals. I was having my hair done, and he came by and hung out with me all day at the salon. By then he had the bodyguard who was watching him, and he told the guy, "No, no, you can go. I'm with Fisher. I'm fine." And I was thinking, well, *that's* not true. Then we went over to this Japanese restaurant on Sunset in Hollywood, and he started drinking sake. And at that point I hadn't been in AA yet. I didn't really know that if you were trying not to do drugs you really shouldn't do anything. But pretty soon I got the feeling that we were in for a bad night.

After dinner we went over to On the Rox, this club on Sunset. We walked in and a bunch of people from "the crowd" were there. I lost John for a second, and then he came back over to me with this panicked look and said, "Oh God, I just did some coke."

I said, "John, we can leave right now. If we leave now everything will be fine."

And he just stared at me in this state of total fear and said, "...I can't."

The next morning I got a call from his manager. "Where's John? You were the last one to see him."

BERNIE BRILLSTEIN:

The morning before they left for Colorado, John really freaked out. He was having some pretty serious doubts. We had a meeting at my house. It was me, Sean Daniel, John and Apted. John had made up his mind and all of a sudden he wanted to back out. "I can't do it. I can't." He was scared of playing a romantic lead. He blamed Blair. He blamed Apted. He had all these reasons why it wasn't going to work. In the end we calmed him down, and he agreed to stick with it.

SMOKEY:

When we got to Colorado, the deal was that Bill took care of his conditioning, and I handled the security. The catch was that whatever John did with diet and exercise, I had to do, too. I was not crazy about it, but it helped him. In the beginning, it was an uphill battle. The diet that Bill had him on was this spartan fruit and cereal routine, the same thing every day. I told him, "If you think keeping your nose clean was hard, this

is going to be even harder. Because your stomach is a much tougher problem to deal with."

Within a week John was like, "Man, you were right. I am so hungry." He hated it. There were times he'd come to the set and be like, "I cannot eat another bowl of fruit and cottage cheese. I can't."

"John, it's either that or you have nothing to eat until dinner."

"Well, can I have twice as much at dinner?"

"You'll never make it. You'll pass out first."

So he would eat. But he got to the point where he was like, "In fifteen minutes I get to have my popcorn, right?" He knew the deal exactly. Then, like everything else, it became a game for him. He'd be showing off for the crew how many push-ups and sit-ups he could do.

MICHAEL APTED:

John was really up for the movie. He worked hard at trying to get the role down and get his body and his mind in shape,

and he did it for a long time. We shot a lot of the film up in the Rockies, and he did really well.

But John would still test you, see how far he could push you. He would always be late and stuff like that. It was irritating. When you look at his earlier films, he had done them with very inexperienced directors—gifted directors, but inexperienced ones. I was very firm with him about it, and he stopped doing it.

But at the same time, I wanted to engage him. I wanted to involve him in the whole process so he wouldn't feel like he was just some actor for hire.

While we were shooting the film, we would look at the dailies together and talk about them and go through them, because it was a challenge doing this kind of stuff. It was a challenge to create this character of Souchak. So in one way, I was firm with him. I told him what I wanted and what I needed, and he respected that. But in another, more positive way I involved him in the process because I respected his talent and intelligence, and I could use his help as well.

JUDITH BELUSHI PISANO:

Smokey, Bill, John and I were this funny little family unit in our daily routine. They would head out pretty early for location, and I was left to fend for myself in the wilderness. So I became the nutritionist. I'd devise these complex diet meals, actually counting calories and weighing food. That took a good part of the day. I'd play drums, read.

By the time I'd hear the whir of the helicopter, I was like the year-rounders on the Vineyard when the summer people return after winter—real glad to see them. Every night we'd all go to the local gym to work out, then return to the house to watch a movie or listen to music. It was pretty low key, but we had fun.

John had grown very fond of Blair, and he trusted Apted, so the work was good. He had a funny perspective on our life in the Rockies. He liked to complain about the lack of everything civilized, the small-town idiosyncrasies. But you could tell he liked being there. I think that grumpy attitude was his way of working on his Ernie Souchak character.

BLAIR BROWN:

We were shooting up near Mt. Saint Helens and every day we had to be helicoptered higher and higher into the mountains because we kept losing snow. So, we're jumping all over from mountaintop to mountaintop, and one day we land at the top of this peak and we see this igloo. We get out and we walk over to it and we find these kids. They were fans of John. They had taken time off from their ski instructor jobs, scaled this mountain, hiked up two days before, built an igloo—and waited.

And of course John was like, "C'mon, let's get in the igloo!" And he went in the igloo and hung out with the kids for a while.

BLAIR BROWN:

I was really happy when we were in Colorado. I was learning to rock climb and having all kinds of fun doing stuff like that. John, of course, was not really having any fun at all. At one point he said, "You really like this, huh? You really like the country?" I was having a good time, but he couldn't fathom it.

Every night after shooting wrapped, I'd go back to this little teeny motel where I was staying. I'd be sitting in my room and I'd hear these little feet—John had little feet—just tap-tap-tapping by outside my window. Bill was having him do laps around the motel. This was around 9 PM and I'd already be in my room having a cocktail or something, but John was out there working and working and working.

The thing that I remember most about John was just the amount of stimulation that he had to have. He'd call me in my room and say, "What are you doing?"

"Well, I'm reading and I'm talking to you."

"Okay, here's what I'm doing: I've got the TV on, I'm listening to music, I'm reading magazines and I'm talking to you."

SMOKEY:

He was a big, big TV watcher. That always helped. We would stay up to the wee hours just watching TV. I brought in all sorts of things—television, drums, pinball machines—because you always wanted to keep him active, keep him occupied, all the time.

In the beginning, when he saw this little town we were filming in, he couldn't believe it. They had one general store that sold groceries and hardware and was also the post office. It was like going into R.F.D. Mayberry. He was like, "What year is this? Did we go through a time warp?"

But whereas before he had problems with crowds in strange places, here he'd go right up to people, go into the little diner and talk to them. He would relate to people more. He wasn't as fidgety and antsy. He became more aware of the simple moments, and it wasn't all one big party. They had this one movie theater that had been closed, because the town was so small they couldn't afford to bring many movies in. So John called the studio and had movies flown in from California so the townspeople could have a night out at the movies again. He was like a whole new person in a whole new world.

BLAIR BROWN:
With some movie stars people just stare into their faces. John was so antic that that never happened. But one day I saw him sitting alone in this rare moment of stillness, and it was one of those moments when you see somebody and you think, I know who you were when you were a little kid. I know who you were when you were growing up.

And it was that moment, for me, when he stopped being "Belushi." I sort of went, "Oh, right. I get it. You're that guy."

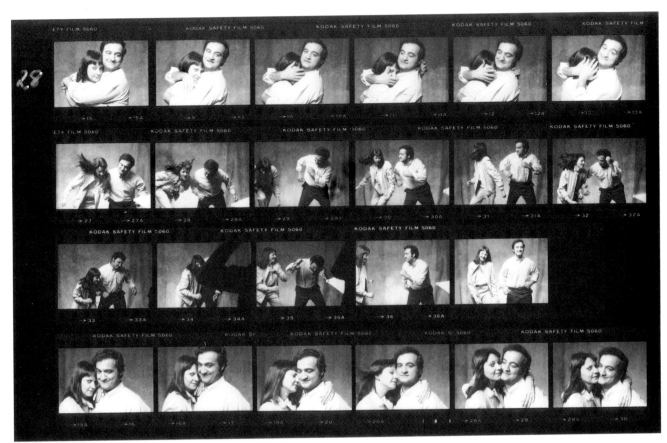

John and Judy, **Continental Divide** *photo session outtakes*

MITCH GLAZER:

Without a doubt he was more fun and more himself when he was straight. For the people around him, it was great to see that guy, because that other guy was a little sweatier and more unhappy, which made him less fun.

BLAIR BROWN:

He was really in a very positive frame of mind the whole time. Smokey and Bill were there keeping him going. Judy, Bernie, everybody was so happy for him.

SMOKEY:

Judy looked at the relationship that John and I had as a very stable one, because John was more stable. There was no more fear of "Where is he? What's he doing? Who's he with?" She knew we were always together, that I was like John's guardian angel making sure he didn't cross against the light.

His relationship with Judy was always a hundred percent. They were joined at the hip, because they'd known each other from a very, very young age. They were friends and then boyfriend and girlfriend and then husband and wife. They were just a cute, funny couple, like Burns and Allen. You'd be hanging out in the house and John would be rattling on about something, and Judy'd be rattling on about whatever he was rattling on about, and they weren't even necessarily in the same room. She'd be in and out, coming and going, but somehow this silly, funny conversation just stayed up in the air. And you'd be sitting there like, "This relationship is working. I have no idea *how* it's working, but it is." They just fit.

For John, she was much more of a family to him than his own family, and he opened up to her in a way that he didn't even to them. It was a nerve that you could hit. If he was wavering or if he was about to go someplace he shouldn't, all you had to say was, "Hey, what would Judy think..." And that was it. It was like a slap in the face. For Judy's part, she loved

him so much that he could do no wrong. She looked past his problems to love him, but she could also see the problems enough to know that something had to be done to fix them if they were going to have a future together. It was never in her game plan not to have him around.

JUDITH BELUSHI PISANO:

One day when John and I were alone, he asked me, sort of out of the blue, if I thought he could get nominated for an Oscar with this role. He was like a kid wondering if he might get that special Christmas present on his list. I said, "You know, this is such a good time of your life. You're happy. You're enjoying your work—I think that's a lot better than any award."

He kind of sat up a little taller, like a lightbulb had gone off. "You're right."

SMOKEY:

He was really getting inspired, looking forward to taking his career in a new direction, playing better parts. He used to go off on the Rod Steiger Napoleon movie, *Waterloo*. He'd always say, "I coulda been a better Napoleon than Rod Steiger. He's too tall to play Napoleon. He probably never even read about Napoleon. I know more about Napoleon than Napoleon knew about himself. Guys like me, we know the Napoleon syndrome."

I thought he was just being dramatic. "What are you talking about?"

"It's the Napoleon syndrome, Smokey. If I was taller, like Jim, this stuff wouldn't happen to me."

"Oh, c'mon."

"It's true. I'm small."

"Yeah, but you're big at heart, John. That goes a long way."

"Yeah, Smokey. Right."

He talked about it a lot. I never really got it, and I never asked him about it. It was the same way some people talk about rock stars.

MICHAEL APTED:

John was great. He was totally focused and worked very hard in Colorado. It started getting a little uglier when we went back to Chicago. Then he was amongst his friends, and, you know, I

One night I heard John turn down coke from someone, and the guy said, "Man, don't you miss it?"
"Every day," John replied.

—Judith Belushi Pisano

began to lose him a little bit. He had the Blues Bar, and he had his mates and all that sort of stuff; it just got a little more difficult for me to connect with him and to be in control of the situation. He would want to party and he would want to show up late and all these kinds of things, so it was just more difficult.

BLAIR BROWN:

I didn't see him much in Chicago. He'd say, "Come to such and such bar at such and such time." That sort of thing. His life was very different then. But he was always there, he always showed up, he was always ready to work no matter where he'd been the night before.

JUDITH BELUSHI PISANO:

We were all worried about how John would handle being back in Chicago, but he was psyched. He kept telling me not to worry, but I'd have to have been insane not to. Against all the odds, he really came through. I think because the Blues Brothers frenzy had cooled off, people seemed more respectful. Maybe it had something to do with the way he dressed, which was pretty much the same as his Souchak character. He looked clean cut. He acted more like a Chicago big shot than a rock star. Smokey and Bill made a big difference, but the real difference was John and his determination.

SMOKEY:

I knew that the temptations were there at the Blues Bar. Judy, as a rule, didn't like to go, but she felt a level of security with Bill and me. Several times I heard John say to people, "No, no, man. I'm okay. I'm cool." He wanted to keep it together and wanted to stay out of the drug scene. The people there knew who I was, that I was the opposition, and the wall between anyone offering drugs and John was constantly tested. Sometimes there were just too many people for me to handle, and I'd say to Bill, "Look, you gotta help me here. We gotta work together."

I always tried to be discreet in handling these people, but Bill's methods were a little like Charles Bronson in *Death Wish*. He wasn't called "Superfoot" Wallace for nothing. He was very fast, and if he even thought some guy was getting too close to John, he'd be on him. I'd go off to sweep the bathroom, hear a commotion and turn around to see some big, tattooed biker guy pinned up against the wall with Bill's foot on his throat. Most guys, if they come at you in a bar they're doing it with their hands or some kind of blunt instrument that you'd expect. Not Bill. This guy's standing there wondering what the hell's going on 'cause he's getting smacked in the cheek with a shoe. I'd have to go over and say, "N-no, Bill, no. This isn't quite what I meant."

BLAIR BROWN:

Was John Bluto or was he Souchak? I would say Souchak, but that's how I know him. The day we shot the love scene was priceless. If you've ever been a part of one of these movie love scenes, they're just deeply peculiar. We were in this little room in a hotel somewhere. It was a closed set. John was there, the camera operator was there, the sound guy, Apted and that's it. Everybody else was away. You're wearing this robe, and all you've got under that is this little bitty underwear that you're going to still be wearing when you do the scene.

I don't think John had ever done a love scene before, and he was clearly nervous about doing it. He just lay there in bed trying to think up all the funny names for penis that he could: the Hose of Horror… Mr. Wiggly… We were weeping with laughter it was so funny. It was just like watching a little kid stalling because he doesn't want to eat his vegetables. "Oh, oh, wait—you know what else? Here's another one…"

After a while we finally had to say, "Okay, okay, John. Now you have to do the love scene." He was just stalling and stalling and stalling because he was so nervous.

MARK CARLSON, *friend*:

One day my wife and I were driving by Judy's old house, and we saw a limo out in front. We figured Belushi must be there so we went home and called the Jacklins. Sure enough,

Back in Chicago (from top left): as Ernie Souchak;
on set with Smokey and Bill; with Judy; filming with Blair Brown

John and Smokey on location in Chicago

John was there. He got on the phone and told me he'd just finished shooting location stuff for this movie called *Continental Divide* and was leaving to shoot the rest of the movie in LA. "It's the best work I've ever done," he said.

BERNIE BRILLSTEIN:

We went to a wrap party for *Continental Divide* at some decorator's house out here in LA. At the end of the party, we went back into a room. John reached in his pocket, pulled out eleven vials of cocaine and tossed them on the bed. That's how much had just been passed to him over the course of the evening by people trying to be his friend. He took them and he flushed them down the toilet.

ED BEGLEY, JR., *co-star*, Goin' South:

I visited him at a house he was renting up in Coldwater Canyon for a New Year's Eve Party. It was me, John, John

Candy and Tom Scott—and we were all clean and sober. We'd all put those problems behind us. We actually toasted at midnight with Martinelli's Apple Cider.

JUDITH BELUSHI PISANO:

Our birthdays were one right after the other, and that January John threw me this great party for my thirtieth. A couple weeks later, for his thirty-second, I found him a '68 Volvo, the same make and model—minus the gaffer's tape—as the one he'd had in college. I tied a ribbon onto the door handle, ran it from the garage through every room in the house, and tied it off with a big bow at the front door. When he got home from work, he had to follow the ribbon around the whole house to see where it'd take him. When he finally got to the end, his expression was priceless.

A couple of weeks later we were back on the Vineyard. He said maybe he'd like to get a motorcycle, too, one like his old BMW that he'd lost when his dad couldn't make the payments on it. He thought that might be a fun reward for staying clean through the shoot. John wasn't a very good driver. I think it had to do with focus, and so the idea of a motorcycle worried me on two levels. Driving safety was one, but the biggest was that I didn't trust that there wouldn't still be relapses. It seemed premature. I suggested that maybe he wait until he'd been sober for a whole year, as a goal. He agreed. We decided he'd get a motorcycle for his one-year anniversary.

SMOKEY:

Martha's Vineyard was a safe haven for John. It's a small island, and everybody knows everybody. That was probably the happiest I've ever seen him. He could go into stores and nobody would bother him. He loved his house up on the beach. He loved the ocean. Whenever we had a chance to go, boom, we were there.

That spring was really a downtime for John. He had a movie lined up to shoot in a couple of months, but for the present he didn't really have anything to do. At that point in my career, I hadn't really looked to stay with any one person forever. It never entered my mind to be a personal assistant to anybody on a permanent basis. I was ready to move on to the next thing, try something else. I had only been in the business for a couple of years at that point, and I wanted to explore other opportunities, other clients. Sometime around March I went in to John and Judy and said, "Look, I think it's time for me to move on." It was like I'd punched him in the face.

"What are you talking about?"

"Well, I think you're doing better now."

And he was, but I hadn't really looked at the overall picture. Celebrities always have somebody that's their crutch or confidant, whether it's a personal assistant, business manager, security guard, lawyer, or just the Guy Who Takes Care of Things. When you're in John's position, the simple job of being you becomes such a huge task that you need someone to help you do it. People like me help you be yourself. I had not absorbed the importance of that, and so I did not, at the time, grasp the significance of my leaving. I was oblivious to it. In my mind, I was just the security guy.

I said to Judy flat out, "Look, no matter what happens, I'll still be here. Just look at it like I'm going on a vacation. If things ever get bad again, if you ever need my help, just pick up the phone and I'll come. I'll be there." But to John, my leaving was like dropping him off alone to survive on a desert island. He was like, "How am I going to do this?"

"You can't go," he said, and he was dead serious. "You can't go. I don't want you to go, and I won't let you. I want you to stay."

"Well, that's not—"

"I'll pay you double."

"I'm flattered, but—"

"I'll buy you a house."

"That has nothing to do with it, John. You're fine now. You kids have got your whole life ahead of you. You've got it all together. It's like you all got reborn. The magic that the two of you have, it's always been there, but it's even stronger now. There's no reason for me to stay. You can do it on your own."

John was upset. I'd really, really hurt him. But Judy, Judy has this thing—and she's gonna kill me for giving this up—that whenever she's really nervous she never looks directly at you. She sort of puts her head down and tilts it from side to side with her hair falling down in her face a bit. So Judy was doing that routine like, "Well, John, you know, if Smokey feels that he has to go then, well, we can get by..." And you can't travel with a person all the time like I did and not know their personality traits. I said to her, "Judy, are you not comfortable with me going?"

She sort of tossed her head a bit and said, "Well, Smokey, we're just, you know, used to having you here and...I mean, sure we're gonna miss you, but..." And then she stopped, looked up, looked me straight in the eye and said, "No, I don't want you to go." ■

Chapter 14

BUT

NOOOooooOOOOOOOooooo

a fight with the neighbors

JIM DOWNEY, *writer*, SNL:

Belushi and Aykroyd told me that they so hated the director of *Neighbors* that they had looked into hiring a hit man to kill him. And they weren't kidding. They had really checked this out. John was really excited about it, very animated. He was like, "Did you know it only costs five thousand dollars?" He couldn't get over how cheap it was. "Five thousand! That's such a bargain!"

"Yes," I said, "but it's wrong. It's wrong to kill."

"Oh, well, sure. Yeah, yeah. Absolutely. But five thousand. That's like a used car."

In March of 1981, Smokey departed, leaving John happy, healthy and seemingly stable. Bill Wallace, John's trainer, stayed on the payroll to help him stay fit for his upcoming movies and would become the de facto replacement for many of Smokey's duties. But despite his best intentions and formidable talents, Bill was a kickboxer, not a former Secret Service agent.

Still, John was in a good place. Filming with Michael Apted had gone well, and everyone's hopes for Continental Divide were high. Studios were itching for the chance to put the blockbuster Belushi/Aykroyd team on the screen again, and the perfect vehicle soon came over the horizon: a dark, black comedy about the stifling conformity of suburbia. Based on a respected, best-selling book, it was the ideal mix of the comedy Belushi fans wanted and the credibility to which John aspired. Neighbors, the novel, was the story of two men locked in a mortal test of wills that drives one of them completely over the edge. Ironic, then, that the filming of Neighbors wound up being a story about the exact same thing.

When Michael Ovitz, John's new agent, first brought the project to Bernie Brillstein's attention, he had every reason to be excited. The producers, David Brown and Richard Zanuck, had just fielded a huge hit with Jaws. The novelist, Thomas Berger, had written the book that inspired the Arthur Penn/Dustin Hoffman classic Little Big Man. The screenwriter, Larry Gelbart, was one of the Emmy-winning creators of M★A★S★H. And the director, John Avildsen, had just won an Academy Award for Rocky. Add to that the box-office popularity of John and Danny, and, within a matter of weeks, the producers had a green light from Columbia Pictures. With Ovitz negotiating on his behalf, John took home a check for $1.25 million. Danny was signed to play the uptight Earl Keese, and John was Vic, the crazy, abusive guy next door. To everyone at the table, it looked like a walk-off World Series home run.

Except that it wasn't.

DAVID BROWN, *producer*:

As we always do, we found a book that interested us, we thought it would make a good movie, and we pursued it. We presented it to Frank Price who was then the head honcho at Columbia. He liked it and said, "Go get a script." We had Larry Gelbart write it and presented that to Frank. He liked it and said, "Go cast it. This is going to be our Christmas movie." It was a kind of process that's unknown in the film business today.

JOHN AVILDSEN, *director*:

I had read the Tom Berger novel and liked it a lot. I went to option it and discovered that Zanuck and Brown had gotten there before me. Then the three of us decided to do it together. My original notion was to cast Rodney Dangerfield in the role of Earl Keese. He was a character that got no respect, and, of course, that was Rodney's signature bit. But no one had heard of him at that point, and the studio said no.

"What about Aykroyd?" they asked. I liked Aykroyd, and he brought along Belushi.

RICHARD ZANUCK, *producer*:

It was their decision, John's and Danny's, to change the roles. That horrified Larry Gelbart, the writer. It horrified all of us, actually. David and I didn't use the kind of judgment that we should have. We thought, well, Belushi and Aykroyd are really skilled at what they do. If this is the way they want to do it, it would be wrong to force them to do otherwise.

The fact is they had accepted the film, and the film had been greenlit, with the casting done the other way around, but we all got caught up in the idea that, "Oh, that's the obvious thing, so let's do something different and unexpected and we'll pull it off." Truth is we should have left it like it was originally.

MITCH GLAZER:

The decision to switch roles in *Neighbors* was just madness. I thought they could do anything, but the choice was perverse. John was obviously the neighbor from hell, and Danny was clearly the put-upon straight man. To switch that just for the sake of it felt wrong.

TIM MATHESON:

I was shooting a picture in New York, and John invited me to drop by their office around the time they were percolating the idea of switching roles, where Danny would play the crazy one and John would play the sane one. And I said, "Wow, what a terrible idea. Why?"

"I don't want to keep doing the same shtick," he said. "I want to mix it up."

BERNIE BRILLSTEIN:

The studio said yes because anyone would do anything to have a John Belushi/Dan Aykroyd movie, but it was not a good decision.

CATHY MORIARTY, *co-star*:

I didn't see a problem with it. I believed in it. That may be part of the reason John and I bonded so quickly. I really did think that John could be working with DeNiro and those guys if he ever got a chance to be taken seriously.

JUDITH BELUSHI PISANO:

It was an incredibly subtle book, and Avildsen didn't get it. Everybody wanted John to play the crazy neighbor, but this was a black comedy. The neighbor had to be crazy in a creepy, disturbing way, and John was crazy in a loveable, endearing way. Danny, on the other hand, could be very creepy. His character was funny because it made you feel so uncomfortable.

RICHARD ZANUCK:

From the very first moment that we sat down and started rehearsals, it was clear that the two guys, and particularly John, didn't care much for Avildsen.

DAVID BROWN:

John and Dan had some reservations about Avildsen as a director. They came by my house on the Upper West Side one night and said, "Let's talk." So we retreated to a Village restaurant, and they said, "He's not funny. You're making a mistake. Get a comedy director. A black comedy is still a comedy."

RICHARD ZANUCK:

John and Dan asked us to can him. Even though we could see that there were problems, we still believed that he was the man for the job, and we stuck by him. There were no grounds to let a guy go like that in the middle of rehearsals, especially one who had just won an Academy Award. Ultimately, I'd say we made a mistake. Not that John Avildsen isn't a good director; he is. But he wasn't the right director for this picture. If we'd had a crystal ball, we would have seen the troubled waters on the horizon.

With Tim Kazurinsky

DAVID BROWN:

We resolved the issue by saying there would be two takes for each shot: one the way Avildsen wanted to do it, and one the way John and Danny wanted to do it. The only problem was Avildsen was also the editor.

HAROLD RAMIS:

John called me before they started *Neighbors* and said, "There's a picture I want you to think about directing."

I said, " Send me the script."

"Well, it's soon."

"How soon?"

"We start shooting next week."

"What, are you talking about *Neighbors*?"

He was afraid that John Avildsen didn't get it. He sounded pretty desperate.

TIM KAZURINSKY:

John had really pushed to get me into the replacement cast for *Saturday Night Live*. I went in and did one show. Then the

writers went on a strike. It looked like it might be the last episode ever, so I was leaving. Before I got on a plane to go back to Chicago, I dropped by the set of *Neighbors* to say goodbye to John.

"You're leaving?" he said. "Why don't you just stick around?"

"Well I gotta go back. I gotta work," I said.

"You can be in the movie. C'mon, there's a part I want you to read for." So he got the director, brought me in and said, "Read for this part. Sound older."

So I read the part, and Avildsen said, "No, John, I don't think he's old enough."

I said, "I know I look young, but I'm actually thirty."

Avildsen just looked at me. "This part is for a sixty-five-year-old man," he said.

"John, you jerk," I said. "I can't do this."

Then John physically dragged me upstairs to the makeup man and said, "Make him look sixty-five." Then he scrounged around and got some clothes, we dirtied them up, and I went back down in this latex makeup and read for the part. I got it, grudgingly.

The neighbors: Kathryn Walker, John, Cathy Moriarty and Dan Aykroyd

Halfway through shooting Avildsen came up to me and said, "You know, I didn't want you to do this part, but John was right. You're good, and the stuff works great between you two. It was a real smart decision, and I should have trusted him."

JUDITH BELUSHI PISANO:

When John got Tim into the cast, he counted it as a minor victory, proof that he knew what worked. John could be a major pain in the ass when he disagreed with you, as all of the *SNL* writers know, but only because his faith in his own instincts was unshakeable. And when it came to his own comedy, he was usually right. But as the weeks wore on, things just got worse and worse. He knew he was on a sinking ship and he began to disagree more openly with Avildsen's decisions. He really wanted to walk.

BERNIE BRILLSTEIN:

I made a bet with John that a fistfight was going to break out before it was all over.

DAVID BROWN:

The mood on the set was such that our production coordinator answered the telephone, "General Hospital." There might have been an occasional truce, but nothing I would call actual peace. I was being interviewed by the *Los Angeles Times* on the set one day. During my interview, in which I was trying to paint a euphoric picture of what was going on, Belushi and Avildsen almost came to blows within earshot of the reporter. Belushi was screaming, "I'm gonna kill that guy!" So I had to scramble and get them to calm down.

BILL WALLACE:

John really did want to kill him.

DAVID BROWN:

Avildsen was very calm about all of this, almost passive. The angrier John got, the more passive he became. He didn't react with emotion to anything. The boys couldn't get a rise out of him. They were looking for somebody they could have a laugh with, but Avildsen was just too much of a solid citizen.

DAN AYKROYD:

John Avildsen did not present himself as a strong presence, and that was the problem. It was a matter of respect. John might disagree with you, but he'd work with you if he respected you. John perceived weakness in Avildsen, and he didn't like that. Pretty soon it was like the Battle of the Bulge. There didn't have to be a war, but the Allied lines were weak and the Panzers rolled right in, right into the weak spot. He wanted Avildsen to stand up to him, to follow his convictions and take command, and Avildsen was not that kind of a director.

TIM KAZURINSKY:

Avildsen would always consult with a lot of people and ask them what they thought, and John interpreted that as someone who didn't have a clear vision of the way he wanted the film to be. If he did, it certainly didn't jibe with John's.

BILL WALLACE:

Avildsen was just a complete dick. As good a director as he was supposed to be, he couldn't make up his mind about things. Finally, he really pushed the limit. John and Danny were standing there ready to shoot. John had his lines down, Danny had his lines down, and Avildsen couldn't decide where he was gonna put the cameras. And it wasn't that important of a scene, wasn't that big a deal, just a little transition from one part to another, but it was just the straw on the camel's back. John said, "Okay, you motherfucker, you let me know when you're gonna shoot it." He stormed off and got in his car, and he and his driver took off. That's about when the trouble started.

RICHARD ZANUCK:

Our first question to Bernie when we submitted the script to him was, "Is John okay? Has he cleaned up his act?"

"Absolutely," Bernie said. "Totally cleaned up."

I checked out *Continental Divide*. John looked fine, and he was fine. We had no problems at all, and everything seemed great. Then we started the night shooting.

DAN AYKROYD:

When we got to the night shoots, all the grips, the electricians, the tradespeople, were being fueled by coke. It was like the coffee of its time; you'd do it just to stay up. And so once John, with all his frustrations and weaknesses, and without Smokey, was back in that environment, things just got out of control again.

BERNIE BRILLSTEIN:

Avildsen figured he could limit John's drug use if he made him sit around and wait on location, but getting drugs on a movie set is even easier than getting them in prison.

RICHARD ZANUCK:

It was pretty horrifying, quite frankly. His behavior was awful, very unprofessional. I liked John very much, but this wasn't John. It was not the John that I had witnessed on any previous occasion. He refused to come out of his trailer. They kept calling him and calling him. We had 150 people standing around waiting.

I'd go in his trailer, and the music would be blasting at full decibels. He'd be in his undershorts and just totally out of it. I'd plead with him. "John, we've got all these people waiting, all the other actors are ready and we've got to shoot and you've got to get out there." He insisted that he would only come out if Avildsen left the location, and I'd say, "But John, he's the director…" And we'd have these nonsensical discussions that went on forever.

Eventually he'd come around to shoot the scene, then he'd be fine for a day, and then he'd relapse again. Finally, one night I took a long walk with Dan in the woods surrounding the location and said, "Look, I need your help with this."

DAVID BROWN:

Without Danny we couldn't have finished the picture. He was the pacifier. They were so close that he was the only one John would listen to.

He was very crude and very loud once he was in that condition. His language left a lot to be desired. But underneath all of that I found him to be a nice, gentle guy. I never stopped liking him, and this was during a time when I was ready to kill him.

—Richard Zanuck

RICHARD ZANUCK:

It's hard to imagine, looking back, how awful it was. But it really was terrible. At that point it looked like a picture totally out of control; it wasn't. We were able to shoot around John during these episodes, and the episodes were not a continuous thing. They were spotty, sporadic, and only lasted for a week. Once we got back into the day shooting, it was fine.

TIM KAZURINSKY:

I was there for five weeks, and he had one bad week. But even when he knew that it wasn't going to work, he still came back and did his job, did take after take after take, knowing that it wasn't going to turn out the way he wanted.

JUDITH BELUSHI PISANO:

At that point there were a little over two weeks of filming left. The only thing that got John through it without killing

John and Judy during first visit to Martha's Vineyard, 1974

Avildsen or himself was the promise that we were to have two solid months on the Vineyard once shooting completed. Within hours of the last take, we were on a plane. As soon as he set foot on the island his blood pressure dropped and he went into Vineyard mode.

Martha's Vineyard is a small island off the coast of Massachusetts, founded over three hundred years ago as a fishing and whaling colony. Like many fishing and whaling colonies, it is now a summer resort destination for the superwealthy. The Vineyard is a strange place, idyllic and charming and utterly unique. Unlike the tony enclaves of Palm Beach or the Hamptons, it has a simple, unassuming vibe that belies its reputation as a trust-fund playground. Stop in somewhere for a sandwich and you might find yourself at the counter with a billionaire, a movie star and a fisherman—and yet you'd be hard pressed to tell the difference between them. Probably because none of them bothered to shave that morning, and at least one of them isn't wearing any shoes.

John and Judy discovered Martha's Vineyard during a break from The National Lampoon Radio Hour *in 1974 and became regulars by the second year of* Saturday Night Live. *The effect of the island on John is hard to describe, but it seemed to bring him a peace of mind that he found nowhere else. As he said to his bodyguard Smokey one day on the beach, "This is where I like being me." In October of 1979, he and Judy bought a vacation home in the town of Chilmark. The ocean-front property came with a private beach and had belonged to former Secretary of Defense Robert McNamara. A few weeks later, Danny bought a house of his own, sight unseen, just up the road. John was on pilings atop the ocean cliffs. Danny was on bedrock up behind the tree line. Soon they had matching jeeps with sequential license plate numbers, which is really all that two best friends could ever need.*

JAMES TAYLOR, *singer*:

I first met John on the Vineyard, just after he'd finished shooting *Animal House*. It was always difficult for John to relax. He was so fired up all the time. I often got the feeling he was trying desperately to put on the brakes. It was humorous, too, to see him sort of skidding in for a landing. We went fishing, which was comic, and we partied a lot. I guess it wasn't much like relaxation, but it passed for relaxation in between times of intense concentration.

KATHRYN WALKER:

That summer, after Doug had died and we'd shot *Neighbors*, John and Danny brought me to the Vineyard and found me a house. For the first few days I was there, they were over all of the time, taking care of me in a sort of hearty, jostling, hilarious way. Some sort of bug was having one of those ten-year resurgences; they were everywhere, underfoot, dropping from trees. John was always doing this bit with two birds gorged on insects: "You want a bug?" "Jeez, I couldn't. But I'll split one with you." It was a truly fun summer, very idyllic, and a precursor to more of the same. For me it was the beginning of moving on, and I have John and Danny to thank for that.

JAMES TAYLOR:

He and Danny would go by at least once a day just to check on Kathryn and help her to relax and feel at ease. Their excuse was always that they were making sure she had an automobile that worked. They would come over with a car and swap the car out with another car every day, just to have an excuse to sort of check in on her and say, "Everything okay with you?" It got to be pretty funny.

LARRY BILZARIAN, *friend*:

I met John through James Taylor back in 1979. I have a shop on Martha's Vineyard called Take It Easy, Baby. And whenever John was on the island, he'd always come by and help out, taking care of customers and selling merchandise. People were always a little surprised that John Belushi was waiting on them, but they'd usually end up buying something. He was a pretty good salesman, and the locals loved him.

He had a lot of friends on the Vineyard. Nobody bothered him there, you know. That's the way the Vineyard is. He loved to organize cookouts and barbecues, loved playing host. We played Monopoly or backgammon just about every night. That was his time to come down, July and August. That was his time to rest, just eat and rub his stomach and watch TV. We watched a lot of *SCTV*. He loved *SCTV*.

On the Vineyard (from top left): the Chilmark House; with John Landis and James Taylor; with fish; on beach with Judy; relaxing with Mitch Glazer.

LARRY BILZARIAN:

We put this rope in so we could climb down the cliff to the beach. There are these mud holes in the clay cliffs down there where we used to have "mud parties." You'd just mix up the mud, and it would form a little pool that you could soak in. It's really great for your skin and all that. The sun would just bake it onto you, and then you'd wash it off a half hour later or so. It was actually refreshing, because it was so hot out anyways. It was like a cold spring after a while. At first he couldn't believe that I was gonna lie there in it and let it harden on me. Well, after that, he used to do it every day. You know, that was like the big thing.

John loved to let the mud and sand cake all over him to where he looked like a giant clay monster with some horrible disease, and then he'd run down the beach with a club or a stick, terrorizing people. He loved sneaking up on Danny like that if he was down on the beach with a girlfriend or something. It was a lot of fun.

Sometimes we'd hop in the car and start driving around with clubs in our hands. It was like, "Let's go for a monster ride!" We'd have our Blues Brothers glasses on and clay and sand all over us, riding into town to buy stuff for the barbecue. People thought we were completely nuts.

DAN AYKROYD:

Every single day of that summer was great. John and Judy would come over and wake us up around eleven. We would take a drive down to Larry's store, and John would sit behind the desk and move the merchandise. Then we'd go grab lunch somewhere, and then off to the beach for a swim and back to my place for a nap. James Taylor was there, Carly Simon. We had so many friends on the island. Every day we'd pop by somebody's house for tea or lunch.

It was clear to everyone at that point that John had a problem, a physical problem, with cocaine. And all those hangers-on and folks that were constantly feeding him that stuff, they just weren't allowed. John made it very clear that people weren't welcome if they were bringing it. We just swam and surfed every day in the sunshine.

JUDITH BELUSHI PISANO:

John and I were alone on the beach one afternoon and some guy walked past along the water's edge. Suddenly he recognized John sitting there. He yelled out, "Hey, Belushi! You want some cocaine?" We both just stared at him for a minute, dumbfounded.

Then John said, "Get the hell off my beach and don't ever come back."

LARRY BILZARIAN:

The Fourth of July was always a festive time. He'd invite a bunch of islanders and a bunch of off-islanders, a real fun crowd. He and I built this plywood launchpad, and every year we'd buy about five-hundred-dollars worth of fireworks and set them off over the ocean. He was always the field marshal, directing which rockets we'd set off and when. I think we may have burnt a few of the neighbors' houses down, but people cheered and it was great.

I never wanted him to leave. He never wanted to leave. At the end of August he always used to say, "I have to go back." That meant summer was over. No more barbecues.

That last summer, he kept stalling and stalling and stalling. Finally we said goodbye and he left to go catch this private jet back to New York. That night, I'd gone to see the Taylor family perform at the Hot Tin Roof, this music joint we have. Around midnight John showed up. He'd grabbed the pilot and the whole flight crew off the plane, delayed the flight at the airport, and dragged them back to the bar for the show. Then he got up onstage and sang. He just didn't want to go.

DAN AYKROYD:

Unquestionably, that was the happiest time for John. He was totally clean, reading all kinds of books, hanging out with William and Rose Styron and people like that. He basked in the beautiful golden glow of Styron's lawn down there on Vineyard Haven, relaxing with all the luminaries of American culture and just walking back and forth along the dock and eating hot dogs. He was accepted as a peer and as an equal in this great, great fraternity of artists and really exceptional, outstanding people. That was the greatest summer of his life.

Louis Malle, the renowned French director of My Dinner With André, *had been collaborating for many months on a film with playwright John Guare, the award-winning author of* Six Degrees of Separation. *The movie was a smart, highbrow political satire based on a very real bribery scandal involving several congressmen and the FBI. It was called* Moon Over Miami, *and the stars they wanted for it were John Belushi and Dan Aykroyd.*

The first week of September, John, Judy and Mitch Glazer went to a dinner party with the director and playwright at Malle's Manhattan apartment. In the middle of the meal, John got up from the table and ran out to grab a copy of Time *magazine, which was running one of the first early reviews of* Continental Divide, *due out the following week. The reviewer declared the film "superior," applauded John's transformation as an actor and lauded him with favorable comparisons to Spencer Tracy. John was ecstatic.*

Then, a few days later, for reasons that seemingly had nothing to do with anything but probably had everything to do with everything, John suffered a major relapse. The following week, Continental Divide *was released. The reviews were overwhelmingly positive, but the audiences stayed home. The movie grossed less than $16 million and was quickly shelved, a turn of events that certainly didn't help John's state of mind.* Continental Divide *wasn't the end of the world. There were less-successful movies released in the fall and winter of 1981. Unfortunately, one of them was* Neighbors.

SEAN DANIEL:

The reason we all finally went with John as a romantic lead for *Continental Divide* is because John is loveable, and we all loved John. So we thought if we put this up on-screen the audience would fall in love with him the same way we did. We were wrong. It was a very painful moment. You could analyze it in terms of the marketplace and see, rationally, why it had happened. But for John it was a rejection, and, well, that wasn't good.

BLAIR BROWN:

I was doing an interview, and the reporter said to me, literally, "Ewww, how could you kiss him?" There was this incredible resistance among the press to accepting John as a man, as a grown-up. On top of that, Universal was so stupid about how to market it. At one point they wanted to call it *Cabin Fever*, as if that had anything to do with the story. They thought *Continental Divide* was too confusing for the average John Belushi fan. They sold it like it was something it wasn't. Then, when they didn't get the box office response they were looking for, they just turned tail and ran.

MICHAEL APTED:

As a piece of marketing, it was pretty calamitous. The movie itself was a romantic comedy, simple as that, end of story. But the studio didn't have the balls to push it as a romantic comedy.

We really did do our best to try and pull it off. And I think we did pull it off. I just think the world wasn't ready for it. He was a brilliant character actor. Whether he was a romantic hero, which is what I asked him to be, I don't know. Maybe that was too big a stretch that we all made. If he had managed to keep going and keep working on both fronts, as a comedian and as a straight actor, then he would have found that balance and he would have pulled it off.

Regardless, it didn't help his state of mind. He'd tried to do something, really worked hard at it, and people were unkind about it. They love to tear you down in this business. The truly disappointing thing is that I thought he'd really picked up on something during the movie, picked up on what he could achieve when he really got clean and he took some interest in his health and in what he was doing. I'd hoped that it would have been a message to him, but ultimately, sadly, that wasn't the case.

DAN AYKROYD:

In early September, John and I went with the producers to a screening room to watch a rough cut of *Neighbors*. John and I were tickled by how different we looked in the movie, but it was not a night of celebration. That was one of those nights of hard, crashing reality, when you realize that all of the hard work you put in might have been wasted. We were just glad it was over. We had a whole bunch of changes we felt should be made. We gave a list of them to Avildsen, some of which he used, some of which he didn't. We weren't too jubilant. Everyone was feeling kicked in the stomach.

BERNIE BRILLSTEIN:

Belushi and Aykroyd weren't happy with Avildsen's rough cut of *Neighbors*, and they let him know about it. Then work on the film moved to Los Angeles. John arrived in late September for looping and other post-production duties.

RICHARD ZANUCK:

When he came back to LA, he went backwards again.

JOHN AVILDSEN:

This biggest problem in postproduction was the score. When one of the executive producers came out of the screening, he said that the music sounded like a documentary about Auschwitz.

DAVID BROWN:

At that point, John wanted to add a song to the closing credits, and he'd become enamored of a punk band called Fear. We hated it.

DAN AYKROYD:

Over the past few months, John had become one of the first punk-rock fans in America. He used to drag me to CBGB's all the time. He knew all of those bands and loved them. He was a heavy-metal fan from the beginning, but back then that meant Allman Brothers and Zeppelin. Now it was Fear.

The first score of the movie was really, really weak. And then Tom Scott tried to do something, and it just didn't work. Then Bill Conti came in and did this comic, tinkly bells-and-xylophones score that wound up being in the movie. John was looking to put a little edge in the thing. He spent hours in the studio recording this punk song to use over the closing credits. I thought the Fear thing worked when I heard it. But I wasn't around for any of it. I was gone that fall researching a movie.

MITCH GLAZER:

There's a moment when you're so in the pocket that your choices are America's choices. That's the way it was with the Blues Brothers. The blues were nowhere, but John liked them, decided that everyone should like them, and everyone did. But toward the end the choices were getting strange, a little too aggressive. At one point he gave me a huge stack of his blues albums. He said, "I don't want to listen to this shit anymore. Fuck this. All I'm going to listen to is Fear and the Dead Kennedys." It just felt wrongheaded.

RICHARD ZANUCK:

I was out at Columbia having a meeting, and he just burst in unannounced. He was in terrible shape. He was screaming and going on about the music and the score and how it was terrible and how much it sucked, and then he burst out again.

Then I took him over to see Richard Berres, the music director at Columbia. John was in one of those uncontrollable states, and he got very wild in the guy's office. He knocked some things off his desk, pounded on it. It was a very uncomfortable situation.

DAVID BROWN:

When John visited the head of Columbia's music department, a man in his sixties or seventies, with one karate chop he practically split his desk in half. He ripped the phone out of the wall. That's how mad he was about not getting to use his punk band.

BERNIE BRILLSTEIN:

By the time he went out to Columbia and trashed the place, he was pretty far gone. The first time Hollywood really let John down was on *Goin' South*. He'd been so excited about working with Jack Nicholson, but the producers were so mean to him that one day he came to my office and he cried, literally cried. Then when he had problems on *Neighbors*, he went on a rampage. That's what had changed.

MITCH GLAZER:

The problem with cocaine is that *the fear* settles in at a certain point. The truth is John could have made ten failed movies in a row, and they still would have gone after him for the eleventh; there was nobody like him. But cocaine puts you in a vulnerable place. You get that jittery feeling of having not slept for days. At the heart of comedy is confidence, and if you need confidence then cocaine is not the drug to be taking. It wasn't like Hollywood did it to him, but he'd eroded all of his natural defenses. When it came to his work, John was always incredibly confident, a classic middle linebacker. Things were just starting to eat at him that never would have bothered him in the past.

DAVID BROWN:

I don't know what it was about LA. When he was in New York or on Martha's Vineyard, he was fine. When he was in Hollywood he was a disaster. He did not relate well to the environment out there. It was probably the corporate nature of the place, because John was a maverick. He couldn't stand it. And he's not the only one. A lot of us can't stand it.

ROBIN WILLIAMS:

John hated to be alone, and in LA you're surrounded by non-friends. As nuts as you can be in New York, you walk outside and there's garbage men goin', "What the fuck are you doin' up?" There's a little bit of a reality quotient that will eventually force you to come around. Whereas in LA, everything is good when it's not. You're surrounded by yes men and it's all kind of surreal. One time I got stopped by a cop, and he gave me a script. It's Mickey-avellian. The ends justify the media. You get too caught up in it, and you start to believe it, and that's when it's dangerous.

JUDITH BELUSHI PISANO:

During the fall of '81, when John began using again, I found myself feeling alternately angry, numb and afraid. It wasn't that he was doing drugs all the time. On the contrary, it was completely sporadic. He insisted he wouldn't fall back into his old ways, but each time, even if it didn't turn into a full-blown binge, I only felt worse. As much as I loved John, as much as I couldn't imagine life without him, I was finding it harder to tolerate him when he was on drugs. I was tired of the battle. I decided to see a therapist.

At the first meeting I told the doctor about John's drug history, how I was desperate to help him and yet resented having to play the cop. The doctor said that even without the drug problem, our life was extremely hectic. I was exhibiting the same symptoms as an overwrought mother with several children. I needed time for myself, he said, suggesting I commit to therapy for at least three months so I could reassess the situation. I was pretty surprised. The focus on me, and not

John's problem, was uncomfortable. He said the caretaker role was unhealthy and that I couldn't really help John until I myself was healthy. I arranged for weekly sessions.

RICHARD ZANUCK:

We had a couple of private previews of *Neighbors* that didn't work so well. That's when the harsh reality set in that it was a troubled picture.

DAVID BROWN:

John's career was on the line. He wanted a good movie. His poor behavior at the end did not change the fact that he'd been right at the beginning. Looking back, we should have listened to him. Zanuck and I made a mistake in sticking with the director. Giving Avildsen full credit for his talents, we should have put our money on Belushi and Aykroyd.

CATHY MORIARTY:

What it could have been and what it turned out to be were two completely different projects. It was a combination of everything. It was everyone's fault.

MARILYN SUZANNE MILLER, *writer*, SNL:

If you look at the string of comedies that followed out of *SNL*, you'll see that it's just unending: *Meatballs, Caddyshack, Animal House, 1941.* They just did one after another after another. It was a time best encapsulated by *ET*. It was a time of boyishness. Not manliness, boyishness, because that's what Hollywood wanted. *Animal House* was the killer; that killed everything else. *Animal House* was a very smart movie because of who wrote it, but as far as the studio was concerned it was just a lot of pie throwing.

Chevy, Danny, Billy, those guys played kids, *were* kids, for years. The endless adolescence of the baby boom can be seen primarily through those movies. They weren't allowed to grow up, and it wrecked their lives. If you look at the performers that came out of the Actor's Studio in the fifties, guys like Brando, all the guys on *SNL* aspired to be actors of that caliber. And they were actors of that caliber, as Danny's and Billy's

Oscar nominations have now shown us. But nobody ever told John, "Why don't you go down and study with Uta Hagen?" Or, "Why don't you just go down and study, period?" Nobody ever said that, because there was too much money to be made off of him. Why do you think they tore Danny from John and dumped him into that goddamned *Dr. Detroit*, the worst movie ever in history? They figured they'd make two separate movies and double their money.

Danny and John chose *Neighbors* because it was so dark and weird. They were really looking to do an important film, but they were too young to know how to get control of the project, to stop Hollywood from botching it. It's impossible. Hollywood eats you alive, especially when the agents and the studios are all in it together. You can't fight that. They were trying, but how were these young, inexperienced guys supposed to get one over on these known shysters?

HAROLD RAMIS:

Watching John's movie career unfold, I always felt that he was not being well served, that the choices were strange and not fully realized in some way. I understood that he wanted to break out of Bluto, but there were so many things he could have done other than *Neighbors* and *Continental Divide*. Part of the problem was that this was the first medium he had encountered that did not immediately fall to his charm and talent. Audiences liked him. People would forgive him anything. But it was questionable as to whether he could make a movie career out of that, especially when his own focus was being so distorted by his personal habits.

You have to have the ability to find meaning in what you do, and I don't know that John was grounded in anything other than his own ambition. I once said to Chevy, "You know, you can't make everybody love you."

And he said, "Oh yes I can."

It's a classic pattern. It's what makes an addict an addict, the expectation that if you just get more, then you'll finally cross over and find some permanent satisfaction. But Hollywood is an empty and horrible place if you have no drive other than to be well liked and successful. ■

ISSUE NO. 361 · JANUARY 21ST 1982 ·

RollingSton

John Belushi

More Than
Just a
Pretty
Face

Chapter 15

NOTHING IS OVER
UNTIL WE DECIDE IT IS

the spin cycle

ELLIOTT GOULD, *host*, SNL:

In 1971, my career really took a left turn. I fell out of the mainstream. Years later someone asked me in an interview if I'd ever had a drug problem. My answer was and still is, "No, I never had a drug problem. I had a problem with reality." Part of the reason I fell out is that I was incapable of and unwilling to compromise with the system around me. That did me a great deal of harm, and I could recognize the same thing in John. For someone as sensitive and as vulnerable as he was, it must have been nearly impossible to fathom the lack of soul and conscience in the industry.

Above: John on the Pacific Coast Highway, February 1982; last known photo

On December 18, 1981, Neighbors *was released. In the flurry of holiday moviegoing it grossed over $28 million before dropping like a stone as word of mouth began to spread.*

That year, John's movie career went through a painful and awkward adolescence, but if his personal problems could be brought under control, there was still ample reason to believe that bright things lay ahead. By December, Louis Malle and John Guare were close to a finished shooting script for Moon Over Miami. *John was also attached to star as the bombastic Ignatius J. Reilly in the film adaptation of the Pulitzer Prize-winning novel* A Confederacy of Dunces, *with Richard Pryor and Eddie Murphy alternately discussed as possible co-stars. Back in New York, Danny was hard at work on another project for the team, a bizarre adventure tale of paranormal exterminators called* Ghostbusters.

In the near term, however, it was decided that the duo should split up, with Danny going to work on Dr. Detroit, *a movie about a college professor turned pimp, and John going to work on* Sweet Deception, *a lighthearted diamond theft caper in which a young man finds himself caught up in a web of international intrigue. It was a fluffy romantic comedy very much in the vein of the Cary Grant/Audrey Hepburn classic* Charade. *In other words, a film that was completely wrong for John Belushi. And for an A-list star it was definitely a B movie.*

But John's new agent, Michael Ovitz, thought otherwise. He put together a package for John to star and Bernie Brillstein to executive produce and sold it to Michael Eisner, then president of Paramount Studios. John would be paid $1.85 million. Ovitz also negotiated a pay-or-play deal, meaning John would be paid whether the picture was made or not. John felt the pay-or-play deal would give him the leverage he'd lacked on Neighbors. *He also thought he could take a smaller project and retain greater control. He was wrong. To say that the film turned into a disaster would be misrepresentation of the facts. It was a catastrophe from the word go.*

JAY SANDRICH, *director:*

I wanted John Ritter, from *Three's Company*, to play the lead in *Sweet Deception*, a caper set against the backdrop of the California wine industry. But at that time none of the studios would greenlight a picture with John Ritter. Somewhere along the line Mike Ovitz, my agent, called me up and said, "What about John Belushi?" And I hung up the phone. Mike called me back and said, "No, no, I'm serious."

I checked out *Continental Divide*, liked it and decided to meet with him. I was very candid with him. I said, "Look, I'm just not that interested. It's not the right part for you, and if you're on drugs then it's never going to work."

"That was a bad time in my life," he said, "but I'm over that now. I have to stay clean. If I don't, my wife is going to leave me." And I believe that at the time he sincerely meant it. A couple of months went by, and I got a call that John had decided to do the picture.

We went to Paramount and met with Michael Eisner and Jeffrey Katzenberg. I thought I was going there to talk about a potential deal, so I was shocked to find out that a deal was already on the table. I had no say in it at all. One of the things that came out of this meeting was that John had the right to hire a writer to rewrite the script with him. I knew John was funny, and it was obvious some changes needed to be made to suit him, so I was willing to go along with it. I didn't have the clout to say no. By that point, there were already millions of dollars on the table, and the deal, strange as it was, was moving under a momentum of its own.

DON NOVELLO, *writer*, SNL:

Bernie Brillstein, John's manager and also mine, called me and said, "John wants you to rewrite a script he's doing, *Sweet Deception*." He said it would only take a month. John and I met for dinner and discussed ways to make it work.

When Bernie and Ovitz brought John *Sweet Deception*, it was pitched to him as a "great deal." It probably was, but it was also a weak, secondhand script, and it was totally wrong for him. The part was something Chevy Chase might have played, and Chevy had already turned it down, as had two major studios. But John took it with the understanding that the script could be rewritten for him.

Everyone involved in the project wanted something different. Sandrich was expecting us just to "polish" his lame script. John and I were under the impression that we had carte blanche to change it. What Bernie, Eisner and Ovitz wanted out of the script, I don't know, because I honestly can't believe

that any of them had actually read it; it was that bad. Bernie wanted more of the slapstick, crowd-pleasing routine. He thought it was "time for John to drop his pants again." Eisner just wanted a John Belushi picture, period. It didn't matter that John and the director had totally different ideas about the film. And Ovitz, all Ovitz wanted was to sell this whole package to Paramount. What I didn't know then—and what I don't think John knew either—was that Michael Ovitz was representing every single person at the table and taking home a piece of everybody else's action.

JUDITH BELUSHI PISANO:

Originally, Don wanted to work in San Francisco; he needed to stay close to home. When a freak rainstorm hit the Bay Area, causing mudslides that closed the Golden Gate Bridge, they settled on LA. My heart sank. It was the last place I wanted John to go.

I knew if I went with John to California I could help keep him on track, but at the same time I couldn't keep playing the caretaker role. I didn't think it was good for John or myself in the long run. And there were rational reasons for me to stay in New York. I was working on a new book with Anne Beatts and Deanne Stillman, and I was committed to my therapy. I trusted Novello. I wasn't worried about Don in terms of drugs, but I still had a gnawing feeling in my stomach. I explained all this to my therapist, and he asked, "What are you afraid of?" *Afraid of?* I hesitated. I didn't want to say what my first thought was, because I didn't really believe it myself. But it was the first thing that came to my mind: "I'm afraid that he'll die."

CAROL CALDWELL, *writer*:

At the same time John was headed to LA to work on *Sweet Deception*, I was going out for a few months to work on a screenplay for MGM. Neither of us had ever written a feature, and we were both fairly nervous. When I had first met John in France with Michael O'Donoghue, he was clean as a whistle, and so the person I knew did not do drugs, but I made a pact with Judy that I would check on him as regularly as I could. We both had deadlines to meet, but we talked by phone almost every night. He would call me when he was through writing, sometimes as late as two in the morning. We talked mostly about the writing, how it was going. It seemed as if everything were okay.

DON NOVELLO:

When John and I met back in LA, I'd been working on the script over Christmas and had lots of new ideas. We met with Sandrich. He liked some of the changes, but he thought we took out too much of the intrigue. We kept throwing funny ideas at him, but he was hung up on the romance and the caper more than the comedy.

JUDITH BELUSHI PISANO:

John would call and tell me the story line they were developing or gags they worked in. He was trying to lose the romantic comedy angle, because that's what everyone didn't like in *Continental Divide*. Danny DeVito was going to play his older brother. They also wrote a small part for Orson Welles, who had recently become the spokesman for Gallo wine. I was pleasantly surprised at how well things seemed to be going at first.

TINO INSANA:

John was tired of staying in a hotel. He asked if he could stay with my wife and me for a while. He slept on the couch for like two weeks. He was gone most of the day working, and then he'd come back and we'd have popcorn and watch movies. We spent a lot of time together in those last two months, casually talking about the old days with the West Compass Players back in Wheaton. He told me that those days were, he felt, the most important for him, just doing good work and flying by the seat of our pants like we did.

ROBIN WILLIAMS:

My most vivid memory of John is him coming to visit the set of *Mork and Mindy* during those last months, when Jonathan Winters was there. We just sat there offstage watching Jonathan riff, and John was saying, "Man, he's the source. He's why we're here." We watched Jonathan go off, which he would do—two little kids watching the master. Somebody saw us and went, "That's weird." To see these two maniacs sitting very still in the corner was just odd, I guess. That was the quietest I ever saw John, and it was kind of wonderful.

DICK BLASUCCI:

John always wanted our high school band, the Ravins, to get together and play again. He talked about it all the time out in LA. Then he called me one day and said, "Hey, I got us a gig!" He'd arranged for us to play the wrap parties for *Police Squad!* and *Taxi*. We went over to Paramount and set everything up ourselves. John, at this point, was a major star, and yet he was down there on the floor setting up his own drum kit. Once we started playing and he got behind the drums, you could just see how happy it made him.

It was just odd that John was suddenly coming back into everyone's lives, getting the band from Wheaton back together. It had absolutely no connection with the Hollywood crap or that after-hours world that he'd gotten into. And John never did any drugs around us. Never. He'd just come over late at night and want to hang out and talk.

BOB WEISS:

After *Blues Brothers*, I had started producing the TV show *Police Squad!* We killed off the guest star in the opening credits of every episode. That way we got the name value of a guest star but didn't have the pain in the ass of actually dealing with them. Florence Henderson, Robert Goulet, we killed them all.

I had asked John to bring his band in to play the wrap party for the show, and also if he wanted to do a celebrity guest death. Eventually we came up with the idea that was actually filmed, the camera looking up underwater as John and a cinderblock slowly float into the frame, showing that he's just been dumped in the river. But before we came up with that, John said—and it still chills me—he said, "Why don't you show me lying dead with a needle stuck in my arm?"

There was nervous laughter in the room, and we said, "John, well, that's not really funny." I think back and I wish I'd heard it a different way. I wish I'd extrapolated what John was really saying and hadn't been so fast to just rewrite it. But I didn't. John died before the footage ever went on the air, and it was put on ice, hopefully forever.

EUGENIE ROSS-LEMING:

He called me in LA shortly before he died. It was very weird, because we hadn't spoken in over a year. He sounded weary, subdued, not like the young, happy John that I knew in the Second City days. I felt like he wanted something from me, so I told him to come over. I gave him directions to my house, and then he never showed up.

MITCH GLAZER:

The last week of January, I was getting married. John called at six o'clock the night before the wedding and told me he wasn't coming. I was furious. I didn't know what was going on in LA. To talk to him on the phone, it just sounded like more of the same, and it made me feel like he was just blowing it off.

"You don't understand what's going on out here," he said. "You just don't understand."

"No, I don't."

"Look, I just can't get on that plane. You don't understand. I can't get on that plane. I can't."

"What the fuck are you talking about? Get on the fucking plane and come here."

"I can't. *I just can't.* Judy and Danny will be there, and I'll make it up to you when I get back."

I didn't know what was going on, and I was just pissed.

RHONDA COULLET:

He called me from LA the weekend of Mitch's wedding. He was just so strung out. He wanted to be there for the wedding, wished he could be there, but felt like he couldn't face it, face Judy and all of us. He was reaching out to me for some kind of friendship or intimate connection. He thought he was losing Judy. He thought she'd leave if he couldn't stay straight, and deep down he was afraid he'd never be able to.

DON NOVELLO:

The original script really had nothing to do with wine at all, and we wanted to add that. One night John and I had dinner in LA with Tommy Smothers, who owned a vineyard up in Sonoma. That night he told us about noble rot. It's a fungus, *botrytis*, that grows on grapes. Normally that's a bad thing, but this kind actually gives the grapes a certain sweetness that's impossible to capture any other way.

After Judy flew in for John's birthday, we went up to tour Tommy's vineyard and got a real crash course in wine. John

was really getting into the whole culture. We spent the week mostly in my office, writing and having a lot of fun kicking around ideas. John came up with this great character, a guy with his own noble rot. He's a little grungy, and everybody underestimates him, but he triumphs in the end. Needless to say, it's a part that John really invested a lot of himself in. After that we decided to make this character the center of the story, and we changed the name of the picture to *Noble Rot*.

ALAN ZWEIBEL, *writer*, SNL:

I'd gone up to San Francisco with my wife and baby to see John and Judy and Novello. I got a sitter, and we all went out to dinner. It was the wildest night in the world. I thought I was going to die. John was driving, and every time he took a hill your head would hit the roof of the car. It was like every San Francisco car chase I'd ever seen in the movies, except that I was in the fucking car. "I want to show you guys the best time ever!" he said. He took us to this nightclub, that restaurant. It was completely nuts, but it was fun.

Was John "out of control"? How the fuck would I know? Before we went out everyone came up to see my baby in the hotel room, and John was just so warm and sweet. Watching him holding my child seemed like the most natural thing in the world. Then ten minutes later we're flying over the hills of San Francisco, and I'm holding on for dear life. That was John. It was a great, great night. It would still stand out in my memory today, even if it wasn't the last time I ever saw him alive.

JAY SANDRICH:

While he and Don were up in the wine country, every couple of days I'd call and say, "Can I see some pages so we can get an idea of how this is going?"

He'd say, "Well, we're not really doing it in any kind of linear way, so we don't really have anything to send to you right now." That bothered me a lot. Plus I had started to hear a lot of stories about John out at clubs and high on coke. I was starting to lose interest in the project. I had more or less decided to pull out.

DON NOVELLO:

Judy flew back to New York, and John went back to LA. I'd been working around the clock in San Francisco piecing everything together. I got to LA, and for the next three days I worked a lot of long, hard hours at his bungalow at the Chateau Marmont. For those three days John was gone a lot of the time. I hardly saw him.

DAVE THOMAS, *writer/performer*, SCTV:

John was having an awful time with it. He would alternate between, "It's going badly," and, "It's going great!"

LORNE MICHAELS:

I saw John at the Playboy Mansion two weeks before he died. I'd gone there with Buck Henry for Hugh Hefner's movie night. John didn't want to watch the movie; he was in the other room playing video games. But he came in to see me and Buck, and throughout the movie he kept sneaking up the aisle and taking handfuls of popcorn out of Hefner's bowl, just to make us laugh. Every time Hefner would go for his popcorn there would be less and less of it there.

After the movie I saw him outside and we hugged and caught up. I think he was happy to see me, because we hadn't seen each other in a while. He was going on and on about *Noble Rot*. He seemed manic to me, on edge. The old John was still there, the sweet, warm John. That guy was always there. But I thought, oh, this is trouble. Not John. I'd stopped thinking that John was trouble. He was just in trouble.

CAROL CALDWELL:

Michael came out to LA sometime in February, and to celebrate we threw a party. John came by at some point, took me aside and said I needed a pick-me-up. He pulled two bags of white powder out of his jacket and laid out a couple of lines from one of them. It was the only time I ever indulged in coke with John, or so I thought. While I snarfed the lines, he went in my bathroom and threw up. I said, "What's the matter with you?"

"I've just been staying up too late."

"How much of this stuff are you doing?"

"Too much."

After I did the lines, with all I'd had to drink that night, I felt very woozy and collapsed on the bed. There was no pick-me-up to be had. Later, someone came in and told me my guests were beginning to go, and shouldn't I get up? I could no more have gotten up than flown to the moon. I later realized what he'd given me, mistakenly, was heroin.

HAROLD RAMIS:

By that time, John's condition had to be as much a chemical response as an emotional one. People say that excessive cocaine use leads to a condition known as anhedonia, the inability to feel pleasure. When I saw him that night at the party, maybe two weeks before he died, he looked exhausted. I said, "How ya doing, John?" He just laid his head on my shoulder and said, "Oh, Harold." That was it. Oh, Harold. It was like he couldn't even articulate anything about his situation. I just sensed total despair.

PENNY MARSHALL:

People always let John call and crash in the middle of the night, in part because they had some of that same aspect to their own personalities. They knew what it was like to be scared, to be up alone at some odd hour. But as time went on, as things got deeper, the same behavior that people initially embraced and enjoyed eventually pushed some of them away. A lot of people saw a reflection of themselves in John, and it scared them, and they pulled back.

DAVE THOMAS:

John went to dark places. When I was with him and Danny at the Blues Bar in New York, John would always want to leave and go someplace else. I would tag along to someplace that was a little darker and a little creepier. And then John would go on and adjourn to another place. And I always stopped. I would think, Jesus Christ, this is getting fucking creepy. It was the same thing in Los Angeles. John would want to go hang out with these seedy people, and I would be like, "Nah, nah, forget it. I'm not going there."

MITCH GLAZER:

Toward the end, the phone would ring at three in the morning and I'd know it was John, and I just couldn't pick up. Part of it was that I had a wife. Part of it was that I just didn't have the strength anymore. I'd just lie there in bed and

Chateau Marmont

Hotel

8221 Sunset Boulevard
Hollywood, Calif. 90046
Telephone: (213) 656-1010

TELEX 9103213006

A SARLOT-KANTARJIAN HOTEL

BOTH MEN SMILE AT ONE ANOTHER, KNOWING FROM HER THE
TONE OF HER VOICE THAT EVERYTHING IS OKAY.

                    GATES
        It sounds as though everything went
        ~~is~~ okay up there with you.

We were counting on you to bring us something back.

                    CHRISTINE
        Everything ~~just~~ is fine. I had a very
        nice moring.
        ~~How are things there~~?   No problems

What just

                    TISDALE
        We expected your call an
        hour ago. WE were starting
        to ~~wx~~ worry.

                    CHRISTINE
    What?

            GATES (TO TISDALE)
        You have to talk louder.

            TISDALE (LOUDER)
        We expected your call an hour
        ago. Steven and I were starting
        to worry.

                    Christine
        I bet. You probably ~~thought x~~ were worried I
        was on my way to South America.

listen to him on the machine, calling from some street corner somewhere. It was heartbreaking. From the minute we met we were never apart very often, but it wasn't a coincidence, truthfully, that I got married five weeks before he died. I don't know if it was self-preservation or just instinct or both, but it wasn't an accident. I know that looking back.

MICHAEL KLENFNER:

I never stopped loving him, but if he was on a roll he wouldn't think twice about coming to your place at three in the morning, thinking you had drugs. And that wasn't cool with a baby, his goddaughter, sleeping in the next bedroom. It became a burden. You didn't want to hear that John was missing and you were the last person to see him, and so you were somehow responsible for letting him go. The truth of the matter is that, at some points, you were not answering your phone because you didn't want to be there anymore.

When he was clean and sober he was the most wonderful man I've ever known. When he was fucked up, he was as big a horror as you ever could imagine. That last Christmas, my wife and I had rented a house in Miami Beach. John and Judy came down to stay with us for the week. One night John was so fucked up that he started screaming at my wife, accusing her of stealing his Quaaludes. My wife didn't do drugs, and she'd never steal from anyone. But he was serious.

Judy stood up to him. She yelled, *"She didn't take your Quaaludes, so get that idea out of your head right now!"* But he didn't listen; he just waved her off and went right on in his mission, searching for drugs. I wish I had a better grasp of the English language, to describe to you the look of sadness that I saw in Judy's face that night. But I don't, and it didn't matter. It didn't matter that Judy was sad. It didn't matter that her heart was broken. He just kept going. It finally came to the point where I told him to get the fuck out of the house.

On Tuesday, February 23, the morning after Carol Caldwell and Michael O'Donoghue's party, bound copies of Noble Rot *were delivered to Paramount. Don Novello flew to Toronto to begin work on* SCTV, *and John boarded an early-morning flight back to New*

York. Upon arriving at JFK, he took a car back to Morton Street and went to sleep. Judy came home, found several grams of cocaine in his luggage and threw them into the fireplace.

BERNIE BRILLSTEIN:

I read the script on a flight to London. It was terrible. It didn't even make sense. I called Ovitz, and he agreed the script was a mess. After I hung up, the phone rang. It was Belushi. I took a deep breath and told him the truth. We agreed to wait for Eisner's reaction. A couple of days later, Ovitz heard from Eisner. He hated it.

JAY SANDRICH:

From my point of view, it was just a disaster. This triangle that I had seen of comedy, adventure and love had become basically a car chase with a lot of very violent scenes. John insisted on talking to me to find out what I thought of it. So I called him in New York and told him, "Look, there's some good stuff here, but a lot of it I have real problems with. The love story needs to be totally reworked, and it's not as funny as it should be." That was the last time I talked to him. He was really crushed. He thought this was just a wonderful script, and everybody disliked it intensely. It delivered a terrible blow to his ego.

DON NOVELLO:

It was a first draft. Did it have problems? Sure. We were still working out how to mesh these two plots, and we had a ways to go. But Bernie had told them the rewrite should only take a month. Maybe if we'd just been giving it a polish like Sandrich expected, then it would only have taken that long, but we were just getting it together. You don't write a screenplay in a month, or even two. But this was supposed to be a Christmas movie. That was the big rush. They had a release date and a start date and a date for us to turn in a draft. They were going to start, ready or not.

MITCH GLAZER:

John came into my apartment and put a huge pile of drugs on the coffee table and picked up the phone and just started screaming, terrorizing Bernie and Ovitz out in California.

Wendie went in the back room and hid. She didn't want to be around him. I didn't realize how bad it was. I felt like I had seen this before, but, clearly, I hadn't.

He was so insane. The next day he gave me a copy of the script to read while we were standing in the middle of a Mink DeVille concert at the Savoy. Then he called me about an hour later and said, "Did you finish it?" I finally read it. I didn't think that much of it, but then I'd told him not to do *Animal House* because I thought he was too old for it.

Seeing him during that week of *Noble Rot*'s rejection was just crazy and sad. Later that night, we were at the Blues Bar. Danny had left. It was like three in the morning, and I didn't want to stay any longer. In the old days I would have stayed until daylight, but I just didn't feel the same. *It* didn't feel the same. Finally I said, "John, I'm going." He begged me to stay there with him, begged me. But I was with my new wife, and I just couldn't do it. He told me to take his car so I'd get home okay. We got in. I told the driver where to go and then turned around and looked out the back window. It was like something out of a movie. He just stood there in the middle of the street, hands at his sides, and watched us drive away. I never saw him again.

JUDITH BELUSHI PISANO:

John decided he had to go back to LA. Danny and I begged him not to go, told him to come up to the Vineyard and relax, but he said if he talked to them in person he could convince them to do the script. He slept most of the next day. Late in the afternoon, he woke up coughing—coughing up blood—coughing so hard I thought he was going to die right there. I just watched him, heartsick, wondering how he could be doing this to himself. He felt me looking at him. "What? What's that look?"

"It's concern, John. I don't know how you can do this to yourself. You know it's the coke. Your body can't take the abuse anymore."

"Oh, is that so? What are you saying? That I'm out of control?"

"Yes!"

"*I'm out of control?*" he yelled, storming out of the room and slamming the door.

MICHAEL KLENFNER:

The last night he was in New York, John, Judy, my wife and I went to the movies. John fell asleep through most of it.

Then we went down to the Odeon for dinner, and John tried to put the Fear cassette in the tape player. He was always trying to get that stuff played all over the place. Then it was over to this nightclub and that nightclub, and eventually it turned into a drug quest and my wife decided to bail. I stayed on for a little bit longer because I was worried. There was no security, and I just wanted to be there because I knew I had my head about me. Finally I was just too spent. I went home.

JUDITH BELUSHI PISANO:

A little after four in the morning, we ended up at this club on Third Avenue and Thirteenth in the East Village. About that time, the energy in the clubs always turns darker, and I was ready to go. I wanted John to come home with me. He wanted to stay out. He walked me to a cab and, even though I was angry, kissed me goodnight. As the cab pulled off, I turned, expecting to see him walking back into the club or talking with someone. But he was just leaning against the building, watching me pull away. He looked exhausted. Startled, I waved to him. I don't know if he saw me, but that was the last time I ever saw him, just watching the cab as it rounded the corner. It was the exact same corner as the very first apartment we shared in New York, ten years before.

John spent the morning at the Tenth Street Baths and caught a flight back to Los Angeles that afternoon, without returning home. That night, he checked into Bungalow Three at the Chateau Marmont. John had come back to Hollywood believing that a face-to-face meeting would convince Michael Eisner and Paramount that Noble Rot *was salvageable. Eisner had a different agenda. John's deal was pay or play, meaning the studio had to fork over his salary to him even if the film were never made. Eisner's goal was to shift John's sizeable financial commitment to a different project,* The Joy of Sex, *a farcical comedy based on the best-selling sex manual.* National Lampoon *publisher Matty Simmons had agreed to co-produce and attach the magazine's name to the film, and* National Lampoon *plus John Belushi plus sex was a surefire success.*

There was only one problem. Joy of Sex *was an industry joke, a legendarily bad script that had languished in development at Paramount for years. It followed a young man from infancy, through puberty and beyond as he "discovered his sexuality and became a man." It was comedy of the lowest order. In one scene, they actually wanted John to play a breast-feeding baby.*

On Monday morning, Eisner met with John at his bungalow and told him that the studio was not going to produce Noble Rot *and that they wanted him to shift his commitment to* Joy of Sex. *They discussed the script and threw around some ideas, but John was noncommittal and less than enthusiastic. With the pay-or-play deal, it was supposedly John's prerogative to say no, take the $1.85 million and walk, but doing so was not as easy as it sounds. Eisner left, and they agreed to meet again.*

DON NOVELLO:

Pay or play doesn't mean what everyone thinks it does. You don't get to walk away with millions of dollars for doing nothing, not really. In most cases what it means is that they've already paid you, so now they have the leverage to keep the same deal in place but change the terms. Same wedding, different bride.

Joy of Sex wasn't any funnier than *Noble Rot*, but it was faster and cheaper and easier to produce and market by Christmas. Studio executives don't read a script the same way you or I do. They're not looking at the humor. They read it and see "Helicopter shot: $50,000. Winery location: $75,000." In retrospect, what John and I had written would have been a very expensive script to produce, lots of locations and sets. But all that gets settled and compromised through rewrites. Scripts are rewritten in Hollywood ten, fifteen times. Nothing is ever rejected, or accepted, on a first draft. *Noble Rot* was rejected and replaced within a day. Bernie never called me with any notes, anything that needed to be fixed or changed, and I was his client. Why? Because it was all bullshit. Michael Eisner wanted John Belushi in a Christmas movie. It didn't matter what it was. The truth is, the studio had been trying to get *Joy of Sex* off the ground for years. They had it in their back pocket the whole time, and it was out on the table a few hours after we turned our script in.

DAVE THOMAS:

Paramount had pitched *Joy of Sex* to John two years before, and he had turned it down. Around the same time, Eisner and Katzenberg offered me the job of directing it. I was surprised, because I had never directed anything before, nor had I ever told anyone that I wanted to be a director. The first thing I said in the meeting was, "Why did you guys bring me in for this? I've never directed anything in my life."

Katzenberg said, "John Belushi thought you'd be a good choice to direct this movie."

I laughed. "So John is so powerful now that on the strength of his say-so you'll bring a guy in and offer him the job of directing one of your movies. That's hilarious."

"Well, we don't think of it that way, Dave," Eisner said. He was getting a little pissed. "You see, the way we view a director is sort of through the metaphor of a vending machine. We have the machine, and the director is kind of like a quarter that we put in and a product comes out."

"Well," I said, "if I were a real director, I'm sure I would be terribly insulted by your metaphor, but since I'm not I'll read the script and let you know."

It was a complete piece of shit, just disgusting sex jokes. Katzenberg called me and I tried to be diplomatic, saying I didn't think I had the skills to pull off what they needed and so forth. Then Katzenberg asked me if I'd like to act in it. I said, "Maybe I'm not making myself clear. I said I didn't want to direct it because I wouldn't want my name associated with it. So I wouldn't want to act in it because I wouldn't want my face—no, no, excuse me—my thirty-five-foot-wide naked ass associated with it either." And I hung up the phone, called John and said, "Hey, thanks a lot for recommending me for that fucking piece of shit *Joy of Sex*."

"Don't do it," he said. "It's a bad movie. Don't do it."

Directing any movie would have been a big step for me, so I guess he thought that he was maybe doing me a favor, but once we both realized how bad it was, he saw it wasn't a good idea. Then later, when his pay-or-play deal on *Noble Rot* fell through and they told him he had to do it, it must have been pretty galling.

JUDITH BELUSHI PISANO:

John called me Thursday morning and said he was sorry for not coming home Sunday. He said he had to stay in LA for one more meeting. He sounded frustrated, depressed. "You wouldn't believe what they want me to do with this *Joy of Sex* script," he said. "You should read it."

"I love you," was the last thing he said. And then he was gone.

BERNIE BRILLSTEIN:

John came to my office to meet with Eisner. I told him he needed a hit, and if he fucked up the Paramount deal and didn't deliver a feature, he'd have trouble getting work. I told him he should do *Joy of Sex*. It'd be a big hit, and then we'd have *Moon Over Miami* and Danny's *Ghostbusters* lined up right after that. He seemed to be warming up, but he was still noncommittal.

Later that day, Eisner showed up for the meeting to push *Joy of Sex*. As a way to smooth things over, he told John he could continue to rewrite *Noble Rot*. This time, John seemed willing to consider the proposal. That afternoon at about five o'clock, he called me at home. He said he'd do *Joy of Sex*. He said he had some ideas for it and we could make it work. Then he called Katzenberg and told him the same. He set up a meeting for ten the next morning to work out the details.

DON NOVELLO:

John called me. I hadn't heard from him for a few days, and so I was getting worried. He said they didn't like the script, but that we could rewrite it if he did the other movie first. He was so depressed about it. "They want me to wear a diaper," he said. John was a rock star. He was on the cover of the *Rolling Stone*, and they wanted him to wear a diaper. They didn't give a shit about him. Just crank out another Elvis movie for Christmas. The deal never made any sense in the first place, but they were treating John like he was the one who was crazy. Where were the people who were supposed to be looking out for him? The people he was paying to be in his corner had carved out corners of their own, and he was all alone out there. He was all by himself.

DAN AYKROYD:

I'd gone into the office Thursday morning to work on the script I was writing for *Ghostbusters*. He was on the answering machine when I checked the messages. It was very slurred. He was fucked up, and he was hurting. I'd never heard him

that bad before. I thought, I'm going to finish this paragraph, and then I'm going to get on a plane and get the fuck out there. And I didn't. I tracked him down that afternoon on the phone instead. He sounded sad and defeated. I said to him, "John, c'mon man, you gotta come home. I'm writing something great for us here that's gonna solve everything. But you've gotta come back." And he said okay. He said he was coming back on the red-eye, and so I didn't go.

CAROL CALDWELL:

That last night, Michael and I had gone to dinner at a friend's house a couple of blocks from the Chateau Marmont. On the way over he said, "Have you heard from John?"

"No, why?"

"He's back in LA."

"What?"

"He came back on Sunday."

"No…no, that's wrong. That can't be. I talked to Judy when he left. She has him in New York. She said she was taking him to a doctor."

And all of a sudden I got very worried. We sat down to dinner with about eight other people, all of them good friends of John, and not one of us had seen him or heard from him for the week that he'd been back.

SMOKEY:

I had been back and forth to Hollywood with different clients, and I'd heard some horror stories about John falling back into his old habits. The afternoon before he died, I got a call from Judy. They were having some serious problems, and could I come back? He was out in LA, and she asked if I could go out and bring him home. I told her, "Absolutely. I'll fly out tomorrow."

John and I used to joke about my shit detector. Anytime I'd catch him doing something, he'd be like, "How'd you know?" "Oh, my shit detector went off." And when I hung up the phone with Judy that day, my shit detector told me to get on the plane. I sat there for a while, thinking I should just drive to the airport and leave right then. I didn't. The next day I was packing my suitcase to leave, and there it was, all over the television. ■

Chapter 16

DON'T LOOK BACK IN ANGER

a lonesome road

BILL WALLACE:

John had told Bernie's office that he needed a typewriter to do some work. They called me, and I picked it up that morning on my way over to the Chateau. I had the typewriter in my hands and already had a key to the door, so I unlocked it and walked in. I put the typewriter on the kitchen table, saw John in the back bedroom and immediately thought, oh shit, something's wrong. John had a bad nasal problem, and the sounds he made when he was asleep the whole world could hear; I couldn't hear anything. I just had one of those feelings. I walked to the back room saying, "John, time to get up." He was in a fetal position on his right side. I shook him, no movement. I shook him again. Still nothing. I rolled him over on his back, and his whole right side had what's called phlebitis—all the blood had settled to the low point in his body. He wasn't breathing at all. I jumped on the bed, clamped my mouth over his and started giving him CPR. I pounded on his chest, breathed, pounded, breathed. He still didn't move. Nothing happened. I just kept trying. I just kept pumping his chest, pounding and pounding with tears in my eyes, crying, "You dumb son of a bitch. You dumb son of a bitch. You dumb son of a bitch."

Chicago Tribune

Saturday, March 6, 1982

135th Year—No. 65 © 1982 Chicago Tribune   W   6 Sections   25¢   5 Star

Comedian John Belushi is found dead

Patent on the outlandish was ticket to stardom

By Gene Siskel
and Larry Kart

THERE ARE some people to whom stardom in the movies comes immediately. By dint of a look or an emotional presence they immediately speak to millions.

John Belushi was one of those people. His moment for movie stardom came at the beginning of his first film, "National Lampoon's Animal House" (1977), in the role of John "Bluto" Blutarsky, the campus pig who majored in food fights and toga parties.

In the middle of a fraternity rush party, a drunken Bluto takes a guitar from the hands of a wimpy classmate who is singing an insipid song about giving his

● Belushi's death shocks the Chicago area, where the comic star grew up and still had close relatives and friends. Page 4.

true love a flower. After listening to the sugarplum music, Bluto fixes the singer with an arched eyebrow, grabs the guitar, and smashes it against the fraternity house wall. Audiences went wild, and "Animal House" became what was then the top-grossing comedy of all time.

THAT WAS Bluto. That was Mr. Belushi, a marvelous physical comedian who appeared to be on a lifelong mission to wreck everything that smacked of pretense and pomposity.

"I hate to admit it," Mr. Belushi said in a Tribune interview at his New York

Coming Sunday

● A report on the life and death of actor-comedian John Belushi will be in the Sunday Chicago Tribune.

home last August, "but it's true. I am Bluto."

In addition to Bluto, Mr. Belushi's stardom derived from his TV appearances on "Saturday Night Live" in such characters as a Samurai warrior, a killer bee and a violent TV news commentator.

He was a member of the first "Saturday Night Live" cast in 1975 and one of the original "Not Ready for Prime Time Players," along with Dan Aykroyd, Garret Morris, Chevy Chase, Jane Curtin, Laraine Newman, and Gilda Radner.

HE WAS the show's top physical comedian, with his partner Dan Aykroyd handling the more cerebral material. Mr. Belushi was the one who did a spastic impersonation of rock singer Joe Cocker. And as the show's hysterical news commentator, he added a phrase to a generation's lexicon: "But nooooo."

Along with Aykroyd he invented the characters known as the Blues Brothers, a soul-singing duo who wore black suits, black hats, and black sunglasses. Aykroyd was the blues freak who turned Mr. Belushi on to the music that was born in part in Chicago.

MR. BELUSHI was born in Chicago on Jan. 24, 1949, the child of Albanian immigrants.

Growing up in Wheaton, he exhibited

Continued on page 4, col. 1

John Belushi, who starred on television and in movies, dead at 33.

Versatile star, 33, may have had heart attack

Chicago Tribune Press Service

ACTOR JOHN BELUSHI, who went from Chicago's Second City to television and movie stardom, died in a Los Angeles hotel Friday, apparently of natural causes. He was 33.

The comedian, who became a national hit on TV's original "Saturday Night Live" and in the movie "Animal House," died in a bungalow he had rented at the Chateau Marmont hotel along Hollywood's Sunset Strip.

Lt. Dan Cooke of the Los Angeles Police Department said a heart attack was a possible cause of death. He said an autopsy would be performed, probably this weekend. A security guard at the hotel said it appeared that Mr. Belushi had choked on some food.

"IT APPEARS to be death by natural causes," Cooke said. "The detectives

● Full page of photos on the actor's career on page 10.

here found nothing to make it seem suspicious."

Cooke said one of Mr. Belushi's friends, later identified as his physical trainer, William Wallace, found the comedian's nude body at 12:15 p.m. on a bed in the bungalow. Wallace, who often traveled with the comedian and actor during filming, trained Mr. Belushi for some of the scenes he did in the film "Continental Divide."

Mr. Belushi appeared to have been dead for two or three hours when Wallace arrived, Cooke said.

"He tried to administer mouth-to-mouth resuscitation, and the paramedics were called," Cooke said.

This story is based on Tribune reports from Aaron Gold and Andy Knott in Chicago and Ronald Yates in California. It was written by Sallie Gaines.

A WOMAN who arrived at the bungalow while authorities were there was handcuffed and taken to a police station for questioning. Police, who did not identify the woman, said she was a potential witness and the handcuffs were just standard procedure.

Reliable sources identified the woman as Wallace's wife, Smoky. She arrived in Mr. Belushi's car, which may have prompted the police action, the sources said. Mrs. Wallace did not know when she arrived that Mr. Belushi was dead, sources said.

Homicide detective Tony Diaz said the woman may have been the last person to see Mr. Belushi alive and, when he became ill, left to get help.

Mr. Belushi, who lived in New York with his wife, Judith, checked into the hotel last Sunday. He was in Los Angeles to make a movie.

BRUCE BECKLER, a hotel gardener and day security guard, said he went into the bungalow with Wallace and saw Mr. Belushi lying on the bed with his head on a pillow, as if he had been sleeping. Beckler said he also tried to resuscitate Mr. Belushi, but he appeared to have choked on food and had swallowed his tongue.

"I've never closed somebody's eyes before

Continued on page 4, col. 1

On Friday March 5, 1982, John Belushi was found dead in his bungalow at the Chateau Marmont Hotel in Los Angeles, California. He was thirty-three years old. John was scheduled to have a meeting at ten o'clock that morning with Michael Eisner and Jeffrey Katzenberg at Paramount. He was late and had not been answering his phone.

After Bill Wallace discovered the body at noon, the police and the LA county coroner rushed to the scene. At 12:45 PM, John was officially pronounced dead. The national media quickly descended into a frenzy. Initial rumors circulating on radio and television indicated that the cause of death was possibly a heart attack or the result of choking on food. Lieutenant Dan Cooke, the officer at the scene, told reporters, "It appears to be death by natural causes. The detectives here found nothing to make it seem suspicious." In fact, the only truly suspicious incident that occurred that afternoon was that a woman arrived at the bungalow shortly after the police and paramedics. She was driving John's car. The woman was handcuffed as a precaution, taken in for questioning and then released within a few hours. Early reports in the press identified her as possibly being Wallace's girlfriend; those reports were erroneous.

JUDITH BELUSHI PISANO:

I woke up and wasn't feeling well; I'd had a series of throat problems and was lying on the couch upstairs in our living room, trying to take it easy and trying to figure what to do about John. When he returned to LA I had felt pretty defeated and uncertain about our prospects, but our last conversation had given me a renewed hope. I had to find new ground in terms of how to deal with John's drug abuse. I knew he could do it, stay straight, but I also knew the problem was bigger than the both of us. I was basically exhausted and didn't know what to do, but I believed in him and believed we would find a solution.

BERNIE BRILLSTEIN:

I'd been trying to reach John all morning about his meeting. There was no answer, but that was typical John. About noon I got a call from Bill Wallace. He sounded crazed. John was having trouble breathing, and he couldn't wake him up. I told Bill that I was sending someone right away; then I had my secretary call the paramedics, and I left for the hospital as fast as I could.

It was only ten minutes from my office to the emergency room at Cedars-Sinai. I drove up, left my car out front, ran in and found a nurse. "Look," I said, "John Belushi is going to be coming in here in a minute. I'm his manager. He's had an accident, and I want to keep it quiet." I paced around, found a bank of phone booths and called my office. There wasn't any news. I gave them the pay phone number to reach me.

I went over to the sliding door, stood halfway in and halfway out and had a cigarette. I was watching for the ambulance and listening for the phone. I finished that cigarette and lit another, pacing and wondering, where the fuck are they? Finally the phone rang. I ran over and grabbed it and it was my assistant, Fran. "Bernie?" she said. And as soon as she said my name, I knew it wasn't okay. When she told me, I actually dropped the phone. I just stood there and then slumped against the wall of the phone booth. Finally I picked it back up, told her I'd be back at the office soon and hung up. Then I called Danny in New York. I was very matter of fact. I said, "Danny, sit down. We don't have time for you to overreact. John is dead. You have to leave the office *now*. Go straight to Judy's house so she doesn't hear it on the radio. You've got to tell her."

"Yes." That was all he said. Then he hung up the phone.

DAN AYKROYD:

It was a beautiful day in New York, one of those spectacular March afternoons, and the streets were full of people out enjoying the first warm weather of the year. The whole time I was walking from Fifth Avenue down to Morton Street I just kept thinking, *I've got to keep walking. I can't get in a cab. I have to keep walking.* I knew if I stopped for a second I would lose it, so I just kept going and going down Fifth and across the Village, trying to get there before Judy heard it from anyone else. I got to their apartment and let myself in. Judy was upstairs in the living room. I ran up the stairs taking three at a time. As soon

as she saw me, she knew something was wrong. I said, "I don't know how to tell you this…"

"Danny, what is it?" I couldn't get the words out. She started to panic. "What is it? Has John been hurt?"

"No, honey. He's dead."

JUDITH BELUSHI PISANO:

Danny was as gentle as he could be, and yet the force of the words pushed me back, knocked me down and literally threw me across the room. He started going on about the details. I could hear him talking, but it was nonsense. Time stopped, emotions disappeared and I was in another dimension, weightless, empty. I remember rolling across the floor, and then later I was sitting in a chair, motionless. Maybe if I didn't move, it wouldn't be real. A few minutes later, Michael Klenfner burst into the room, ran toward me, dropped to his knees and began sobbing. That shook my suspension, brought me back to earth. John was dead.

RHONDA COULLET:

One of the greatest things John gave us, those of us who were a part of his life, was his outrageous sense of the absurd. I was at the house with Judy that day. Chaos was swirling all around—the phone ringing off the hook, people coming and going, the coroner on TV, cops and reporters just everywhere— and in the middle of all of it she looked up at me with tears streaming down her face and said, "I should have killed him myself. He always left a mess."

JOHN LANDIS:

I was at my office at Universal, and I got a call from Danny. I called Sean Daniel and said, "Meet me in John's office. Now." We immediately went over there and did a huge search to make sure there were no drugs or anything personal or incriminating. There wasn't.

TOM DAVIS:

I was up at Broadway Video playing pool with Al Franken. Joe Forestal came in and said, "Did you hear the news?"

"What news?"

"Belushi OD'd."

"Is he going to be okay?"

"No, he's dead."

And it was one of those strange moments when everything familiar seems strange and unfamiliar all of a sudden. It was like walking through a dream. Then we went over to the television set, and they were showing the shrouded body coming out of the back of the Chateau Marmont, and there was no doubt about it.

RICHARD BELZER:

I was filming *Night Shift* out in LA. They found John in the morning, and everybody on the set knew, but no one told me the whole day because they knew he was my friend. Finally someone told my wife, Harlee, and she came into my dressing room, sat down and said, "I have to tell you something." I just lost it. I was numb for about a month.

DICK BLASUCCI:

I was in this little writers' room at *SCTV* with Andrea Martin and Paul Flaherty. Rick Moranis opened the door and said, "Belushi's dead." Nobody believed him. "I'm not kidding you," he said. "Belushi's dead." I just wandered out into the hallway. Candy was beside himself.

CARRIE FISHER:

We were all sitting there waiting to find out what killed him and hoping it wasn't our drug of choice.

TIM MATHESON:

You could sort of see it coming, but it was also a big surprise, because you just thought he was bulletproof. You thought nothing could stop him.

EUGENIE ROSS-LEMING:

Performing with John onstage I'd watched him throw himself headlong into floors and walls. Sometimes it's easier to hit yourself with a two-by-four for a laugh than to deal with other things. In the end, oddly enough, John was a lot more fragile than the rest of us.

JOYCE SLOANE:

It was like a fortress at Second City with the cameras and the reporters. Of course, we didn't let anyone in the theater. I had this young touring company out on the road. I called them immediately and said, "You don't talk to anybody. You don't make any statements." Jim was in *Pirates of Penzance*

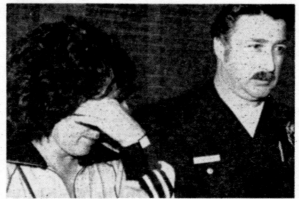

Film and stage star John Belushi dies at 33

Continued from Page 1

Mr. Belushi's nude body before paramedics arrived, said: "When we got to him I could tell he had been left alone a little too long. He was just such a heavy man and his heart evidently failed on him. There was no evidence of anything else."

Beckler tried to revive the actor with mouth-to-mouth resuscitation and said Mr. Belushi apparently had swallowed his tongue.

Mr. Belushi was found at a bungalow behind the Chateau Marmont Hotel, above Sunset Strip, at about 2:15 p.m. (Chicago time) Friday by William Wallace, his physical therapist.

Paramedics pronounced Mr. Belushi dead at the scene and said he had apparently been dead several hours.

ASSISTANT Hotel Manager Thom Rafter said room service made a delivery to Mr. Belushi's bungalow about 8 a.m. The check was signed by an unidentified woman, apparently the last person to see Mr. Belushi alive.

During an hour of questioning, the woman told police that when she woke Mr. Belushi at about 8 a.m., "he was breathing with difficulty from some nasal congestion," Cooke said. "She asked him if he was all right and he said yes. She gave him a glass of water and he went back to sleep."

"She went into the living room, and assuming he was asleep, she went out about an hour later," said Cooke. When the woman returned at 2:15 p.m. in Belushi's Mercedes-Benz, she was met by detectives.

The woman later was released by police.

The whereabouts of the actor's wife, high school sweetheart Judith Jacklin, was not immediately known.

Beckler said the hotel's staff became con-

AN UNIDENTIFIED WOMAN is escorted from a Los Angeles police station Friday after being questioned concerning the death of actor and comedian John Belushi. (AP)

cerned about Mr. Belushi Friday morning when he did not answer his phone.

"We knew he was in the room because he always checked with the desk on his way out," the security guard said. Asked to check the room, he said he found Mr. Belushi's physical therapist already there. "I asked, 'Is Mr. Belushi OK?' He said, 'No, he's dead.' We immediately called the paramedics."

The Chateau Marmont is a legendary Hollywood hotel much used by actors, writers and

musicians. Mr. Belushi checked in last Sunday to work on a new movie, "Noble Rot," for Paramount. His permanent homes were an apartment in New York's Greenwich Village and a bungalow on Martha's Vineyard, Mass.

In Chicago, the actor's younger brother, James, 27, learned of the death on arriving at the Shubert Theater, where he plays the leading role in the musical "The Pirates of Penzance." After the evening show, the younger Belushi said, "We're going to miss him."

The people of Chicago are going to miss him."

John Belushi was the star of two of the most popular film comedies in recent years, "National Lampoon's Animal House" (1978) and "The Blues Brothers" (1980).

He returned to Chicago to film "The Blues Brothers" on location and also filmed much of "Continental Divide" (1981) here. His last film was "Neighbors," released last Christmas. "Neighbors" and "The Blues Brothers" co-starred Dan Aykroyd, a fellow cast member on "Saturday Night Live" who was Mr. Belushi's best friend.

In "Continental Divide," Mr. Belushi played a Chicago newspaper columnist inspired by Sun-Times columnist Mike Royko.

LEARNING OF the death, Royko said, "We were friends. I'm shocked, dismayed and horrified." Royko said he and Mr. Belushi's father and uncle were friends from the days 30 years ago "when the family was running a short-order diner exactly like the one on 'Saturday Night Live.' I met John when he was a little boy."

Royko said he and Mr. Belushi discussed the role of the newspaper columnist several years before the movie was made. "The night of the Chicago premiere, we partied together at John's bar. That was the last time I saw him."

The bar was opened by Mr. Belushi and Aykroyd when they were filming "The Blues Brothers" here. Known as the Sneak Joint or the Blues Bar, it was in an obscure building down a gangway directly across the street from Second City, at North and Wells.

In the Blues Bar hideaway and on movie locations, Mr. Belushi gained a reputation as an ebullient character whose idea of a good

Turn to Page 35

I named my production company Black Rhino after a dream I had. There was a big rhino with John's face chained up in my backyard, way up north in Canada. I took it as a symbol. It was saying, "You're gonna have this guy in your backyard, in your life, for a long time." And also it meant, you know, that John was like a black rhino. He was gonna be good for a ride. And he was. We all took a ride with him. Like tick birds on a rhino. He took us where we'd never been before.

—Dan Aykroyd

at that time, and we took a lead from him. We felt if he could do a performance, we should too. We felt that's what John would have wanted. After the show I went down to be with Jim.

JIM BELUSHI:

I was in the middle of a voice lesson onstage in the Schubert Theater in Chicago. The box office person came backstage and said, "They're saying crazy shit about your brother on the radio." I thought it was some Paul McCartney joke like "Paul's dead," some publicity stunt. I called the radio station, and the guy read me the AP wire he'd received. Three hours later I had a black armband on, and I was back onstage singing the Pirate King in front of twelve hundred people.

After the show there was a press conference in the lobby. I walked out to answer questions. There must have been fifty people there with cameras, video cameras, tape recorders and notepads. I sat down on the ledge of the staircase. I just sat there for at least two minutes, and nobody said a word. I finally said, "Are there any questions?"

Roger Ebert stood up and said, "I'm terribly sorry for your loss." Then it got quiet again, and then I got a smattering of questions about our age difference and where we grew up. They were all softballs. At the time, nobody knew it was a drug overdose, and so the press was still being courteous. That didn't last.

BUCK HENRY:

I'd been in show business all my life, and it still didn't occur to me that anyone could command as much attention as he did. I was just stunned. Nothing was quite as big as Elvis, but it was pretty damn big.

BERNIE BRILLSTEIN:

Roone Arlidge from ABC was the first call I got. He wanted me to do *Nightline* and talk about John. I said, "Are you out of your fucking mind?" It was terrible. You lose a best friend, and you're in the middle of this shit storm.

AL FRANKEN:

The night he died, *Nightline* had Milton Berle on. I was like, "What the fuck?" Milton Berle had done a show with us, one horrible show with us, years before. On the one hand, God bless Milton Berle. But on the other hand, it was really inappropriate that he would come on to speak. It made no sense at all.

ALICE PLAYTEN:

John loved collecting things from places he'd been, like getting a special hat from some guy he worked with. And as I watched his body being taken away by those guys in the jumpsuits that said "LA Coroner," the first thing that I thought—after the shock and sadness—was that if John had been there, alive, he *really* would have wanted one of those jumpsuits. He'd have said to the guy, "Hey, man, can I get one of those?" And the guy would have given it to him, and John would have thought that was really cool.

JOHN LANDIS:

My first reaction to John's death was anger. I was furious with him, just furious, because it meant I didn't get to see him anymore, and how could he do that to me?

TIM KAZURINSKY:

The anger is what got me through the first six months. That's pretty much how everybody felt; we'd all get together and

Death is the slamming of the door in your face, and the sound of bolting on the inside.

C.S. Lewis

Movies Roger Ebert

It was just a year ago, on March 5, that John Belushi went to his last party. According to the fragmented reconstructions of his last night on earth, it began as pretty much a routine evening, for Belushi, of drinking and rock clubs and palling around the Sunset Strip and, at some point in the evening, making a drug connection that would be blamed as the cause of death.

The images from a year ago still are fresh in the memories of those who loved Belushi: The faded Hollywood glory of the Chateau Marmont residential hotel, where his body was found; the pasty-faced "unidentified

woman" being led away in handcuffs by police; his best friend, Dan Aykroyd, dressed in a Chicago cop uniform, leading the funeral procession on a motorcycle. Soon the flowers of a second spring will bloom near John Belushi's grave.

Hardly a week goes by without a reminder of Joh death. He's there on the TV every weekend, on the retu of "Saturday Night Live." A poster from his mo "Continental Divide" hangs in my office. That one where he played a Chicago newspa on the

Arts & Entertainment

A SORELY MISSED FRIEND

one of the great friendships

decade, if not the century'

Chicago Tribune, 1981

ENE SISKEL

"Have you heard the ke?" asked Dan Aykroyd down to join him for he went off to shoot a

between us. I can't think of any argument that ever lasted for more than 24 hours.

"It was one of the great friendships of the decade, if not the century," Aykroyd said with a big smile, "and it will go down as such. I think

John Belushi: Chicagoan
1949-1982

Sunday Sun-Times, March 7, 1982

Actor Jim Belushi talks about his brother, John, at Shubert Theater here, where Jim appears in "The Pirates of Penzance."

IDENTIFIED only as a friend of John Belushi, a woman is escorted from a Los Angeles police station after questioning. (AP)

March fifth, a little bit of all of us "war babies," who are t ber radio but never knew lif knew it was time to take tha plus fatigue jacket and put it

In a 1972 "official" autob Second City, Belushi stated th was to play pro football. He sa ing an actor but that his se

Belushi's full talents
were just emerging

By Roger Ebert
Sun-Times Film Critic

John Belushi's kid brother Jim stood in the lobby of the Shubert Theater late Friday and let a cigarette burn down between his fingers

56

Belushi a tough k

HARDLY KNEW YOU

was in town, and his friends, or those who thought ...mselves as his friends, dropped in to have a drink ...John.

...loved to play host. For some rea...... ...to be the...

in the life-and-death things, and maybe it was no accident ...went out W... that he seemed to get into more trouble wh... around. That...

The Washington Post STYLE

The A...

March 6, 1982

The Comet Named Belushi Fall:

By Tom Shales

"I guess I want everything," John Belushi once said. But lives lived to excess, lives virtually devoted to it, sometimes end early. John Belushi's did, yesterday. He was 33 and by all accounts, his appetites were still de... ...tly enormous. He was not easily ...in con-

prietor of a greasy Greek diner (where Belushi introduced, among other catch phrases, the cry of "Chee-burger, chee-burger" and the wilting "No Coke, Pepsi"), and the ultimate on... con... era... him...

"Saturday Night Live," when, following the completion of the broadcast and the more-or-less official cast party at one New York bar or anoth... ...Belu...

Night Live"—in the early days people couldn't believe anythi... funny and irreverent would b... ...written...

ARIETY

Wednesday, March 10, 19...

...mic John Belushi, 33, Dies In H'wood Of Unknown Causes

Hollywood, March 9.
...se of death is still undeter- ...for John Belushi, manic ...an whose body was found ...riday (5) afternoon at the ...u Marmont Hotel i... ...ood.

...topsy prove ...s Angeles C ...T. Noguchi ...public spec ...stigations, lin ...the informat ...death has no ...l," and tha ...ormation wil ...her medical ...have been co... ..., 33-year-old ...to fame on th ...turday Night ...such films a ...s Animal H ...s Brothers," h ...per-day bung ...28 and reporte ...e script for a F ...ly a...

On Friday, police briefly took into custody an unnamed woman who admitted that she had signed for room service breakfast at about 9 a.m. and that...

The friends you remember
My Belushi pals

Mike Royko

Like so many Chicagoans, last Thursday night I was watching a rerun of the original "Saturday Night Live" show.

I was rewarded when John Belushi came on to do one of his outrageous skits.

As happened whenever I saw John perform, I felt

★★★ 17

NEW YORK POST, MONDAY, MARCH 8, 1982

NEW YORK POST On the Town
BELUSHI: FINAL GASP OF DYING ERA

By STEPHEN M. SILVERMAN
PART I OF A SERIES ON A ZANY STAR

pressed and America had a new star.
The debut of *Saturday Night Live* coincided ...tion ...the

...er.
...said "chizboog ...hn later did. Hi ...eek. But it wa ...r neighborhood. ...n Belushi was s ...rill. Everybody ...rican dream. A ...rants have alw ...never mind ho ...ur arms.

...e'd probably w ...my attic flat, ...he things we ...t that weekly ...d Adam coul ...to the restaura

...e night a few ...opened. Adam ...ace had thick c ...ngs, a piano pl ...I've ever had. ...on Dempster. ...xican restaura ...It was a lon ...and they had ...Before long

Sunday Sun-Times, March 7, 1982

th marshmallow center

talk about how pissed off we were, and that's how we coped. The day that the news broke, I saw this one old lady at a newsstand. She had to be about seventy years old. She was buying a paper with the headline about John on it, and she said to the newsman, "Goddamn him! I really liked him, and I'm just so mad at him!" I had to laugh.

JUDITH BELUSHI PISANO:

The summer before, John and I had driven past the Chilmark cemetery near our house on Martha's Vineyard. I said that I would like to be buried there. John turned to me and smiled. "Nah, I think I want a Viking funeral."

He'd said it half jokingly, but it seemed like something to go on. Then John's mother called. She was very sweet and very loving. She said, "Judy, whatever arrangements you make, they'll be fine with me."

"Thank you, Agnes."

"Have you made any plans yet?"

"Well, John had said he wanted to have a Viking funeral."

"That's fine, dear. That'll be fine. What is a Viking funeral?"

"That's where they put the corpse on a boat and set it on fire in the ocean."

"*What?! He'll go straight to hell!*"

Apparently, you can't be cremated in the Albanian Orthodox religion. So I agreed we'd have a traditional service, like the one they'd had for John's grandmother, Nena. There was never any question about where we would have it.

DAN AYKROYD:

The Vineyard was the only place John ever slept well.

SMOKEY:

I got a call from Judy's sister, Pam. She said Judy wanted me to come to New York and help handle all the funeral arrangements and deal with the security for Martha's Vineyard. That was a fiasco. There were so many people coming into that little airport, all these jets. I had to deal with the local police, the state troopers, the fire department. It was the off-season, so the whole island was understaffed.

JOYCE SLOANE:

By the time we made it to Martha's Vineyard, the press had already rented every single car on the island. So I went around to some of the people who worked at the airport, the locals, and they were nice enough to let us borrow their cars.

MICHAEL KLENFNER:

Judy's family didn't quite know what to do to get the body back to the East Coast. I called Ahmet Ertegun at Atlantic Records, and he was able to get one of Warner Brothers' corporate jets for us; otherwise the body would have been flown in the cargo hold of some United Airlines 707. If he'd had to go through Boston and be driven down to take the ferry, it would have been a complete circus.

BERNIE BRILLSTEIN:

Two days after John died I flew with his body back east. The plane was a small seven-seater, too small to put a coffin in the cargo hold, so they put John's body in a canvas body bag and laid it out across two seats. I sat in the row next to him and we took off. If it had been a movie, where people always talk to dead bodies, I probably would have given one of those stupid "How could you do this?" speeches. But it wasn't, so I just did my best to try and sleep. It was the worst seven and a half hours of my life.

MITCH GLAZER:

Danny, Klenfner and I were waiting on the tarmac. It was freezing that night, just bitter cold. The plane engines were screaming in our ears, and it was pitch black except for the red strobe lights on the runway. The jet taxied over, and they took John's body off. He wasn't in a coffin, and as they wheeled him over to the hearse on the gurney, the wind was whipping the body bag around so hard I was afraid somehow it would blow right off. Finally somebody grabbed it and held it fast. Bernie looked exhausted.

LAILA NABULSI:

It was very strange, all of us gathering at Judy's house and then driving up to the Vineyard together. Everybody was there. It was like this big party was happening. It was the same party

The whole thing was like a Bergman film, just a very gray experience. John was so colorful and so unpredictable, and we were there to do a very predictable thing.

—Rhonda Coullet

we'd all been going to all those years with all the same people, only one person was missing, and we were going to meet him.

SMOKEY:

The press was all over the ferry, because it was the last one out to the island that day. They're gonna know who you are when you're the only limo on a ferry full of old cars and pickup trucks. So I got out and I asked them to please respect her privacy, which they did. Judy got out. We got some coffee. Some total strangers came over and offered their condolences.

HAROLD RAMIS:

It was spring, but there was a freakish cold snap and a heavy snowstorm was looming, so the island was very bleak. It was an odd mix of people: the folks from the early days, the Hollywood friends, the hangers-on, the people who were just there to be seen—and an army of press, both on the ground and circling in helicopters above.

JIM BELUSHI:

My family, when it comes to mourning, gets pretty hysterical. We have all these aunts and uncles from the old country. They're really into keening, screaming and moaning, all that stuff you see in *Zorba the Greek*. So now I was the head of the family, which I was not prepared for. I had to be the one to keep things under control. I knew there was going to be a ton of press at the funeral, which worried me. So I brought a bunch of 10mg Valiums with me, just in case anyone got too out there.

At the funeral home, during the private showing of John for the family, my aunt started screaming, "*Oh Johnny! Oh Johnny!*" and threw herself onto his body in the casket. After I managed to pull her away from the coffin, I slipped a Valium into her mouth and sat her down. *That* wasn't going to happen again. Her fit had messed up John's hair. With great care, Judy combed it. We stood there looking at John, silent for a long time, kind of taking in the fact that he was gone. Then Judy smiled slightly,

as if finding something good in all this, and said, "I'm so glad I never gave him a hard time about smoking."

LAILA NABULSI:

It was very, very intense in the church, because, for one thing, there was a lot of incense. You also couldn't understand what the priests were saying, because the ceremony was in Albanian. And it was an open casket. They had an icon propped up in the casket, and you had to go up single file and either kiss the icon or kiss the body.

ANNE BEATTS:

When Lorne saw John in his coffin, he said, "I've seen him look worse." And it was true. We had. You just always thought he would bounce back.

LORNE MICHAELS:

He looked good. I was terrified of the open casket. We were all filing past, and I thought I was going to lose it. But then when I saw him, my thought was, oh, Judy dressed him. He was in his high-tops and his tweed jacket; she didn't put him in some navy suit. She'd taken great care to give him his own style and his dignity.

DAN AYKROYD:

I touched his forehead and it was like marble. But he looked great. He looked good in his army pants. I slipped some cigarettes and a couple hundred-dollar bills into his pocket. And of course, Agnes did not disappoint. She got to the front of the church and threw herself on the coffin.

JUDITH BELUSHI PISANO:

It was very strange, first of all, just having this Eastern Orthodox ceremony in a New England Congregational church. On top of that, you had a bunch of Hollywood celebrities sharing the pews with John's relatives, all these

tiny Mediterranean women covered head to toe in black, sobbing and wailing. The whole service was dreamlike, and yet I found it comforting.

JIM BELUSHI:

Judy was very thoughtful and understanding of the world she was in. There's a tradition that a crucifix is placed in the coffin, and when they close it they take the crucifix and give it to the wife. When they gave it to Judy, she turned and gave it to my mother.

LAILA NABULSI:

At one point, I felt this strange sensation. I turned around, and I swear to God I saw John standing there at the back door of the church, just like he always did, with the eyebrow up that said, "C'mon, time to go."

DAN AYKROYD:

After the service I led the cortège over to the Abel's Hill cemetery. That's where they bury all the whalers, the Indians,

the smugglers and the pirates, so it was a good place for John. I was on my bike, and the hearse, the Bluesmobile and all the family cars were behind me. I gunned the engine as loud as I could the whole way, just in case John could hear me.

HAROLD RAMIS:

Judy had asked me to speak, and with this huge crowd I didn't want to shout some long speech, especially with the helicopters whirring overhead. So I just told the story of John when he played an angel at Second City, how he wore the little cardboard wings and could make everyone laugh by making them flap when he walked across the stage. I thought it was funny and would be a nice image of John to leave people with. James Taylor and his sister Kate sang "That Lonesome Road," this beautiful traditional song. We put John in the ground just as it began to snow. As we were

---

Above (from top left): Dan Aykroyd, Billy Belushi, Steve Beshekas, Tino Insana, and Jim Belushi; Judy and Smokey; Rhonda Coullet; leading the funeral procession; Lorne Michaels; Jim, Agnes and Adam Belushi

walking away from the grave, some reporter ran up to me and yelled, "Howard! Howard! Who's that guy who just sang?"

BERNIE BRILLSTEIN:

After the funeral, if you wanted to leave the island you had to do it in a hurry, because the snowstorm was picking up. Lorne had some planes arranged for us.

I drove to this private airstrip with a couple of executives from a record label. Passing the cemetery where we'd just buried John, in the backseat of the car, they were doing lines of cocaine.

DAN AYKROYD:

I didn't go to the reception after. I went home. The house was completely empty, and I was all by myself. The clouds were low, and the snow was coming down heavy now, big, fat, white powdery flakes of it. That's when I really broke down for the first time. I just fell to my knees and wept.

JAMES TAYLOR:

It was a tragedy and a waste. The thing that resulted in John's death is something that happened to me in my life I can't remember how many times. There but for the grace of God or some other such easy phrase. As strong as my life is now, and as far as I've come from that sort of thing, I can easily see that John could have come through and survived in the same way. I think of it like an automobile wreck on the highway. It didn't have to happen, but it did.

SMOKEY:

Later that night, after everything was winding down from the funeral, we went back to the house. It was Bill Murray, me, Danny, Jimmy and Judy. We were all sitting there, and Danny said to me, "Smokey, you okay?"

"Not really. When Judy called me, given the time difference, I could have been out there that same day, and I just feel like I let John down by not going when I knew I should have."

Above: Bill Murray

Billy sat me down and said, "Listen, Smokey, if you'd gotten on that plane you could have been in the air going from east coast to west, and it could have happened then. You could have been in the cab on your way to the Chateau, and it could have happened then. You could have been coming up in the elevator, and it could have happened then. And there's nothing you could have done about it. Don't think for a second that John isn't here because of you. John isn't here because of John."

DAN AYKROYD:

He was his own man. He was the captain of his own ship, and he made his own choices. But he needed me, and I didn't get to him in time. And I carry that with me to this day. It's just something that he and I are going to have to settle in the next dimension. I know that he's going to be the first person waiting for me when I cross over, and, when I do, he and I are going to sit down and sort that out.

CARRIE FISHER:

We were up on Martha's Vineyard one weekend, me, John, Judy and Danny. And I remember John and I were outside that night, and he said, "You and I are alike, Fisher. We're addicts. *I'm an addict!*" He was stripped to the waist, yelling, almost howling at the moon. But he wasn't just talking about drugs. He was talking about life, about everything.

PETER RIEGERT:

You read these biographies of famous people, you string twenty of them together and eventually they all say the same thing. Because to have that kind of success you have to have some demented idea that you're Christopher Columbus. That the world isn't flat, and you're gonna find the route to the East Indies. And you have to have a deep, deep well of need to overcome the obstacles that stand in your way, even to make a living, let alone succeed. And some people have a well of need that's so deep it can never be filled. It can't be filled by your spouse, your parents, your friends, the business. But it drives you; it enables you to survive all the rejection and crap you have to go through. The amazing thing, and the thing that's different about John, was that his generosity belied whatever his need was. He was just a warm, generous guy, and that's rare. And that's why we all remember him so fondly.

ALAN ZWEIBEL:

When I saw John again that year, I thought, "Great! John's fat again. He must not be doing cocaine anymore." What did I know? For all the trouble we'd seen John go through, the idea of anything terrible actually happening to him had never occurred to us. To any of us. That's the thing about a clown. When he falls down, he's going to get back up.

MITCH GLAZER:

He called it the spin cycle. He knew what it was. He'd be fine until something came along and triggered it, and then he'd go out again. Maybe it was the rejection of *Noble Rot*, maybe simple inactivity, maybe a lethal boredom. Whatever it was, it was always a cycle he expected to survive.

DAVE THOMAS:

He fucked up. John was moody and he was self-destructive, but as bad as it would get, he always believed he would rise up and live to fight another day. He was supposed to come up and do some sketches as a guest star on *SCTV* that very next week. We'd been talking about it on the phone, and he was excited about it, really up for it. There were two parts that he wanted to play, and I think his choices speak volumes about his state of mind at the time. One of the characters he wanted to play was himself, as a former circus geek who'd hit the big time but whose career had been so destroyed by the Hollywood studios that he'd been forced back into the circus to bite the heads off of chickens. The other was Napoleon. ■

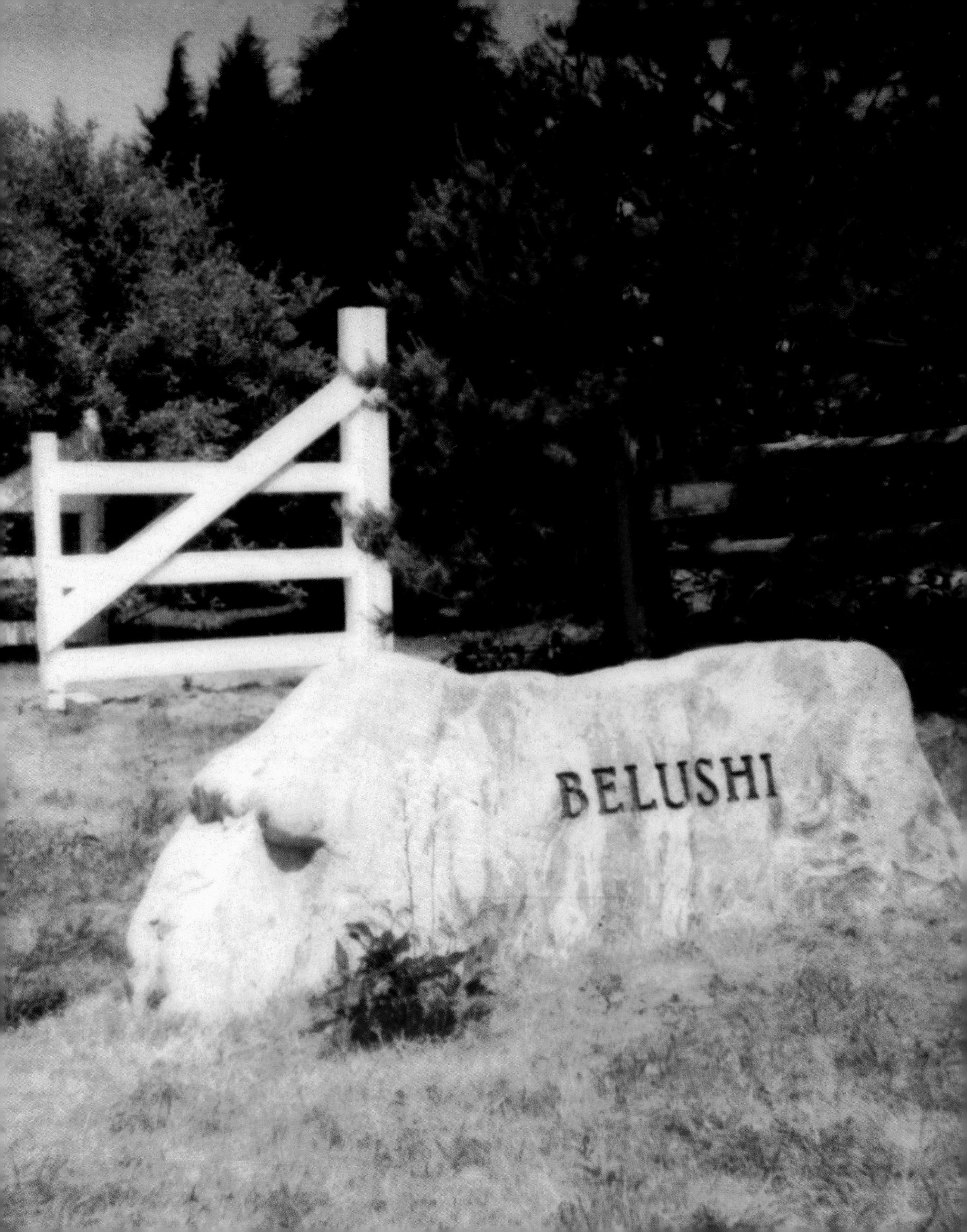
BELUSHI

EPILOGUE

viking funeral

On March 10, 1982, the Wednesday following John's funeral, the Los Angeles coroner's office held a press conference announcing that he had died from a lethal injection of cocaine and heroin. Less than five minutes after a perfunctory phone call to Bernie Brillstein, coroner Thomas Nagouchi was standing before reporters. Both Judy and John's family learned the news along with the rest of America, on television.

Subsequent investigations revealed that, for the week he'd been back in Los Angeles, John had spent most of his time in the company of a few hangers-on and Cathy Evelyn Smith—the woman driving his car at the Chateau Marmont that day, and a known heroin dealer.

Removed as they were, John's parents and extended family were largely unaware of his drug problems and still believed that his death had been from natural causes. After the grief of burying him on Martha's Vineyard, hearing the news of the overdose was akin to watching him die all over again. Even for those who knew John's history all too well, the news that heroin was involved was shocking. None of them had witnessed him using it on any occasion. With so many questions left unanswered at the time, conspiracy theories abounded; none were ever proven. Today, the extent to which John did or did not use heroin outside of those final days remains an open question, and largely an academic one.

On the one-year anniversary of John's death, Judy drove down to a beach known as Dog Fish Bar near the Gay Head cliffs of Martha's Vineyard. Joining her were her siblings Pat and Rob, friends Mike and Carol Klenfner, Kate and Huey Taylor, Laila Nabulsi and Walter Wlodkya, a local lobster fisherman. Together, they unloaded onto the beach a small dinghy that, as of that morning, had been rechristened the Black Hole, after one of John's many nicknames.

Lashed to the bow of the craft, in lieu of a mermaid, was a pink lawn flamingo once given to John by his brother-in-law. Flanking the bird were two small Albanian national flags. The boat had been outfitted with a square-rigged sail, and in its center was a large bale of hay, doused with kerosene. Onto the bale of hay the congregation ceremoniously placed a scrapbook that Judy had made for John's twenty-ninth birthday, a pack of cigarettes, a flower, a cross, a necklace, a guitar pick, a blues harp, a microphone and an unpaid IOU, from John, made out to Bill Murray.

At sunset, Walter tied the Black Hole to his fishing boat with a length of rope and rowed out from the beach in the falling tide. Once a safe distance away, he took a torch fashioned from old T-shirts, set the ship ablaze and cut it loose. The small band of friends sat on the beach, bracing themselves against the cold ocean air with Jack Daniels whiskey and watching the ship as it slowly drifted away. Twenty minutes later, leaving only a skyward trail of black smoke, it disappeared over the horizon and out to sea.

The following year, in the summer of 1984, Danny's Ghostbusters was released. It was directed by National Lampoon Show producer Ivan Reitman. Rounding out the team of paranormal exterminators with Danny were Harold Ramis as Dr. Egon Spengler and Bill Murray as Dr. Peter Venkman, the role originally created for John. In a matter of months, the blockbuster film pulled in over $238 million, easily surpassing Animal House and setting a new record as the highest-grossing comedy of its time.

On September 2, 1986, following a grand jury indictment and a lengthy extradition from her native Canada, Cathy Evelyn Smith pleaded no contest to charges of involuntary manslaughter and three counts of furnishing and administering illegal drugs. John's death had initially been ruled an accident, but the Belushi estate had for some time been petitioning the district attorney's office to open a criminal investigation. Instrumental in launching the inquiry was the confession of Smith herself, which she had sold to the National Enquirer. In the article, she admitted to selling John drugs, as well as injecting him with the fatal overdose, saying quite plainly, "I killed John Belushi." She was paid $15,000 for her story, and was sentenced to three years in prison.

Not long after John's death, Judy moved permanently to a new home on Martha's Vineyard. On October 7, 1990, she married writer/producer Victor Pisano, becoming a stepmother to three young girls. The following year, she gave birth to a son, Luke.

DAN AYKROYD:

It's strange how things work. The morning after we buried John on Martha's Vineyard, I was on the Concorde winging my way over to London. I was going to see a man I had never met. And I believe, I honestly do, that at that moment, as I was flying high across the Atlantic, John was getting his audience with the higher powers. God, Allah, Buddha, Vishnu, the Cosmic Engineer, whomever you believe is actually up there and has some control over these things. And John said, "Look, I was somebody in that last place. I was someone, and I really messed up. And there are some people that you have to take care of for me."

And the man that I met that week was Isaac Tigrit. He was one of the owners and founders of the Hard Rock Café in London. He had also lost two brothers, one to accident and one to suicide. Larry Bilzarian had said to me, "Go over and meet this guy. He can help you with your grief." And so I went.

Not only did he help me with my grief, but Isaac really pushed me to put the original band back together as the Elwood Blues Revue, which I was very nervous to do without John, but I did and people loved it. We came back to New York and opened up the Hard Rock Café here. After that we used the band to open several more of the Hard Rocks in Dallas and other places.

From that, Judy and Larry decided we should start another chain of nightclubs in the spirit of the original Blues Bar. Isaac thought that was a great idea. We went to the Harvard Endowment, got the financing and built the first House of Blues right there in Cambridge, Massachusetts. After that the private equity community got onboard, and now, fifteen years later, Judy, Victor and I oversee a multinational business with ten nightclubs, 2,300 employees and a topline budget of $450 million. There's a casino, live stage productions, and we're expanding into even more venues through 2007. House of Blues is now the third-largest concert booking entity in the country, churning over a half a billion dollars every year. And every night people all over the country are going out to great shows to hear this great music that John loved. All that from this idea that we came up with thirty years ago at the 505 Club in Toronto.

And with our licensing deal, we derive a royalty stream from that, from giving this company the use of the name and the Blues Brothers image. We get a payment, quarter after quarter, hopefully year after year, just like the guy who invented the three-way wiper blade for Ford Motors. ■

ACKNOWLEDGEMENTS

The authors would jointly like to thank: Shawn Coyne and Web Stone; Jay Naughton; Timothy Hsu; Zoe Feigenbaum; Joe DiMento; Alexa Bedell-Healy; Anna Thorngate; Mike Bosze and Joey Handy at Broadway Video; Roni Lubliner and Deidre Theiman at Universal; Edie Baskin and Amber Noland; Joanne Strohmeyer; and all of the agents, managers, agents' assistants, managers' assistants and assistants' assistants who helped us navigate the labyrinth of Hollywood to reach the people we needed to find.

Judy would like to thank: Jim Belushi, Anne Beatts and Jessica Pisano, for putting eye to page along the way; Billy Belushi, for his help in the photo department; Kali Wingood, for being my memory "backup" and assistant extraordinaire; Allen Rongood and EduComp, for kamikaze tech support; Victor, for personal and creative support; Dan Aykroyd, for being a great partner, first to John and then to me.

And an extra special note of appreciation to all the folks who shared their time, energy and memories to provide the core of this book. Not long ago I made a similar request, one that ultimately bore a rather bitter fruit. It is a testimony to faith over experience that any of those who blindly followed me before trusted me again, and I am touched by the generosity of spirit I encountered along the way. Tanner and I both regret we were unable to include everyone we spoke to, but all the interviewees' remembrances enriched our understanding and added to the success of the project.

Tanner would like to thank: Alan Donnes, for getting me through the trenches and out, older and wiser, on the other side; Mom, Dad, Mason, Jenni, Gus and Lena, for enduring my interminable absence; Rex Reed, for his guidance and real estate; Jerry Daigle, for his faith in adversity; Jay Forman, for his way with words; Brett McCallon, for his last-minute save; Matthew Atkatz, for his impeccable eye; Mach Arom and Joan Rentz, for their lifesaving phone calls; Tex Clary, Mike Daisey and Brendan Greeley, for their lackluster accounting skills; Mitch Glazer, for passing the baton.

And John. If only we could have met under better circumstances.

NOTES ON SOURCES
AND METHOD

Full credit for initiating this project must be given to Mitch Glazer and the late Timothy White, who conducted the first oral history of John's life for the *Rolling Stone* tribute published in April of 1982. For certain subjects who were currently unavailable and/or presently deceased, quotes from those *Rolling Stone* interviews have been used as needed.

Subsequent to that piece, in the spring and summer of 1983, the first interviews that laid the groundwork for this book took place. They were conducted by Judith Belushi Pisano and Mr. White. The remaining present-day interviews were conducted, transcribed and edited by Ms. Belushi Pisano and Tanner Colby between September of 2004 and June of 2005. Most of these interviews took place over the telephone. Two of them took place over alcohol, however, and at least one took place over breakfast, as discerning readers will note.

This book is not objective. It contains little in the way of actual, verifiable fact. What it does contain is a sprawling canvas of unreliable first-person narrative, biased opinion, unsubstantiated allegation and foggy, fumbling recollection—all of which adds up to something surprisingly close to the truth. In assembling this canvas, the authors relied heavily, almost exclusively, on human memory. While the passage of time may do wonders for real estate values, the same cannot be said for the mind, a fact which posed certain challenges. The John Belushi era began well over thirty years ago. Over the course of our research, the advancing median age of the interviewees led to as much bemused frustration as actual anecdote. The following, in reference to the Blues Brothers 1978 concert at the Universal Amphitheater, represents a typical exchange:

Famous Person: It was an incredible night. Everybody who was anybody in Hollywood was there.
Author: Really? Like who?
Famous Person: Oh I have no idea.

In spite of such obstacles, the authors did their best to construct a complete and honest narrative. Fortunately, over the passage of three decades, the memories that survive are the most vivid, the most relevant and the most revealing. In the research and preparation of this manuscript, several patterns of human nature emerged, patterns that seem to comprise a relatively sound rule of thumb for the working biographer. And that is that in recounting personal histories, for the most part, people only lie about themselves. They're usually more than happy to tell you the unvarnished truth (as they see it) about others, even about people who are not remotely the subject of your interview, and especially if that person is Chevy Chase.

For matters of historical record, dates and events were cross-checked with secondary sources and contemporary reports, and diligent efforts were made to excise any comments found to be demonstrably false or factually inaccurate. By and large, however, the statements of the interviewees have been allowed to stand on their own—even, in many cases, where one or both of the authors disagreed with them wholeheartedly. In instances where we encountered substantial difference of opinion about a certain event, both perspectives were juxtaposed in the text to indicate as much.

Also, in order to eliminate needless repetition of shopworn tales, portions of Tony Hendra's and Bernie Brillstein's comments have been taken, with their generous permission, from their very detailed and helpful memoirs (listed below).

Finally, for general reference and historical background, the following sources were indispensable:

Going Too Far: The Rise and Fall of Sick, Gross, Black, Sophomoric, Weirdo, Pinko, Anarchist, Underground, Anti-Establishment Humor, by Tony Hendra (Doubleday, 1987).

Live From New York: An Uncensored History of Saturday Night Live, by Tom Shales and James Andrew Miller (Little, Brown, 2002).

Mr. Mike: The Life and Work of Michael O'Donoghue, From National Lampoon to Saturday Night Live, The Man Who Made Comedy Dangerous, by Dennis Perrin (Avon Books, 1998).

Samurai Widow, by Judith Belushi Pisano (Carroll & Graf, 1990).

Saturday Night: A Backstage History of Saturday Night Live, by Doug Hill and Jeff Weingrad (William Morrow & Co., 1986).

The Second City: Backstage at the World's Greatest Comedy Theater, by Sheldon Patinkin (Sourcebooks, 2000).

Where Did I Go Right?: You're No One in Hollywood Unless Someone Wants You Dead, by Bernie Brillstein with Dennis Perrin (Little, Brown, 1999)

And, yes:

Wired: The Short Life and Fast Times of John Belushi, by Bob Woodward (Simon & Schuster, 1984).

THE –OGRAPHIES

FILMOGRAPHY

1975

Tarzoon: Shame of the Jungle, dir. Picha
    voice of the Perfect Master

1978

National Lampoon's Animal House, dir. John Landis
    John "Bluto" Blutarsky

Goin' South, dir. Jack Nicholson
    Deputy Hector

Old Boyfriends, dir. Joan Tewkesbury
    Eric Katz

1979

1941, dir. Steven Spielberg
    Captain Wild Bill Kelso

1980

Blues Brothers, dir. John Landis
    Joliet Jake Blues

1981

Continental Divide, dir. Michael Apted
    Ernie Souchak

Neighbors, dir. John Avildsen
    Earl Keese

DISCOGRAPHY

1973

Lemmings: Original Off-Broadway Cast Recording, Sony

1974

The Missing White House Tapes, Sony

1975

Gold Turkey: The Greatest Hits of the National Lampoon Radio Hour, Sony

1976

Saturday Night Live: The Not Ready for Primetime Players (Live), Arista

1978

Briefcase Full of Blues, Atlantic Records
    1. Opening: I Can't Turn You Loose
    2. Hey, Bartender
    3. Messin' With The Kid
    4. (I Got Every Thing I Need) Almost
    5. Rubber Biscuit
    6. Shotgun Blues
    7. Groove Me
    8. I Don't Know
    9. Soul Man
    10. B Movie Boxcar Blues
    11. Flip, Flop & Fly
    12. Closing: I Can't Turn You Loose

1980

The Blues Brothers: Original Soundtrack Recording, Atlantic Records
1. She Caught The Katy
2. Peter Gunn Theme
3. Gimme Some Lovin'
4. Shake A Tail Feather
5. Everybody Needs Somebody To Love
6. The Old Landmark
7. Think
8. Theme From Rawhide
9. Minnie The Moocher
10. Sweet Home Chicago
11. Jailhouse Rock

Made in America, Atlantic Records
1. Soul Finger (including "Funky Broadway")
2. Who's Making Love?
3. Do You Love Me (including "Mother Popcorn (You Got To Have A Mother For Me)")
4. Guilty
5. Perry Mason Theme
6. Riot In Cell Block Number Nine
7. Green Onions
8. I Ain't Got You
9. From The Bottom (I'm Hollywood Bound)
10. Going Back To Miami

SELECTED VIDEOGRAPHY

Saturday Night Live (notable appearances):

1975-76 Season

10/11/1975, Host: George Carlin
"Wolverines," as the Immigrant
"Bee Hospital," as a bee

10/25/1975, Host: Rob Reiner
"With a Little Help From My Friends," as Joe Cocker

11/22/1975, Host: Lily Tomlin
"Beethoven," as Beethoven

12/13/1975, Host: Richard Pryor
"Samurai Hotel," as the Samurai

01/10/1976, Host: Elliott Gould
"Godfather Group Therapy," as Vito Corleone

01/17/1976, Host: Buck Henry
"Samurai Delicatessen," as the Samurai
"King Bee," as a bee

02/14/1976, Host: Peter Boyle
"Samurai Divorce Court," as the Samurai
"Dueling Brandos," as Marlon Brando

03/13/1976, Host: Anthony Perkins
"The Weatherman: In Like a Lion, Out Like a Lamb," as himself

04/24/1976, Host: Raquel Welch
"One Flew Over the Hornet's Nest," as a bee

05/08/1976, Host: Madeline Kahn
"Nixon's Final Days," as Henry Kissinger

05/22/1976, Host: Buck Henry
"Samurai Tailor," as the Samurai

05/29/1976, Host: Elliott Gould
"The Last Voyage of the Starship Enterprise," as Captain James T. Kirk
"The Honeymooners," as a bee

06/24/1976, Host: Louise Lasser
"The John Belushi Line of Clothing," as himself

07/31/1976, Host: Kris Kristofferson
"Samurai General Practitioner," as the Samurai

1976-77 Season

10/02/1976, Host: Eric Idle
"Feelin' All Right," as Joe Cocker with Joe Cocker

10/23/1976, Host: Steve Martin
"Plato's Cave," as Shelley Bayliss

10/30/1976, Host: Buck Henry
"Samurai Stockbroker," as the Samurai

12/11/1976, Host: Candice Bergen
Opening monologue: *Casablanca* parody, as Humphrey Bogart
"Santi-wrap," as Santa
"Adopt Belushi for Christmas," as himself
"Let's Kill Gary Gilmore for Christmas," as himself

01/29/1977, Host: Fran Tarkenton
"Preshow Pep Talk," as the Coach

03/12/1977, Host: Sissy Spacek
  "Romance," as the Husband

03/19/1977, Host: Broderick Crawford
  "Samurai Hitman," as the Samurai
  "The Weatherman: The Luck of the Irish," as himself

03/26/1977, Host: Jack Burns
  "John Belushi Holds *SNL* Hostage," as himself
  "The Farbers Meet the Coneheads," as Larry Farber

04/16/1977, Host: Elliott Gould
  "The Castration Walk," as Backup Dancer
  "You've Come a Long Way, Buddy,"
  as Rapist Hotline Operator

05/21/1977, Host: Buck Henry
  "Samurai B.M.O.C.," as the Samurai
  "Return of the Coneheads," as the High Master

1977-78 Season

10/29/1977, Host: Charles Grodin
  "Samurai Dry Cleaners," as the Samurai

11/19/1977, Host: Buck Henry
  "Little Chocolate Donuts," as himself
  "Samurai Psychiatrist," as the Samurai
  "The Rickey Rat Club," as Sleazeball

01/21/1978, Host: Steve Martin
  "What If Napoleon Had a B-52?" as Napoleon

01/28/1978, Host: Robert Klein
  "Olympia Diner," as Pete Dionasopolis

02/25/1978, Host: OJ Simpson
  "Samurai Night Fever," as the Samurai

03/11/1978, Host: Art Garfunkel
  "Don't Look Back in Anger," as himself

03/25/1978, Host: Christopher Lee
  "The Thing That Wouldn't Leave," as the Thing

04/22/1978, Host: Steve Martin
  "The Blues Brothers," performing "Hey, Bartender"
  and "I Don't Know," as Joliet Jake Blues

05/28/1978, Host: Buck Henry
  "Samurai TV Repairman," as the Samurai
  "Sodom Chamber of Commerce," as Ashnor
  "Olympia Diner: Guard Dogs," as Pete Dionasopolis

1978-79 Season

10/14/1978, Host: Fred Willard
  "Aging Stuntman: Cliff Preston," as Cliff Preston
  "Scotch Boutique," as Kevin

11/11/1978, Host: Buck Henry
  "Samurai Optometrist," as the Samurai
  "Celebrity Corner: Elizabeth Taylor,"
  as Elizabeth Taylor
  "St. Mickey's Knights of Columbus,"
  as the Grand Knight

11/18/1978, Host: Carrie Fisher
  "The Blues Brothers," performing "Soul Man,"
  "(I Got Everything I Need) Almost" and
  "B Movie Boxcar Blues," as Joliet Jake Blues

12/02/1978, Host: Walter Matthau
  "The Bad News Bees," as a bee
  "Olympia Diner: Coca-Cola Salesman,"
  as Pete Dionasopolis

12/16/1978, Host: Elliott Gould
  "The Widettes," as Jeff

01/27/1979, Host: Michael Palin
  "The Adventures of Miles Cowperthwaite,"
  as Captain Ned

02/24/1979, Host: Kate Jackson
  "Fred Silverman Sabotages NBC," as Fred Silverman

03/17/1979, Host: Margot Kidder
  "Superman's Party," as the Incredible Hulk

05/12/1979, Host: Michael Palin
  "The Adventures of Miles Cowperthwaite: Part II,"
  as Captain Ned

05/26/1979, Host: Buck Henry
  "Samurai Bakery," as the Samurai

Other appearances:

1977

The Richard Pryor Special, as himself

1981

Steve Martin's Best Show Ever, as himself

CAST OF
CHARACTERS

in alphabetical order

ALLEN, KAREN: Actress. Starred opposite John in *Animal House* as Katy, Boon's girlfriend.

APTED, MICHAEL: Director. Worked with John on *Continental Divide*.

AVILDSEN, JOHN: Director. Worked with John on *Neighbors*.

AYKROYD, DAN: See Blues, Elwood.

BACON, KEVIN: Actor. Made his film debut opposite John in *Animal House* as the smarmy Omega pledge Chip Diller.

BEATTS, ANNE: Writer. Worked with John on *The National Lampoon Radio Hour* and then on *Saturday Night Live*. Coauthored, with Judy and Deanne Stillman, the books *Titters* and *Titters 101* and *The Mom Book*.

BEGLEY, ED, JR.: Actor. Starred opposite John in *Goin' South* as the criminal Whitey.

BELUSHI, AGNES: John's mother.

BELUSHI, BILLY: John's youngest brother.

BELUSHI, JIM: John's younger brother. Inspired by John to join Second City and now a successful actor in his own right.

BELUSHI, MARIAN: John's older sister.

BELZER, RICHARD: Comedian and actor. Worked with John on *The National Lampoon Radio Hour* and the *National Lampoon Show*. Through John's encouragement, landed a gig as the first warm-up comic for the *SNL* audiences and was a featured player in several sketches.

BERGEN, CANDICE: Actress. One of *Saturday Night Live*'s first and favorite recurring hosts.

BESHEKAS, STEVE: Member of the West Compass Players and manager of the Chicago Blues Bar.

BILZARIAN, LARRY: Proprietor of the Take It Easy, Baby clothing store on Martha's Vineyard and a featured extra in *Neighbors*. Currently a partner in House of Blues.

BLASUCCI, DICK: Writer and director. Played guitar in John's high-school band, the Ravins. With John's help, auditioned for and joined the touring company of Second City. Later joined the writing staff of *SCTV*.

BLUES, ELWOOD: See Aykroyd, Dan.

BRILLSTEIN, BERNIE: John's manager. Also represented Lorne Michaels and many of *Saturday Night Live*'s writers and performers. Credits John's success in *Animal House* with "putting him in the movie business."

BROKAW, TOM: Former anchor for *NBC Nightly News*. Became friendly with John and many of the *SNL* players while coanchor of the *Today* show, which also taped in Rockefeller Center.

BROWN, BLAIR: Actress. Starred opposite John in *Continental Divide* as the reclusive bird-watcher Nell Porter.

BROWN, DAVID: Producer. Worked with John on *Neighbors*.

BROWN, JAMES: Godfather of soul. Starred opposite John in *Blues Brothers* as the Reverend Cleophus James. Also sang "The Landmark Church" for the motion picture soundtrack.

CALDWELL, CAROL: Writer. Met John through *SNL* writer Michael O'Donoghue.

CARLSON, MARK: High-school football teammate. Currently owns and operates Carlson's Hardware in Wheaton, Illinois.

CHARLES, RAY: Musician. Starred opposite John in *Blues Brothers* as the gun-toting owner of Ray's Music Exchange. Also sang "Shake a Tail Feather" for the motion picture soundtrack.

CHASE, CHEVY: Actor. Worked with John in *Lemmings* as well as *The National Lampoon Radio Hour* and later on *Saturday Night Live*.

CLOSE, DEL: Second City director and guru.

COOPERMAN, MORT: Owner of the Lone Star, a popular downtown New York music venue that John frequented and performed at.

COULLET, RHONDA: Actress and writer. Starred opposite John in the touring company of *Lemmings*. Performed Jackson Browne's "For a Dancer" at John's memorial service at the Cathedral of St. John the Divine in New York City.

CROPPER, STEVE "THE COLONEL": Musician. Rhythm guitar player in the Blues Brothers Band. One-half of the famous Cropper and Dunn rhythm section from the days of Memphis Stax/Volt movement. Still tours with the Blues Brothers Band today.

DANIEL, SEAN: Producer. Worked as an executive in various escalating positions at Universal Studios during the production of many of John's films, including *Animal House*, *1941*, *Blues Brothers* and *Continental Divide*.

DAVIS, TOM: Writer. Worked with John at *Saturday Night Live*.

DIMAS, GUS: John's older cousin on his mother's side.

DOWNEY, JIM: Writer. Worked with John at *Saturday Night Live*.

DOYLE-MURRAY, BRIAN: Writer and actor. Created many of the original scenes and characters that John took over when he joined the replacement cast of Second City. Was the first of John's Second City friends to join him in New York as part of the *National Lampoon* company. Went on to become a writer and featured player on *Saturday Night Live*.

DUNN, DONALD "DUCK": Musician. Bassist in the Blues Brothers Band. One-half of the famous Cropper and Dunn rhythm section from the days of Memphis Stax/Volt movement. Still tours with the Blues Brothers Band today.

DUNNE, MURPHY: Actor and musician. Substituted for Paul Shaffer in *Blues Brothers* when scheduling conflicts prevented Shaffer from being in the movie. Also recruited by John for his fictional band in *Old Boyfriends*.

EBERSOL, DICK: NBC executive during the early years of *Saturday Night Live*.

FISHER, CARRIE: Actress and writer. Hosted *SNL* for the Blues Brothers' second appearance as musical guests. Starred opposite John in *Blues Brothers* as the "Mystery Woman." Engaged, and subsequently unengaged, to Dan Aykroyd.

FISHER, JIM: Actor. Cast member of Second City's main company with John.

FLAHERTY, JOE: Actor. Cast member of Second City's main company with John. Later joined him in *The National Lampoon Radio Hour*, the *National Lampoon Show* and *1941*. Also part of the founding ensemble of Second City's *SCTV*.

FLAHERTY, JUDY: Actress. Joined the Second City replacement cast with John.

FLAHERTY, PAUL: Writer, musician and director. John's roommate and the substitute musician at Second City. Also hired by John to be a part of his fictional band in *Old Boyfriends*.

FONTANO, RED: Proprietor of Fontano's Subs in Chicago, makers of a damn fine meatball sandwich.

FRANKEN, AL: Writer. Worked with John at *Saturday Night Live*.

FURST, STEPHEN: Actor. Starred opposite John in *Animal House* as the naïve, portly Delta pledge, Flounder.

GLAZER, MITCH: Writer. Wrote the first media profile of John for *Crawdaddy*. On John's recommendation, was hired by Universal to write a screenplay for *Kingpin*, a film project about a professional smuggler. Is now a screenwriter in Los Angeles.

GOODROW, GARY: Actor. Starred opposite John in *Lemmings*.

GOULD, ELLIOTT: Actor. Hosted *Saturday Night Live* several times during its first five years. Starred opposite John in the famous "Godfather Group Therapy" sketch.

GUEST, CHRISTOPHER: Actor, musician, writer and director. Worked with John in *Lemmings* and again at *The National Lampoon Radio Hour*.

HENDRA, TONY: Writer. Worked as an editor at the *National Lampoon*. Directed John in *Lemmings*.

HENRY, BUCK: Writer and actor. By far the most prolific host of *Saturday Night Live*'s early years. Starred opposite John in ten of the fourteen Samurai sketches.

HIRSCH, JANIS: Writer. Worked with John as group ticket sales manager for *Lemmings* and as publicist for the *Radio Hour*.

INSANA, TINO: Writer and actor. Also a member of the West Compass Players. At John's insistence, was hired for a small part as Perry Greavy in *Neighbors*, and was also working on various screenplays with John at the time of his death.

JACKLIN, JEAN: John's mother-in-law.

JACKLIN, PAM: John's sister-in-law. Also the attorney for the Belushi estate.

JACKLIN, ROB: John's brother-in-law. Also an artist. Made Judy's wedding band.

JACOBS, PAUL: Musician and composer. Starred opposite John in *Lemmings*. Cowrote the music for the Joe Cocker parody "Bottom of the Barrel" and worked as a studio musician on the *Radio Hour*.

KAZ, FRED: Second City musical director.

KAZURINSKY, TIM: Actor and writer. Met John while a cast member at Second City. Through John's efforts, was later chosen to join the replacement cast at *Saturday Night Live* and the cast of *Neighbors* as the cantankerous Pa Greavy.

KELLER, SUE: Middle- and high-school friend of John, with whom she costarred in many a theatrical production. Also on swim team together.

KELLY, SEAN: Writer. Worked as an editor at the *National Lampoon*. Worked with John in *Lemmings*, at *The National Lampoon Radio Hour* and, loosely, on the *National Lampoon Show*.

KLENFNER, MICHAEL: Executive at Atlantic Records. Instrumental in signing the deal for the first Blues Brothers album. Has a cameo appearance in *Blues Brothers*. Made John and Danny co-godfathers to his daughter, Kate.

KORTCHMAR, DANNY: Musician. A performer, session player and producer. Met John through various connections in the Los Angeles music and entertainment scene.

KRENITSKY, KAREN: Secretary. Worked for John, Danny and Judy at the Phantom Enterprises/Black Rhino office. Was the inspiration for the receptionist in *Ghostbusters*.

LANDIS, JOHN: Director. Helmed the cult classics *Schlock* and *Kentucky Fried Movie* before hitting mainstream success with John in *Animal House* and *Blues Brothers*.

LEE, FRANNE: *Saturday Night Live* costume designer.

MARSHALL, PENNY: Director and actress. Met John during *Lemmings* and became a close friend. Was discussed as the director for *Joy of Sex* at the time of John's death.

MATHESON, TIM: Actor. Starred opposite John in *Animal House* as the lothario Otter.

McGILL, BRUCE: Actor. Starred opposite John in *Animal House* as the loose cannon D-Day.

McKEAN, MICHAEL: Actor. Starred in the sitcom *Laverne and Shirley*. Friends with John through Penny Marshall and Christopher Guest.

METCALF, MARK: Actor. Starred opposite John in *Animal House* as the sadistic ROTC captain Douglas C. Neidermeyer.

MICHAELS, LORNE: *Saturday Night Live* producer and creator.

MILLER, CHRIS: Writer. Cowrote, with Harold Ramis and Doug Kenney, the screenplay for *Animal House*. Came up with the iconic character of Bluto for John.

MILLER, MARILYN SUZANNE: Writer. Worked with John at *Saturday Night Live*.

MORIARTY, CATHY: Actress. Starred opposite John in *Neighbors* as the vamp Ramona.

MURPHY, MATT "GUITAR": Musician. Lead-guitar player for the Blues Brothers Band.

MURRAY, BILL: Actor. Recruited by John out of Second City to join the company of *The National Lampoon Radio Hour* and the *National Lampoon Show*. Joined the cast of *Saturday Night Live* in its second year. Replaced John as Dr. Peter Venkman in *Ghostbusters*.

NABULSI, LAILA: Producer. Met John through Christopher Guest during the *Lampoon* years. At John's insistence, became a production assistant to Tom Schiller on many of the *Saturday Night Live* short films.

NEWMAN, LARAINE: Actress. Original cast member of *Saturday Night Live*.

NICHOLSON, JACK: Actor and director. Directed John in *Goin' South*.

NOVELLO, DON: Writer. Worked with John at *Saturday Night Live*, where he wrote the famous "Olympia Diner" sketches. Later cowrote the screenplay for *Sweet Deception/Noble Rot* with John.

O'DONOGHUE, MICHAEL: Writer. Worked with John at *The National Lampoon Radio Hour* and later at *Saturday Night Live*.

ORMAN, SUZE: Judy's college roommate. Also a best-selling financial guru.

PALIN, MICHAEL: Actor, writer and founding member of British comedy group Monty Python. Hosted *SNL* three times during John's tenure, costarring with him in the legendarily long "Miles Cowperthwaite" sketch.

PAYNE, DAN: John's high-school drama teacher, surrogate father.

PAYNE, JUANITA: Wife of Dan Payne, surrogate mother.

PISANO, JUDITH BELUSHI: Writer and designer. High-school sweetheart, live-in girlfriend, wife and widow.

PLAYTEN, ALICE: Actress. Won an Obie award for her role opposite John in *Lemmings*. Was also quite famous for an Alka-Seltzer commercial at the time.

POMUS, "DOC": Singer and songwriter. A major influence in helping John and Danny form the Blues Brothers band.

RAMIS, HAROLD: Director, writer and actor. Worked with John as a cast member at Second City and also as part of the *National Lampoon* radio and stage show companies. After cowriting *Animal House* with Doug Kenney and Chris Miller, went on to direct many of the early *SNL/Lampoon* movies, including *Caddyshack* and *Vacation*.

REITMAN, IVAN: Producer. Worked with John on both the *National Lampoon Show* and *Animal House*, the success of which led to his directing the classic comedies *Meatballs*, *Stripes* and *Ghostbusters*.

RIEGERT, PETER: Actor. Starred opposite John in *Animal House* as the jazz-loving, anti-authoritarian frat brother Boon, boyfriend of Katy and Otter's constant companion.

ROSS-LEMING, EUGENIE: Cast member of Second City's main company with John.

RUBIN, ALAN: Musician. Trumpet player in the Blues Brothers Band. Still tours with the band today.

SAHLINS, BERNIE: Second City co-owner and director. Auditioned John and placed him in the main company.

SANDRICH, JAY: Director. Slated to work with John on *Sweet Deception/Noble Rot*.

SCHILLER, TOM: Writer. Worked with John at *Saturday Night Live*. Wrote and directed the iconic short film "Don't Look Back in Anger" starring John as an old man visiting the graves of his *SNL* castmates.

SCHUSTER, ROSIE: Writer. Worked with John at *Saturday Night Live*. Created the evil bee sketches.

SHAFFER, PAUL: Musician. Member of the original *Saturday Night Live* band. Hired by John to be the bandleader for the Blues Brothers and instrumental in creating both the band's lineup and signature sound.

SIMMONS, MATTY: Founder and publisher of *National Lampoon*.

SLOANE, JOYCE: Producer. Met John at the College of DuPage and encouraged him to audition at Second City.

SMOKEY: Bodyguard. Hired by John to help control his drug problem. Worked with John from April of 1980 through March of 1981.

STEENBURGEN, MARY: Actress. Made her film debut opposite John in *Goin' South* as the gold-prospecting Julia Tate.

STILLMAN, DEANNE: Writer. Along with Judy and Anne Beatts, coauthored the humor collections *Titters* and *Titters 101*.

SWEARINGEN, EARL: John's next-door neighbor and junior-high science teacher in Wheaton. Also the inspiration for the Larry Farber character from *Saturday Night Live*.

TAYLOR, JAMES: Musician. Sang "That Lonesome Road" with his siblings at John's funeral.

TEWKESBURY, JOAN: Director. Worked with John in *Old Boyfriends*.

THOMAS, DAVE: Actor and writer. Original cast member of *SCTV*. Writing partner of Dan Aykroyd on several film projects, including *Spies Like Us*, another Belushi/Aykroyd vehicle in the works at the time of John's death.

TISCHLER, BOB: Sound engineer and producer. Worked with John on *The National Lampoon Radio Hour* and later on both the two live Blues Brothers albums and the motion picture soundtrack.

WALKER, KATHRYN: Actress and girlfriend of *Animal House* writer Doug Kenney. Through John, she landed the part of Enid Keese, his wife in *Neighbors*, and also met her future husband, James Taylor.

WALLACE, BILL: Former kickboxing world champion and John's personal trainer. Worked with John from the summer of 1980 until his death.

WEISS, BOB: Producer. Worked with John on *Blues Brothers* and later on the television series *Police Squad!* for John's never-seen celebrity guest death scene.

WENDELL, RICHARD "SMOKEY": See Smokey.

WENNER, JANN: Publisher of *Rolling Stone* magazine. Hired John and Danny to write a piece on their cross-country road trip in 1976. Also put John on the cover of *Rolling Stone* four times in five years, including the tribute after his death.

WIDDOES, JAMES: Actor and director. Starred opposite John in *Animal House* as Delta House president Robert Hoover.

WILLIAMS, ROBIN: Actor and comedian. Met John through the New York comedy scene at Catch a Rising Star and backstage at *Saturday Night Live*. Describes his own career at the time as "following in John's wake." Along with actor Robert DeNiro, was one of the last to see John alive the night before he died. Later testified for the grand jury opening the criminal investigation into John's death.

WILLIAMS, TREAT: Actor. Starred opposite John in *1941* as the girl-chasing Corporal Sitarski.

ZANUCK, RICHARD: Producer. Worked with John on *Neighbors*.

ZWEIBEL, ALAN: Writer. Worked with John at *Saturday Night Live*. Was in line to cowrite *Sweet Deception/Noble Rot* with John, but had to back out due to scheduling conflicts.

PHOTO INDEX

All photos in this book ©2005 Judith Belushi Pisano except the following, used by permission:

Courtesy David Alexander
Pages 148, 162

Courtesy Edie Baskin
Pages 94, 96, 99, 100, 101, 102, 105, 107, 111, 114, 117, 118, 121, 124, 129, 152, 176

Courtesy Billy Belushi
Page ix, 16

Courtesy Broadway Video
150, 155, 157, 175

Courtesy Mark Carlson
Page 22

Courtesy Corbis Images
Pages 10, 11

Courtesy Lynn Goldsmith
Pages 200, 207, 210, 212

Courtesy Christopher Guest
Page 58

Courtesy National Lampoon
Pages 61, 62, 64, 66, 70, 73, 75, 79, 88

Courtesy NBC/Universal
Cover; Pages ii, xvi, 2, 5, 7, 13, 130, 132, 135, 137, 138, 140, 141, 142, 144, 145, 171, 172 182, 184, 188, 190, 192, 193, 194, 196, 197, 214, 216, 219, 220, 221, 222, 224, 227, 228, 271

Courtesy Paramount Pictures
Page 122

Courtesy Alberto Rizzo
Page 127

Courtesy Second City
Pages 40, 42, 44, 45, 46, 48, 49, 50, 54

Courtesy Norman Sieff
Page 223

Courtesy Sony Pictures
Pages 232, 234, 235, 236, 237, 244

Courtesy Joanne Strohmeyer/*Boston Herald*
Page 258, 268, 269

Courtesy Tom Zito
Page 144